Salt of the Mountain

Salt of the Mountain

Campa Asháninka History and Resistance in the Peruvian Jungle

By
Stefano Varese

Translated by
Susan Giersbach Rascón

Foreword by
Darcy Ribeiro

University of Oklahoma Press : Norman

Library of Congress Cataloging-in-Publication Data

Varese, Stefano.
[Sal de los cerros. English]
Salt of the mountain : Campa Asháninka history and resistance in the Peruvian jungle / by Stefano Varese ; translated by Susan Giersbach Rascón ; foreword by Darcy Ribeiro.
p. cm.
Includes bibliographical references and index.
ISBN 0-8061-3446-1 (alk. paper)
1. Campa Indians—History—Sources. 2. Asháninka Indians—History—Sources. 3. Asháninka Indians—Politics and government. 4. Asháninka Indians—Social life and customs. I. Title.

F3430.1.C3 V3713 2002
985'.004983—dc21

2002019424

The paper in this book meets the guidelines for permanence and durability of the Committee on Production Guidelines for Book Longevity of the Council on Library Resources, Inc. ∞

Originally published as La Sal de los Cerros, © 1968 Universidad Peruana de Ciencias y Tecnologías, Lima, Peru; and as *La Sal de los Cerros: Una aproximación al mundo Campa*, 2d ed., Retablo de Papel Ediciones, © 1973 Instituto Nacional de Investigación y Desarrollo de la Educación, Lima, Peru.

1 2 3 4 5 6 7 8 9 10

To Rita, who showed me the way and helped me to follow.
To my father, who made it possible.
To Linda, Vanessa, and André, more than thirty years later.

Contents

ILLUSTRATIONS

FIGURES

PHOTOGRAPHS

All photographs were taken by the author.

Foreword

Why do I venture to write the foreword to the new edition of Stefano Varese's book? I dare to do so because Peruvians, more than anyone, know who Stefano is and know his immense worth. I can only say that I view him as one of the best contemporary anthropologists.

He is not just good; he is also better because the important work that he owes us lies in the future. He is better because he has placed himself in the vanguard of the few of us who attempt to rethink anthropology and commit it to the struggle to remake our societies and cultures. This new anthropology takes pride in being a science placed at the service of the revolution, just as all academic anthropologies were and are—to their joy or sorrow—weapons of external colonialism and internal oligarchic oppression. Stefano is better, too, because, besides being an ethnologist with the mysterious power of getting inside the skin of the people he studies to see the world through their eyes, he does it with the greatest feeling of respect and love toward them.

Another of Stefano's qualities is the courage of his utopian thought. He accepts as the mission of applied anthropology, not the dirty work that has been called that in the past and that fills us with shame, but the challenge of rethinking the human as a project in order to reconstruct it, in order to reinvent life in ways that liberate the best potential in every human.

Salt of the Mountain is clear and direct proof of what Stefano can do. As a scholarly study, it is the historical re-creation of the drama of the Asháninka in their confrontation with civilization. As ethnological fieldwork, it is the result of his effort and joy in living the life of the Asháninka in order to give us their vision of the world, of themselves, and of us, their Others and decimators.

I once spoke with Claude Lévi-Strauss about the precariousness of all theoretical work as an incidental, almost faddish, effort to revise whatever dissatisfies us in the conceptual framework of anthropology, and contrarily, about the permanent value of a good ethnographic work that never ages. So it is that every year we republish the classic chroniclers and ethnologists and will continue to republish them, whereas the theorists, with some exceptions, age rapidly.

The former will be the destiny of *Salt of the Mountain* because, like the classic works, it provides a portrait of a people, a distinctive face of the human phenomenon, ever more precious because it is a unique image in a world that is increasingly uniform. In addition to the verbal image reconstructed through the magic of Stefano's words, Salt of the Mountain gives us the vision and emotion of the drama of the Asháninka, who are declining as a society and culture as civilization advances, surrounding, contaminating, and degrading them.

Stefano gives us more than the academic ethnologists offer—the Asháninka's own efforts to explain, within the framework of their culture, the transcendental event of their lives: the unexpected appearance of the white supertribe that fell upon them like a scourge of rotten, ignorant, brutish demons. If the reader is willing to accept my advice, I will suggest that he or she begin reading *Salt of the Mountain* with the last chapter—to see that he or she may also be a scourge, from the Asháninka viewpoint—before entering into the intimacy of their lives.

I ask even more of Stefano. I ask him to give us one of the works that the Peruvian revolution needs most and that he, better than anyone, can offer. I refer to the critical study of the multiethnic nature of Peruvian society, or at least of its biethnic nature, its two, large, distinct, though complementary groups: Hispanic-Peruvians and Quechua-Peruvians.

This work should be simultaneously a truthful analysis of the terrible price the indigenous peoples have paid, and a compelling study of the awful consequences that may affect all of us in the future because Peru, a multiethnic society, was not established as a multinational state. Everything that could have been done to cast all Peruvians in a single mold has already been done. The weapons used for this purpose included plagues, wars, slavery, and catechism. Nevertheless, there are millions of living Quechua speakers; any anthropologist can demonstrate that they will not diminish in numbers, but quite the contrary. In any year in the foreseeable future, there will be more Quechua speakers than there are now, just as today there are more Basque or Catalan speakers than in the past.

Why should we continue oppressing the Quechua, as the Spaniards do with the Basques? We oppress them by not accepting them as a people in their own right—with their own language, tradition, and culture—a people who have the right to live and prosper. I told Don Huillca, the admirable peasant leader, that his grandchildren's grandchildren would speak Quechua as he does, but that is not why they will be poorer and more oppressed than other Peruvians, as they are now. Being Welsh in England or Croat in Yugoslavia no longer means irremediable inferiority, as is the present lot of the Quechua, and no one hopes or desires that the Welsh or Croatians disappear.

The Peruvian revolution already took a fundamental step in this direction with the agrarian reform that gave Quechua peasants their lands back. Another decisive step was making Túpac Amaru, the hero-martyr of the Quechua, the hero-symbol of modern Peru. Above all, after centuries of racism, we are finally beginning to acknowledge in the Quechua face—the face of most Peruvians—its strength, beauty, and human dignity.

Other steps remain, nevertheless, for native Peruvians of all racial and cultural origins to reencounter each other and to be reconciled as equals—though they be different—and as Peruvians.

What are those steps, Stefano?

Darcy Ribeiro

Preface to the English Edition

I wrote this book in Spanish many years ago. In the first and second editions, I acknowledged all the peoples in Peru who helped me and supported my work. Since the Spanish publications were issued, three beloved friends, who inspired my research and my activist commitment, have passed away. May this English edition of *La Sal de los Cerros* be a small tribute to three enormous memories: Bernard Lelong, who from his Lamistas territory in Chachapoyas had begun the French translation of the book and could only complete a few pages and a couple of articles before illness destroyed his tremendous creativity; Guillermo Bonfil Batalla, who showed me the mysterious complexities of "México Profundo" and accepted my expatriation to his country with an overwhelming generosity; and finally, Darcy Ribeiro, heterodox intellectual and heretic revolutionary, whose utopian dreams about a just society nurtured me and scores of Latin Americans.

My interest in publishing *La Sal de los Cerros* in English grew out of my experience as a professor in the Department of Native American Studies at the University of California, Davis. Teaching courses on indigenous peoples of Latin America can be a daunting bibliographical task if the goal is to overcome the limits of traditional ethnographic analyses and offer a more multidisciplinary and comparative approach that focuses on indigenous perspectives and voices. English linguistic parochialism among undergraduate students is becoming epidemic, even in California, where more than half of the population comes from non–English-speaking communities. My friend and colleague Guillermo Delgado at the University of California, Santa Cruz, has been insisting for years that *Salt of the Mountain* should be made available to undergraduate students in English. I want to thank him for his perseverance. I am particularly thankful to all my colleagues in the Department of Native American Studies for their encouragement and support: David Risling, Jack Forbes, George Longfish, Martha Macri, Steve Crum, and Zoila Mendoza. I want to thank especially Inés Hernández-Avila for the innumerable hours we spent together, planning projects and mutually revising our English and Spanish writings. Víctor Montejo deserves a special recognition for his generous concession of his outstanding translator, Susan Giersbach Rascón, who had to postpone her translation of one of Víctor Montejo's manuscripts in order to complete mine. To Susan Rascón, I give my earnest thanks for her patience and persistence in dealing so skillfully with my elaborate Spanish. Steve Kemp, graduate student at California State University, Sacramento, has patiently edited my English preface. Chris Corkrey, computer expert for the Department of Native American Studies, was able to digitalize the maps and graphics for the book. I am grateful for his assistance. I also thank Elizabeth Langland, Dean of Humanities, Arts, and Cultural Studies and of the Committee on Research at the University of California, Davis, for financial assistance.

Salt of the Mountain is a book that straddles many disciplinary boundaries—history being the most obvious—as many of my historian friends have critically reminded me throughout the years. I want to thank my friend, the Peruvian historian Pablo Macera, who acknowledged many years ago my attempt to produce an ethnohistorical study from within the Campa Asháninka society. Arnold J. Bauer at the University of California, Davis, and David Sweet at the University of California, Santa Cruz, have helped me to reconcile myself with the plausibility of writing progressive, if not revolutionary, Latin American history from within the confines of the Empire.

Finally, this book is a delayed tribute of devotion and carinõ to my friend, lover, and compañera Linda Ayre, who for years has kept me close to earth as we both flew in search of the splendor of life.

Preface to the First Edition

The months of January, February, and March are the rainy months on the Gran Pajonal. During this time there are many opportunities for the ethnologist to lie on the platform in the shelter of the Asháninka home and listen to mythical stories mingled with jokes, toasted corn, cassava, and risqué songs. The present study is intended to be a simple introduction to the Asháninka world and stems from fieldwork carried out in the summers of 1963, 1964, and 1967.

I consider it unfruitful to try to understand a society and its culture in exclusively synchronic terms. In this sense, I believe to be fundamental the recent theoretical contributions of ethnohistorians and anthropologists that have stressed the importance of looking at societies as historical phenomena. An approach to the culture of the Campa Asháninka society of the Peruvian jungle should be, first and foremost, a study of its history, a hermeneutic analysis of the written sources and therefore analyses of the patterns of contact between native society and whites—a history of the object, the Asháninka, but also a history of our society's interest in the object because the sources point out, according to the era in which they were conceived, changes in attitude and attention toward the indigenous group. This reveals the relative nature of all observation, a situation from which the authors of the historical documents that concern this study were not exempt and from which the best current ethnological thought is not exempt. Three and a half centuries of history have witnessed the confrontation between the members of a traditional society and the conquistadors or colonizers in an unequal struggle on the battlefield, by all appearances lost from the outset by the Asháninka, but which nevertheless has not yet ended with the defeat of the tribal society. The reasons for a resistance of this type, clearly perceived on a historical level, should also be retrieved synchronically or at least in a comparison of the two perspectives of approach. Only through the comparative journey down these two paths could I approach the "significant structures" of the Asháninka world, the units of "internal coherence," which I was sure meant something in relation not only to the present but also to the past and perhaps to the future. Ethnology arrives at the "synchronic laws" through a historical initiation.

This study, however, is just an introduction to the cultural universe of the Asháninka; the bulk of it thus consists of the initiation corpus, the history. Some brief ethnographic notes are offered to the reader to aid in situating the native society. In the section dealing with the sixteenth and seventeenth centuries, perhaps too lengthy and detailed, I have tried to visualize some aspects of the historical ethnographic map, with which I hope to alleviate the dryness of the reading. The third chapter analyzes the rebellion of Juan Santos Atahualpa almost exclusively from the viewpoint of external history. Only in the reading of the last few paragraphs of the fourth chapter will many interpretive aspects be clarified.

Of the various cultural topics that I could have examined on an ethnological level, I chose some religious topics. The selection has an empirical basis. In daily contact with Asháninka men and women, I clearly noticed some of the profound reasons for a spiritual order that constitute the essence of the fundamental divergence between two ways of confronting the world and life: on the one hand, an indigenous society that considers the intruding colonizers as desecrators of the cosmos; and on the other hand, the vanguard of a profane society that, at the very least, has been limiting its horizons of the sacred more and more—placed face-to-face in a sometimes military, but always cultural, confrontation. The resistance of this native jungle society is, from the perspective of this study, an essentially spiritual matter. Naturally there are other factors that contribute to this adherence to autochthonous and traditional ways of life and thought, but it is useful to remember that—although to modern western society, "nature" has suffered a process of secularization—we cannot apply the same *forma mentis* to other cultures. They are above all two cosmologies that enter into tension when a tribal society is culturally assaulted by ours. And Asháninka cosmology is essentially sacred, hence the necessity to undertake this study from that perspective. I am, however, fully conscious of the limitations implicit in any fragmentation of the unitary reality of a culture. The spiritual perspective is not the only one, nor can it be isolated from the functional whole. After all, we are dealing with levels of comprehension of a phenomenon that have to be separated out of analytical necessity; hence the anamnestic nature of this study, a necessary step but not sufficient in and of itself. I aspire to reunify the whole if future and further research so permit.

One note: All the fieldwork was carried out during three stays in the central region of the Gran Pajonal; the ethnological data are therefore limited to this area, although the historical portion of this study considers other regions of Asháninka territory.

There are many people without whose help the realization of this work would have been impossible. I wish to make special mention of the Franciscan priests, the missionaries in the central jungle, and the sisters of the former Oventeni mission. The authorities of the Universidad Peruana de Ciencias y Tecnología made possible the most recent fieldwork on the Gran Pajonal. The initial impetus and constant stimulus in this research are owed to Professor Jehan A. Vellard. Professor Onorio Ferrero has been a tireless adviser on religious matters. Professor Jorge Puccinelli, Director of the Instituto Raúl Porras Barrenechea of the Universidad Nacional Mayor de San Marcos, has had the kind patience to review the manuscript. My thanks go out to all of them. To my Asháninka friends, generous teachers, in remembrance of the nights of full moon.

Introduction to the English Edition

The last time I was in Gran Pajonal, in the eastern upper Amazon region of Peru, was at the end of 1967. As I was flying out of the small Franciscan mission compound of Oventeni in a taxi airplane, I was making plans for returning to the Campa Asháninka territory to settle, build a slightly modified Campa house at the edge of a *keezi*[1] (a rolling, green savanna), plant a small garden, and complete the Asháninka ethnography that I had dreamt of since I had set foot for the first time on these beautiful jungle uplands. For years, since 1963, I had come to these forests and grasslands for monthly periods to live with the Campa Asháninka, try to learn from them, practice my poor knowledge of their language, and strive to understand the mysterious strength of their culture, which had made it possible for them to survive centuries of aggression and violence while they adapted and maintained a strong sense of ethnic autonomy. At that time I had just finished writing the final pages of my doctoral dissertation, a study that I had reluctantly transformed into an ethnohistorical account rather than the *summa ethnographica* I presumptuously had in mind at the beginning of my research project. I had found two reasons to exonerate myself from writing the definitive Campa Asháninka ethnology. In the first place, I was disturbed by what I perceived as my lack of depth and insight in the few hundred pages of field notes, daily journal, kinship system analysis, pictures, and transcribed tapes that I had gathered throughout those years. All these materials seemed to reflect a rather superficial knowledge of the complexity of the Kéesihatzi (the Gran Pajonal Campa Asháninka) culture and society. I kept comparing my corpus of information to the classic ethnographies written by anthropologists that I had studied in my university courses and to an emerging body of research projects on the Campa that were being carried out in those times by financially well-supported North American scholars, such as John Bodley (1969, 1970, 1972), William Denevan (1971), John Elick (1969), Jay Lehnertz (1969, 1972, 1974), and Gerrald Weiss (1969, 1972).[2]

The second excuse that I found, perhaps a rationalization of my ethnographical anxiety, was built around my combined academic background as a historian and anthropologist. I had arrived to anthropology from the academic field of history and from the less respectable curiosity for exoticism that I had brought to Peru in my European baggage. The two scholars who had a fundamental influence on my training at the Catholic University of Peru, the French Institute of Andean Studies, and the Instituto Riva Agüero were Onorio Ferrero and Jehan A. Vellard. Onorio Ferrero was an Italian historian and philosopher schooled in the neo-Hegelian historicism of Benedetto Croce and the phenomenology of religion. Ferrero, who had been a militant antifascist in Italy and had fought as a partisan in World War II, taught me the basic tools of historical research and philosophical speculation, a passion for the mysterious beauty of symbolic and spiritual thought, and a very pragmatic sense of social justice. As a young Italian immigrant myself, ideologically and politically trained as a teenager in the postwar Socialist, Gramscian, and anticlerical schools and *dopo lavoro* clubs, I came to develop a strong admiration for this liberal, idealist professor, who did not need to be antireligious or Marxist to be an activist in social justice and a supporter of cultural pluralism.

Jehan A. Vellard, however, was a French *pied noire* educated in colonial Algeria, trained as a physician in Paris, and turned into an ethnographer during his travels throughout Brazil with the scientific mission headed by Claude Lévi-Strauss. Vellard's political conservatism and staunch Catholicism did not interfere at all with his tremendous ethnographic skills and vast practical knowledge of South American ethnology. His approach to anthropological fieldwork was more functionalist than structuralist, with a rather disdainful attitude toward his colleague and travel companion Claude Lévi-Strauss's early speculations in *Tristes tropique* and *Pansée sauvage*. Vellard's empiricism was in complementary opposition to Ferrero's speculative mind. Vellard's first recommendation, when I informed him that I had decided to do my fieldwork and research among the Campa, was to insist that I avoid reading any Campa ethnology or history because he thought that I would be influenced by other people's perceptions of this indigenous group, thus ruining the opportunity for a "true, objective, empirical, data-gathering process."

I did not follow Vellard's recommendations. Instead, at the beginning of my fieldwork, I meticulously concentrated on very detailed descriptions of the Campa's "material culture." In my candid interpretation of ethnographic empiricism I adopted a materialistic approach—tangible and measurable observations are easier to grasp—rather than concentrating on spirituality and ideology, whose verification I perceived as uncertain. As I look back at my field notes I can see drawings of bows and arrows with exact measurements, descriptions of houses, details of construction, baskets and ceramic pieces, and the whole array of Campa technology that would satisfy the rigorous ethnographic curiosity of Professor Vellard. But alas, after my first few months in the Gran Pajonal, my notebooks revealed little about the Campa Asháninka intangible culture and an overburdening amount of material culture details that were not exceedingly meaningful and were actually hindering my understanding of the people with whom I was living.

It was the realization of the poverty of this type of ethnographic empiricism and its power to cloud that pushed me back into the arms of the historical approach and the phenomenological analysis of the Kéesihatzi's spirituality and cosmological exegesis. The historical approach was necessarily external, grounded on exogenous primary and secondary sources: writings *about* the Campa, not *by* the Campa. The endogenous Indian history was instead spoken in the words of myths, beliefs, and visionary journeys of the *shiripiári*, the "husband of tobacco," the shaman, whose place in Campa Asháninka cosmogony, cosmology, and social life I soon found to be absolutely central.

When I met Poshano, the *shiripiári* who lived in the forested hills of Chenkári, beyond the savanna of Kishimasháwo, I had no idea that this small, thin man with penetrating dark eyes and a passion for teaching was going to provoke a radical change in my vision of the Asháninka and in my research project. For months I had asked the family members—Coronado, Pashúka, and Omága—with whom I was living on the banks of the Chitani Creek to take me to meet this famous *shiripiári*, who had threatened the missionaries, the military, and the colonists with all kinds of hostile mystical actions. His reputation, which was reaching Campa hamlets far beyond the territories under Franciscan administration and those under evangelical control of the Summer Institute of Linguistics, had captured my imagination and had made my residence in Chitani somehow jittery. My intuition told me that knowing and talking to Poshano could enlighten many of the aspects of my study that were still obscure and vague. I was right: Poshano became my fortuitous third professor and guide.

In the 25, 26, and 27 February 1967 entries in my field diary, I wrote the following about Poshano:

> It is almost impossible to describe the impression Poshano caused on me. Maybe what I had imagined beforehand influenced this positive impression. I had imagined a presumptuous, introverted, somehow conceited individual. . . . Who ever said that shamans must be neurotics, mentally disturbed, or at least epileptics? Poshano, on the other hand, inspires a feeling of safety and peace. I feel that I am with a therapist. The old man is dirty, with long, tangled hairs that disguise a beginning balding head. He carries a thin headband of *chachahuasca*. He walks straight, with firm steps that appear light, almost as

if he does not touch the ground. And his smile is always there, as if he does not take himself or us too seriously. But he is not vain or superficial, and he shows it when we establish conversation and I ask questions. What keeps me astonished is his extreme simplicity . . . his deep eyes, ironic, warm . . . his accessibility . . . ; he answers everything I ask: There are no mysteries to protect; nothing of what I ask seems to annoy him. . . . What amazes me of this wise man is his extreme openness and clarity. It seems as if he is extremely learned about what exists beyond the rational, sensible, and physical world. During the taping of his sacred songs Poshano asked me, "When I die, are my songs going to stay?" I suddenly fear that I will not have time to learn from him. . . . There is something in all this so profound and mysterious that I cannot imagine myself able to receive any support from my academic training. How can I understand any of this? . . . As we walk to the *chacra* behind his *intómoe* to gather the sacred plants that he uses to heal and travel throughout the universe, he whispers to me, "I jump to the sky. And I always come back."

Coronado, Omága, and I left the house of Poshano in the early morning. "Poshano will accompany us on our trip back," Omága told me. After the first stretch down the Chenkári hill, we stopped to rest in a *purma*, an old cultivated plot on which the Asháninka gather fruits and hunt small game that come to feed on the fruit trees. A woodpecker flew trustfully toward me and landed at my side, over the stump of the felled tree on which I was resting. Omága told me that the bird was Poshano. On two other occasions during our journey back we saw a woodpecker. After these three instances, I did not see any woodpeckers during the remainder of my stay in the Gran Pajonal, but neither did I see Poshano again.[3]

By early 1968 the first Spanish edition of *Salt of the Mountain* was published by a newly founded Peruvian university of science and technology, where I was teaching anthropology.[4] In October of the same year a military coup brought to power a small group of young generals and colonels, who initiated one of the most daring social and political reform programs ever undertaken in Peru. Army General Juan Velasco Alvarado's revolution expropriated and nationalized the International Petroleum Company, a branch of the Standard Oil Company of New Jersey;[5] declared and implemented agrarian reform in the coastal region of the country by expropriating sugarcane plantations from a gentrified oligarchy, creating peasant-run cooperatives; and announced the expansion of land reform initiatives in the Andes and Amazon regions. Surprised by this unusual military regime that used progressive discourses and professed its intentions to combat poverty, social injustice, and ethnic-racial discrimination, some of us young intellectuals accepted the challenge of confronting our dreams of social justice by accepting positions within the state apparatus.[6]

In 1969 Mario Vásquez, a Quechua anthropologist from the northern Andean region of Ancash, invited me to join him in the recently created General Directorate of Peasant Communities in the Ministry of Agriculture and Agrarian Reform. Vásquez was part of a small number of Peruvian anthropologists who had been recruited by Allan Holmberg, founder and director of the applied anthropology Vicus Project, to study at Cornell University. There, Vásquez, a Quechua Indian from a small provincial town of the northern Andes, earned a doctoral degree in anthropology and the greatly needed prestige and protection from racial and ethnic discrimination so common in Peru during those years. Vásquez challenged me with the formidable task of extending the land reform process initiated by the military revolution in the coast and sierra to the Amazon region of Peru. In a remarkable meeting with Carlos Delgado, another Cornell University alumnus anthropologist, who was recently appointed Minister of SINAMOS (National System of Social Mobilization), a few other social scientists, lawyers, and army colonels, Vásquez presented me with the challenge of defining the needs of the "tribal Indians" of the Amazon jungle, developing a legal framework for protecting their territorial rights, and guaranteeing their language, cultural, and political rights—all of which, Vásquez reminded me, had to be done swiftly and with scarce financial and technical resources. Most importantly, these studies had to take place against the backdrop of long-held cultural and racial prejudices against the indigenous peoples of the Amazon, prejudices that were shared by the majority of criollo and mestizo Peruvians, the politically cornered oligarchy, the state bureaucracy, and even some of the progressive military who were running a government intended to bring social and cultural democracy to all Peruvians.

I accepted the challenge, and in 1969 I founded the Division of Native Communities of the Jungle as a branch of the Ministries of Agriculture, Agrarian Reform, and SINAMOS. Housed in a horrendous and dilapidated office in the old Ministry of Labor building and staffed with a few of my former anthropology students, a "constitutional" lawyer, an agronomist, and a Peruvian sociologist of Chinese descent, whose cousin had been in the Ernesto "Che" Guevara guerrilla movement in Bolivia, the division started its mission by producing a social diagnostic of the indigenous peoples of Peru's Amazon region. With no reliable demographic data or information about territorial occupation, land tenure, and resource management, the survey task soon became an overwhelming challenge. Peru's academia and governmental administration had no tradition whatsoever of social studies or censuses of the region. This area encompassing more than half of the national territory that constitutes the Amazon had never been seriously considered by the ruling elites or academia. The ethnic surveys that we were initiating had to rely on missionary sources—archives of Catholic orders such as the Jesuits, Franciscans, and Dominicans or of Protestant sects; documentation prepared by groups such as the Summer Institute of Linguistics/Wycliff Bible Translators; the New Tribes Missions; and various other evangelical missions—all of which became our most important sources of information. The desolate landscape that the state administration inherited after more than a century and a half of systematic neglect of the peoples and lands of the Amazon began to burden us. What were the key problems of the Amazon Indian communities? What were their claims? What were their demands? Were there some forms of indigenously generated political programs and platforms? Who and where were the indigenous leaders, the representatives of dozens of ethnic groups and literally thousands of local communities?

During the final months of 1969 and part of 1970, the team of social scientists of the Division of Native Communities carried out a pilot study of the Aguaruna communities of the Alto Marañón River.[7] Through this study we were able to show the subordinate position of the Aguaruna and Huambiza peoples within the regional market economy and political system, as well as the dramatic loss of Indian territorial possessions and control at the hands of the state-planned military colonization, which encouraged colonization of Indian lands by Peruvian civilians and demobilized army personnel. A larger diagnostic study of the indigenous peoples of Peru's Amazon jungle was concluded in 1971 and was promptly stowed away as a "confidential document" in the bureaucratic maze of the Ministry of Agriculture.[8] I used part of the information for a few articles,[9] as did my colleagues and collaborators Alberto Chirif and Carlos Mora, who published a monumental first attempt to systematize the basic ethnography of the Peruvian Amazon.[10]

The accumulation of this small and still precarious body of knowledge on the Amazon region's indigenous communities, as well as the increasing political pressure and mobilization of a few Indian organizations, constituted the basis for the enactment of the Law of Native Communities (Legal Decree 20653), which introduced sweeping reforms and radical changes in the situation of the indigenous peoples of the jungle.

> The statute recognized "native communities" (*comunidades nativas*) as social units with a high degree of autonomy, including a legal right to maintain local customs. More important[ly], native communities could seek land titles, which were to be inalienable and held collectively by community members. As soon as the law went into effect, employees of the government's social mobilization agency, SINAMOS, traveled to Asháninka villages to explain how Indians could begin the complex process of laying claim to their lands. . . . In the first years after

> the law was in effect, the government titled Asháninka communities at a brisk pace. As of 1976, thirty-four communities had received titles to territories varying in size from 188 hectares to more than 10,000.[11]

In 1975 the revolutionary government of Juan Velasco Alvarado came to an abrupt end. "El Chino Velasco," as he was affectionately called by the people, died after a short illness, and a countercoup put into power a conservative sector of the army. The political environment moved quickly to the right and toward the systematic eradication of years of social reforms. In response, the indigenous peoples of the Amazon and the Campa Asháninka of the central jungle threw themselves into politics and activism, which resulted in reactivating local intracommunal organizations, forming and expanding regional ethnic and multiethnic federations, and making the Law of Native Communities their banner of ethnopolitical struggle.

The reestablishment of extremist neoliberal economic policies that accompanied the counterrevolution exacted a tremendous toll on the popular classes, peasants, and indigenous peoples, all of whom suffered a lowering of their already meager income and standards of living as they witnessed renewed attacks on their lands and resources. The systematic contraction of the already deficient welfare state and the cancellation of any government investment in rural areas, especially the Amazon, left the region open to the only "industry" that is highly profitable and environmentally sound: coca/"pasta"/cocaine. Modest cultivation of coca for family consumption had existed for millennia among indigenous peoples of the Andean Amazon, but it was not until the early 1980s that cocaine producers from the coastal and Andean regions massively expanded their business and filled the indigenous territories with plantations of coca and rustic laboratories of "pasta," the first unrefined cocaine product.

By the mid 1980s the Maoist guerrilla movement Shining Path had moved from the Andes into the upper Amazon region; into indigenous Peruvian territory, particularly the Mantaro, Ene, and

Tambo River valleys; and into Campa Asháninka lands. It is estimated that as many as five thousand Asháninka who resisted forced recruitment by Shining Path or could not seek refuge deep in the jungle were killed by the guerrilla forces.[12] In April 1990 as many as forty Asháninka were massacred by Shining Path forces in the village of Naylamp in the province of Satipo.[13] At the same time, drug traffickers, sometimes under the careful eyes of Shining Path, occupied dozens of Asháninka villages, enslaved the people, and forced them to slash-and-burn the forest to provide space for coca and clandestine landing strips.[14]

Toward the end of the 1980s another guerrilla movement, the Movimiento Revolucionario Túpac Amaru (MRTA) expanded its armed actions into the northern Asháninka territory in the valleys of the Pichis and Pachitea Rivers. In 1989 the relations of the Campa Asháninka with the MRTA took a tragic turn. Alejandro Calderón Espinosa, an Asháninka leader from Puerto Bermúdez, was kidnapped, judged by a revolutionary tribunal for his alleged participation in an antiguerrilla movement more than twenty years earlier, found guilty, and summarily executed for events that had taken place in 1965.[15] The reaction of the Asháninka to the killing was swift and radical. The day after Christmas in 1989, hundreds of Asháninka men occupied the town of Puerto Bermúdez, detained the town officials, rounded up dozens of MRTA supporters and members of the guerrilla group, subjected them to "popular tribunals," and punished some of those who had taken a first-hand part in the killing of Alejandro Calderón Espinoza.[16]

In an interview given in 1995 to the Indian journal *Abya Yala News*, Campa Asháninka activist and leader Mino Eusebio Castro confirmed the increasingly disastrous and tragic experience of his people since the mid-1970s at the hands of land squatters; lumber companies; ranchers; drug traffickers; the two major guerrilla groups, Shining Path and MRTA; and finally, the Peruvian army and police force.

> Presently, we have more than 39 communities that have disappeared. Many people have been displaced and are refu-

> gees. . . . [M]any of those killed have been as a result of the military. . . . This is not our war. . . . The military does not know who is who. . . . Who cares when an indigenous person is killed? No one. When one of the military dies, then it is another story. They are made into heroes. When an indigenous person dies in defense of his territory, no one says anything.[17]

Peru's "return to democracy" in 1980 ended in the late 1990s with a decade of the increasingly autocratic, corrupt, and violent regime of Alberto Fujimori, which systematically dismantled every single piece of legal protection for the rights of indigenous peoples. The assault, especially severe in relation to land and territorial rights, began subtly in 1978 during the administration of Fernando Belaúnde Terry with Decree 22175, which retained the main content of the Law of Native Communities (Decree 20653) but restricted communal property rights on the majority of forested lands in order to award concessions to outside interests. In 1979 Decree 20653 abolished the Law of Native Communities, established limits to common property, and created the conditions that facilitated the privatization of communal lands. One year later, in 1980, Decree 02 reduced the lands of indigenous communities and allowed investors to expand their control over Amazon lands. In 1992 Fujimori's administration managed to enact a new constitution, which, in convoluted rhetoric, combines a series of favorable and unfavorable measures affecting indigenous peoples. Although the state defines Peru as a multicultural nation and recognizes the cultural rights of indigenous peoples (their rights to receive bilingual education in Spanish and their native language, as well as the legitimacy of community common law), it also restricts communal jurisdiction over lands by abolishing the protective status of communal lands, thus allowing land to be sold or dispersed in other ways. Indigenous communal lands can be considered by government agencies to be "abandoned," whereas in reality they are lying fallow. This is a serious threat to the indigenous peoples, particularly the Amazon communities and the Campa Asháninka, because slash-and-burn agriculture requires long fallow periods in order to restore the fertility of the soil. "In the new Peruvian Constitution—declares Mino Eusebio Castro—articles 82 and 83 have decreed that our lands can be seized if they are deemed 'abandoned' by the state. They can then be bought by those who have the most economic power, like petroleum companies. . . . [F]or us there are no abandoned lands, because we view land space in an integral manner."[18]

More than thirty-five years ago, my younger brother Luis and I, guided by two Asháninka men, whose names I cannot remember, were climbing the formidable chain of forested mountains that separates, on the east, the lower Perené River from the Gran Pajonal. It took the two of us—young urban students—three days of painful marching through thick tropical rain forest, on muddy and slippery trails and across torrential rivers, to walk the distance that the Campa Asháninka salt traders would walk in a day and a half. I wanted to have the personal, physical experience of entering the Gran Pajonal through the same route that the Asháninka had used for millennia to carry salt from Tzivíniki, the Mountain of Salt, to Kéhesi, the Gran Pajonal. The third day, as our party was leaving the dark protection of the forest and entering the savanna, we met a group of Asháninka Kéesihatzi. Their faces and kushma tunics painted with red achiote; the black dotted lines of huito spreading from their noses to their ears; their long, black hair framing their faces; and their bows, arrows, and shotguns completed, unequivocally, the boundary that separated us white Peruvian intruders from them, the people of the Gran Pajonal. The long, elaborated etiquette that followed—filled with screamed words uttered in high falsetto while bare feet stomped the ground and accompanied by menacing movements of the bows and shotguns—confirmed that I had made the right decision when I chose the Gran Pajonal as my field site to study a traditional indigenous region in resistance. These Campa Asháninka did not seem to be intimidated by our presence, nor were they renouncing their prerogative to contest and oppose our intrusion into their lands.

At that time I could not have imagined that the lives of these men and thousands of other Asháninka and indigenous peoples would be altered in very dramatic ways just a few months later by the guerrilla Movement of the Revolutionary Left (Movimiento de Izquierda Revolucionaria, or MIR), which was brewing in the central jungle of Peru. In the month of May 1963, Javier Heraud, a young promising poet and a peer of mine at the Catholic University of Lima, had been killed by the police in Puerto Maldonado as he was trying to return to Peru from Cuba with six other members of the Army of National Liberation, another revolutionary guerrilla group. He was shot in a canoe as he was floating on the Manu River, just as he had prophetically written in one of his poems: *Me moriré entre flores y pájaros* ("I will die among flowers and birds"). I also could not have guessed that guerrilla commander Héctor Béjar, who in 1965 opened a front of the Army of National Liberation in the Campa Asháninka territory in the jungle of Ayacucho, was going to become in 1970 one of my supervisors in SINAMOS and the agrarian reform process during Velasco's revolutionary regime.

Many paths were being symbolically crossed that day at the entryway to the Gran Pajonal: my somewhat naïve fascination for ethnographic discovery; my firmer conviction that history was an undertaking of consciousness; the passion for social justice that my brother Luis and I were nurturing as the most precious gift of our Italian immigrant father; the outrage that students, workers, and intellectuals of my generation were feeling at the dismal conditions of exploitation, oppression, and racism imposed upon the great majority of Peru's peoples; and finally, the incipient sentiment among a few social scientists still being trained in Peru that the cultural pluralism and ethnic diversity of our country was an extraordinary asset for the new social system that most of us were seeking. My generation and I were both on the brink of fundamental cultural and societal reconfigurations and self-awareness, which would explode with force during the following years. The Campa Asháninka and other innumerable indigenous peoples from the Andes and the Amazon of Peru who died, were uprooted, became refugees in their own land, or endured a miserable life in the cities during the years after 1960s are all part of a common history of Latin America. That history of a devastated past and a hopeful future engaged some of us, from the beginning of our social lives, in the moral promise of intellectual, political, and practical activism.

I cannot remember with precision what my thoughts were at that time. There was certainly no prophetic enlightenment in my mind. What I know is that it took me a few more years after that day in the Gran Pajonal to formulate an analytical understanding of indigenous peoples' resistance and autonomous movements that was free from the Eurocentric perspective that indigenous historical subjects responded in "prepolitical" and "primitive" ways, devoid of rationality and agency. Eric Hobsbawn's analysis, *Primitive Rebels*, was published more than ten years later,[19] and the fundamental revision of indigenous and peasant resistance movements was not initiated by Indian and western scholars under the Gramscian banner of "Subaltern Studies"[20] until the early 1980s.

There I was in the early 1960s, naïvely facing the tremendous challenge of interpreting, translating, and telling the story of four centuries of Campa Asháninka resistance and rebellion, with no tools other than a series of precarious and biased epistemological principles, a fragmented understanding of Asháninka semantics, and a huge collection of western (mis)interpretations registered in less than seducing religious and bureaucratic documents. The task was never fully accomplished. Its conclusion haunted me for decades as I spent more and more time engaged in the study and the struggle of indigenous peoples of the Americas for self-determination, autonomy, and the construction of their sovereignties.

Salt of the Mountain

CHAPTER ONE

Ethnology

This Mountain of Salt is very famous for the large groups of heathen Indians who go there for salt from the most remote jungle nations.

—JOSÉ AMICH, 1771

LOCATION, LANGUAGE, AND DEMOGRAPHY

Between the tenth and fourteenth parallels (southern latitude) and the seventy-second and seventy-sixth meridians (west of Greenwich), in an area more than one hundred thousand square kilometers in size, live the Campa Asháninka, one of the largest indigenous groups in the Peruvian jungle. Most of these Indians inhabit the areas surrounding the Apurímac, Ene, Perené, Tambo, and upper Ucayali Rivers and their tributaries. Groups of Asháninka are also found throughout the Gran Pajonal highlands and along the eastern bank of the Pachitea River. Their western border is imposed by the slopes of the Andes, more than fifteen hundred meters in altitude. Above these Andean spurs still covered with tropical forest, cultivation of cassava is difficult; so too, therefore, is the life of the Asháninka who depend on this plant.

Their territory is bounded on the east and north by other indigenous groups: the Machiguenga, the Piro, the Cunibo, and the Cashibo. To the west, between the Andes and the Asháninka, are the Amuesha.

In terms of linguistic classification, the Campa (Asháninka) have always been considered members of the Arawak family. As early as 1891 Daniel Brinton classified them as members of the "Arahuaco" linguistic stock and even ventured the hypothesis that the Gran Pajonal zone and adjacent rivers could constitute the center of dispersion of the entire stock.[1] Years later, Paul Rivet and Charles Tastevin proposed the designation "pre-Andean Arawaks" for four linguistic groups found at the foot of the Andes. They are (1) the Piro or Chontakiro of the Ucayali River, the Kuniba of the Jurúa, and the Kanamaria; (2) the Kampa, Anti, Machiganga, or Katongo; (3) the Ipuriná and the Marawan; and (4) the Mareteneri, Inapari, and Pajaguara dialect.[2]

The term "pre-Andean" is also used by Chestmir Loukotka in his classification of South American languages.[3] Campa is included among the fourteen languages enumerated by the Czechoslovakian linguist under the label of pre-Andean Arawak languages and, together with Amoise (Amuesha), is the group located farthest west. Loukotka does not name the Machiguenga and probably includes them under the general term "Kampa." Alden Mason, however, in his 1950 classification specifically separates the Campa from the Machiguenga and the Piro.[4] Julian Steward and Louis Faron, relying on a schematic classification proposed by Joseph Greenberg, classify Campa within the Arawak subfamily and include the latter, in turn, in the Andean-Equatorial family.[5] In a long article published in 1958, Olive Shell[6] proposed the following members of the pre-Andean Arawak family: Piro, Machiguenga, Campa, Masco (Mashco), Amuesha, and Nomatsiguenga (the last one is considered a Campa subgroup).

None of the scholars who have worked on linguistic classification of the Campa has ever doubted their membership in the Arawak family; there is less clarity and more discrepancy, however, in the names and number of subgroups. Rivet and Loukotka,[7] for example, consider that in the Ucayali River Basin there are only two important Arawak-speaking "tribes": the Chontakiro (Piro) and the Kampa; and under this latter name, they enumerate a series of ethnic names that cannot be considered groups per se. Anti, Kamatika, Kimbiri, Pangoa, Katongo, Tampa, Ungonino, etc., are terms that do not have the same content or meaning. In some cases they are places (e.g., Pangoa); in others they are phonetic distortions (e.g., Tampa-Campa); in still others they are names, perhaps of Andean origin (e.g., Anti). The name *Katongo*, for example, is a contraction of *katongosates*, a term that refers to the Campa who live on the upper part of a river; those who live downriver are called *kiringasates*. Similarly, those who live along the Perené are Parenis. Furthermore, there is no basis for the two scholars' incorporation of the Machiguenga group within the Campa. Even from an exclusively linguistic point of view, this simplification is not justifiable. As a matter of fact, the division of "idiomatic groups" is based on two conditions explained by Shell[8] in this way: (1) An idiomatic group is an ethnic group that speaks a language that is not comprehensible to speakers of other languages; and (2) The phonological system of their language requires the formulation of an alphabet distinct from those of other languages. Under this definition, Machiguenga forms an independent group from Campa, although there is some similarity and minimal comprehension between the two languages.[9]

Alden Mason and Antonio Tovar[10] also set forth long lists of Campa subgroups, which at times are nothing more than synonymous terms or names devoid of ethnic meaning. Mason refers to the Atiri (Tovar's Atzíri) as a subdivision; in reality, this is a term the Campa themselves use to refer to human beings. The Campa call themselves *Asháninka* (men, people). The term *Campa*, as we will see, appears belatedly in written sources and has a derogatory sound to the Asháninka ear.[11]

Unfortunately for ethnology, each source sets forth lists of tribal names that further confuse the panorama and require meticulous analyses to determine their exact meaning. We forego here a listing of all subgroup names appearing in modern sources, that is, since the beginning of this century, but it is interesting to point out that in most cases the generalization of including the Machiguenga linguistic group within the Campa is repeated.[12] Furthermore, we must not forget that the word *tribe* is not univocal and at times is used to designate a simple group of indigenous families to whom the author gives the name of a nearby river or of the indigenous person with the most hierarchical authority. In some cases the name may even designate a single family, resulting in an excessive proliferation of ethnic names, which certainly do not correspond to *tribes* in the traditional meaning of the term.[13]

Regarding the size of the Campa population, the data are contradictory. In 1896 Claudio Osambela[14] estimated their numbers at 20,000 but included members of other indigenous groups in his calculation. According to César Cipriani,[15] there were fewer, 2,000 at most, but his calculation was based exclusively on the Chanchamayo and Gran Pajonal areas. The estimates of Jorge Von Hassel, Charles Eberhardt, and Otto Nordenskjold,[16] however, were on the order of 10,000 and 15,000. Kenneth Grubb and Pedro Fast were more optimistic, stating that the Campa population was between 30,000 and 40,000.[17] The 1940 census indicates the total number of Indians living in the jungle (350,000) but does not specify the population of each linguistic group. The census data are disputed by anthropologist John Rowe, who argues that they are approximate calculations and of little value.[18] It is difficult to support any one of these estimates, but we believe that the numbers that most accurately reflect reality are those in the range of 20,000, taking into account that the Machiguenga are excluded because they are a separate linguistic group.[19]

ECOLOGICAL RELATIONSHIPS

The Campa Asháninka, like most tribal populations of the tropical rain forests of South America, practice slash-and-burn agriculture, which in Peru is called *agricultura de roza*. The most important plant in their subsistence economy is the cassava (*Manihot esculenta*), called *kaniri* in their language; it constitutes the basis of their daily nutrition, whether plain, simply cooked, or as a fermented beverage called *piárintzi* in Campa and *masato* in the Spanish spoken in the jungle. Nevertheless, a large number of other plants, both native and non-native, complement the diet. The Asháninka recognize approximately thirty-two varieties of cassava, ten of bananas, four of peanuts, seven of *frejol* (haricot bean; *Phaesulus vulgaris*), and many other plants with nutritional or other uses, such as cotton, annatto (*Bixa orellana*), poisons used for fishing, tobacco, hallucinogenic plants, and medicinal and ritual plants. The *chacra* (small farm) of a Gran Pajonal Campa family may have as many as fifty different species of cultivated plants, although of some there may be only one specimen.

The groups that live near the main rivers rely more on fishing and hunting, activities which, due to ecological constraints, are less common in the upper interfluvial regions and the Gran Pajonal savanna. The interfluvial areas are poor in animal life because the mammals of the tropical forests are concentrated near the rivers. Gathering is also an extremely important activity and occupies a significant portion of the time of Campa children and adults of both sexes; nevertheless, it is difficult to state, without quantitative studies, what real importance wild animal products and gathered vegetables have in daily nutrition.[20]

Ethnology and human geography have pointed out an association between swidden agriculture and the mobility of the social unit, which after a certain period of time (two, three, or more years), has to abandon its cultivated fields because their fertility has been exhausted and clear a new *chacra*, or small farm, in primary forest land. What is not clear, however, is the precise relationship that exists between the moving of cultivated lands, the "latterization" of the soil, and other social and religious causes that induce these itinerant practices among the Asháninka. In some cases that we observed, the ecological cause seemed obvious, whereas in others it was not. Preconceived ideas nourished by the reading of a specialized bibliography at times seemed to steer our observation toward the ethnologically orthodox explanation: The change of fields and dwelling seemed to be caused exclusively by the exhaustion of the fertility of the land. Betty Meggers analyzed and explained the cultural characteristics of the societies of the South American tropical forest in this manner in a 1956 article.[21] In the same year another opinion was expressed on the same topic. According to Robert Carneiro,[22] it was necessary to reexamine the common idea that the new location of the swidden horticulturists' village was due exclusively and necessarily to the exhaustion of the land, because a human group of low density (fewer than five hundred people) can actually live sedentarily by practicing crop rotation.[23] In our fieldwork we have been able to establish that the movements of the Campa social unit (ideally the nuclear family) are not always in response to ecological reasons but oftentimes to social and religious causes. In the category of social causes, it is important to point out postmarriage change of residence, which is never a definitive change but is always subject to modification over time. We will not enter here into a detailed analysis of the modalities of residence in the Campa social relationships system, but suffice it to say that many of the changes of dwelling, and consequently of cultivated land, are due to these types of causes, which obviously are rooted in social and economic, as well as ecological, aspects of society.

Among the religious causes of a change of residence, the most common is the abandonment of house and fields because an adult member of the family has died there. It might appear that these social and religious reasons for an itinerant agricultural system could be a posteriori "rationalizations" of causes that have to do fundamentally with poor soil. Nevertheless, many of the cases that were directly observed demonstrate that a Campa family may live as long as ten years in the same place by planting the land in a rotating fashion. In some cases the dwellings have shifted a few (seventy to two hundred) meters from their original locations, apparently for reasons of contingency—fires, natural wear of the dwelling, or the death of a nursing baby—but these changes of dwelling have always been made within the area of cultivated land and, naturally, without abandoning the crops.

The basis of Campa society and economy is the nuclear or conjugal family, which includes the husband, wife, and their sons and daughters. This social unit, which is obviously fluid, can grow, shrink, or disintegrate and rarely remains unchanged to the death of its founders. The nuclear family is enlarged through polygynous marriage, which, though not a general practice among the Asháninka, is found with relative frequency.[24] In this case the family occupies several dwellings. There is another way to enlarge the nuclear family, however; this is related to the norms of postmarriage residence.

Ideally Campa culture requires uxorilocal residence for a certain period of time. In this situation the conjugal family is joined by a son-in-law, who will contribute his services, especially in the economic sphere. For this same reason, the nuclear family will be deprived of its adult sons or sons of marriageable age, who will go to reside with the families of their wives. In the case of a nuclear family with no daughters, there is a serious social and economic problem that can lead to the failure of the marriage because the husband will seek a solution through a union with a second wife who can give him daughters. This arrangement seems to be rejected by all Campa women, who prefer dissolution of the union to accepting a compromise of this nature.

The nuclear family is also included within a network of social relationships, which extends from the ties of the kinship system to the commercial relationships that each adult man[25] may have with members of other Campa-speaking groups, Andean settlers, or whites.

The Asháninka kinship system can be classified as belonging to the Iroquoian type. The preferred and ideal marriage is between cross cousins (symmetrical or matrilateral), although the norm is not strictly followed in practice. With regard to the type of lineage, it is difficult to make a definitive statement, but an emphasis on the maternal side is evident.

It is important to recall some basic characteristics of the slash-and-burn system practiced by Campa society, especially because of the social implications that have been evident, historically as well as at present, in the confrontation between the native society and the national society. The intimate ties between the ecological relationship of a human group and its ideological system are obvious. The manner in which a society interacts with the environment is not only to be understood in terms of a greater or lesser application of rationality to its use of the environment; but it also entails an entire system of behavior that is related to and nourished by a specific ideology, a peculiar visualization, valuation, and perception of nature, and a particular conceptualization of the universe. Historically two types of societies, and consequently two models of socioeconomic, ecological, and ideological organization, have clashed: on the one hand, local segments of colonial and national society with a basically capitalist-mercantilist mode of production and ideology; and on the other hand, the tribal society with "family or domestic modes of production."[26] One of the most important aspects of the struggle of Campa society has been and still is the defense of its territorial integrity against invasions by members of the national society. This phenomenon can be analyzed from several perspectives, but in this case an examination of its ecological aspect and some ideological links is appropriate in order to contribute to a better understanding of the historical portion of our study.

The most salient and positive characteristic of the slash-and-burn agriculture practiced by the Asháninka is its ability to maintain the general structure of the preexisting natural ecosystem. An ecosystem can be defined synthetically as "a system of biotic and environmental interaction."[27] More than a modification of the environment, the Campa cultivation system seeks an integration of the cultivated parcel into the environment; rather than redesigning the landscape, it seeks to imitate it. A Campa *chacra* begins by imitating or mimicking the jungle through the degree of generalization of the cultivated species of plants. The tropical forest in its natural state is a *generalized ecosystem*, that is, one in which a great and very diversified variety of species exists in a situation of dynamic equilibrium. A *specialized ecosystem*, however, is one in which there are a few species concentrated in high numbers. Most recent human utilizations of natural habitats consist of changing generalized ecosystems into specialized ecosystems. We say recent utilizations in a relative sense because it is obvious that only with a certain type of economic development came the need to establish intensive cultivation or single crop cultivation. Within a domestic mode of production like that of the Asháninka, there is no room for the establishment of a specialized ecosystem. In this aspect the Asháninka are typologically related to the thousands of other human groups in the tropical forests of the world that establish a similar type of ecological relationship with the environment. Thirty-six million square kilometers of the earth's surface are covered by tropical forests, and in them live two hundred million people who practice a type of slash-and-burn agriculture with the same general characteristics as those of Campa horticulture.[28] The extreme efficiency of slash-and-burn cultivation is based on using the habitat without substantially modifying the preexisting plant diversity index, and maintaining its natural composition while substituting a selection of plants of human interest. It basically involves the functional introduction of plants useful to humans into the niches of the preexisting biotic communities. Obviously there is an alteration of the original ecosystem, but one that is produced by a systematic substitution that attempts to reproduce the original pattern.

The development of this basically mimetic type of agriculture does not respond to coincidental circumstances. It is not a result of chance; it is instead a rational application of knowledge and experimentation, a science. Anthropology and human ecology have worked toward clarifying these facts in recent years, and it has become ever more clear that the rationale of indigenous slash-and-burn agriculture results from a profound and refined knowledge of the environment, its animal and vegetable resources, biological and seasonal cycles, climatology, soils, etc. As an example, we can state that the Asháninka classify more than seventy varieties of *ivénki*, a magical and medicinal plant that to academic botany is just one: *Cyperus piripiri*. Likewise, when we state that the agriculture practiced by the Asháninka is an imitation of the original forest, we are implying that the ecological knowledge of this group includes complete control and awareness of the cycles of the jungle. There is full knowledge of that paradox of the jungle: a very delicate layer of fertile soil, constantly threatened by erosion but capable of sustaining abundant animal and plant life through quick and very well defined cycles, in which material and energy are constantly transformed. And there is knowledge that in order to avoid erosion, it is indispensable to maintain this cycle through all those practices that members of the national society define as "primitive" and that can be summarized schematically as follows.

(1) The size of the parcel should be small, and the parcel must be surrounded by forest to keep the soil temperature relatively low and to slow the biochemical process of proliferation of bacteria and the disappearance of mushrooms, which causes "latterization," or mineralization of the soils. The maintenance of a relatively low temperature is aided by the presence of trees within the cultivated parcel; they produce shade and slow erosion.

(2) The slashing and burning of the trees is not only a way to clear the land but is also a process of transferring to the soil the rich nutrients stored in the vegetation.

(3) The regeneration that occurs in the cultivated parcel through the process of secondary succession is assisted by the practice of not weeding the field; nothing is taken from the parcel other than edible plants.

(4) In the cultivated parcel, the Asháninka reproduce the same type of "architecture" that the forest possesses: an abundance of shade, the presence of stumps of cut trees, which slow erosion with their roots, and the accumulation in the soil of decomposing material.

(5) The parcel contains a great variety of cultivated plants with different growth cycles (from three to eighteen months for corn, haricot bean, and cassava) and different soil nutrient requirements.

All of these characteristics are summarized by a specialist as follows: Indigenous slash-and-burn agriculture is a system in which "the natural forest is transformed into a harvestable forest."[29]

This type of ecological adaptation, whose most salient characteristics we have described, has permitted Campa society to live and prosper for centuries in an extremely delicate and difficult environment. Nevertheless, the long process of territorial invasion initiated by the Spaniards more than four centuries ago and continued to the present day by the national society has altered the situation, especially for those Campa Asháninka subgroups that have suffered the brunt of colonization and have been forced to retreat to ever smaller territories. The change occurs especially in terms of quantity and quality of available land. Local segments of Peruvian society have always tried to occupy the areas along the rivers because they are the richest in productive soil: alluvial lands whose fertility is renewed by yearly flooding appropriate for permanent agriculture. This territorial occupation has meant, for the Asháninka, a retreat to the poorest high mountainous areas, and consequently a deterioration of ecological relationships and of their economy in general. It is a process that has been accurately examined by archaeologist Donald Lathrap,[30] who has demonstrated with archaeological evidence that before the European invasion, the banks of the navigable rivers of the Peruvian jungle were densely populated by native societies that based their economy on cultivating alluvial soils, fishing, and hunting mammals, which abound in the tropical forests near waterways.

It is obvious, therefore, that it would be deceptive to interpret contemporary Asháninka society based on the assumption that its ecological relationships and economy have remained relatively stable and suffered few substantial changes. Even the Campa Asháninka groups of the Gran Pajonal, who along with those of the Ene River can be considered the most isolated, have undergone a long process of economic deterioration and resulting adaptation; they too are a product of the long process of colonialism. But it is above all the confrontation with the various types of expanding internal Peruvian frontiers that has necessitated a number of adaptations: the Spanish system of *encomiendas* (natives granted to Spanish conquistadors by royal decree) and *obrajes* (sweatshops); the missions; the *haciendas* (large landed estates); the harvesting of rubber and wood; and the capillary invasion of tribal lands by dispossessed Andean peasants. These are all phenomena that, on the one hand, can be classified as manifestations of a unique historical process of growth in the national market economy, and on the other hand, can create different conditions for Campa society, and consequently peculiar adaptive responses in each case.[31]

The members of national society who occupy tribal territories—whether they be missionaries or large landowners, wood harvesters or small settlers—carry out a series of drastic changes and practices that are a cultural extension of a fundamentally "European," capitalist, ecological relationship, in which a classist socioeconomic structure and an extreme division of labor are combined with a conceptualization of the use of the environment in terms of monoculture, that is, a *specialized ecosystem*. This type of ecosystem tends to produce rapid deterioration of the natural resources of the forest, especially the soil. The forest is perceived as an enemy that must be destroyed and razed, not as an ally to be protected. Resources may be destroyed because the national economic system has required and promoted such action historically and up to the present day. The ideal goal is to replace the forest completely with the product currently imposed by an arbitrary and irrational national market precisely because it is colonized and dependent. Thus the sugarcane of the colony or the coffee, rice, and fruit trees alternate in the role of destroyer of the fragile equilibrium of the tropical forest.

It is the economic and political organization of the country that necessarily establishes the ecological relationship in terms of specialized ecosystems for those segments of national society that occupy native lands. The consequences are not long in coming. The disappearance of the forest (which ironically, in their ignorance, the settlers consider a sign of progress); the appearance, in its place, of barren savannah; the destruction of the fauna; and the consequent disappearance of the ecological equilibrium—in a word, *ecocide*—inevitably and constantly pushes settlers to expand the territories they occupy. In their march toward indigenous lands, the invaders leave in their wake eroded jungle, barren plains, or huge estates, which, due to the volume of economic investment, are the only ways to exploit the resources that can endure the damage caused by the establishment of a specialized ecosystem. It therefore seems false to allege that this ecocide and the resulting ethnocide are the inevitable price that must be paid for "modernization" of the indigenous territories; rather, they are the concomitant and structural condition of a society that is capitalist in its mode of production and colonialist in its political organization. The history of Campa Asháninka society demonstrates that this is a forced, secular, and dramatic participation—at times direct and at times indirect—in the development process of the capitalist world.

SOCIAL ORGANIZATION

One of the most fascinating and complex aspects of Campa Asháninka culture is, without a doubt, its social structure. It is important to bear in mind that we are dealing with a relatively numerous tribal society, almost certainly the largest native group of the South American tropical forest, and one that is scattered over a vast territory. These are conditions that make anthropological generalizations difficult. An initial, basic typological division of the group can be established on ecological grounds: the Asháninka of the river banks versus those of the Gran Pajonal highlands and the interfluvial mountainous zones. From a linguistic and cultural point of view, four regions can be tentatively established: Three areas correspond to river valleys (the Ene, the Perené, and the Tambo), and the fourth area is the Gran Pajonal.[32] To date there have been only partial studies carried out in one or another of the different regions; therefore, the construction of a "Campa Asháninka sociocultural model" is still difficult. Since the time of our fieldwork, however, new studies have been done, and many points have been clarified.[33]

If we wish to produce quantifiable sociological formulations beyond a pure anthropological model, we should consider other variables, including aspects related to the presence of the economic and demographic frontier of national society. It is obvious that cultural characteristics, especially those related to the social organization of Campa Asháninka groups that are in close contact with agents of change, should be interpreted according to the new social and economic framework that includes these groups. Anthropologist John Bodley mentions three types of modern adaptations in this regard. The Asháninka of the first group are those who attempt to maintain their independence and traditional lifestyle through isolation in areas of the interior not yet reached by the national economy. The second group is composed of those who have established a relationship of *enganche*, or "company store" debt, with settlers; they work in the "boss's" fields or give him products of the jungle in exchange for manufactured goods. The Asháninka in the third group attempt to acquire economic independence within the local economy. Some have joined Catholic or Protestant missions, and others cultivate small amounts of commercial products that they sell at local markets. The measure to which these different socioeconomic situations modify the traditional model of social organization is a point that can be clarified only through research comparing quantifiable sociological data with the ideal anthropological model.

It should be clear that the great, omnipresent dynamic of change—to which the Campa subgroups are subjected through their interaction with various, expanding, Peruvian economic and demographic fronts—makes us skeptical about the absolute validity of an anthropological model that, by its very nature, is static and ideal. We realize that this argument undermines our case and questions the very principle of the elaboration of anthropological models, but the Asháninka constitute an interesting and extreme example in this sense. Some of the characteristics of their social structure can be adduced as proof of the capacity of this society to adapt to the most diverse historical demands. The same Asháninka who knew how to be flexible when dealing with the conquistadors, missionaries, and *encomenderos* (colonists granted Indians to work for them) and who adapted to new conditions, in our day have found a way to adapt to modern economic boundaries while maintaining elements that ensure their self-identification as members of Campa Asháninka society and culture. This ability to maintain their own ethnic identity, together with a high degree of elasticity and flexibility in their social organization, may explain, at least in part, the success of their secular resistance to the aggression of the surrounding society. This resistance is all the more amazing when we consider that the vast majority of tribal societies in the South American tropical forest have been unable to successfully overcome the crises of the first coercive contacts with whites. It should be possible to examine this phenomenon from three main angles: the aspect of relative biological immunity, the socioeconomic and ecological perspective, and the ideological level. In our study, less ambitiously, we will deal only with some of the ideological topics.

Some Social Characteristics

As explained above, the nuclear family is the basic unit of Campa society. Along with the nuclear family, there exists an extended family resulting from polygynous marriage. In our research in the Gran Pajonal we confirmed only sororal polygyny or preventive sororate. A man marries two or more sisters, some of whom may not yet have reached puberty. Later studies by Bodley demonstrate that less than 3 percent of marriages are polygynous and that the great majority of these are limited to two wives.[34] In polygynous marriages all wives, whether or not they are sisters, have their own fires and sometimes their own houses. This type of compound family offers some advantages: more sons and sons-in-law to help with crops and in the subsistence economy in general, as well as more *masato*, or fermented drink, prepared by the women. This latter element is essential to the social prestige of the head of household.

The subject of postmarriage residence reveals an essential characteristic of Campa society: mobility. In all social units, from the family to the so-called modern communities that have formed near haciendas or certain missions, mobility fulfills a primordial function and at the same time demands great elasticity of social organization because each movement tends to produce a certain degree of readjustment and reorganization. In the life cycle of a Campa man or woman, changes of residence, journeys lasting several months, and returns after many years to the same place one lived as a child are all normal events and, as will be seen, all of Campa culture is functionally organized around this characteristic. There are several reasons for this mobility; although we separate them for analytical clarity, they are all functionally linked and are based on a structural nexus between the society and its ecological relationships.

We have seen that marriage means movement of the husband to the residence of his wife's family of socialization. This matrilocal or uxorilocal residence can be classified as a service of the son-in-law to his wife's parents through farmwork and a contribution to the family economy. But it can also be considered an accumulation of experience for the young candidate, a conclusion to the socialization process. The duration of this period may vary, but usually the new husband and wife move into their own home at the birth of their first child. Bodley mentions as an ideal norm a period of virilocal residence after the uxorilocal residence.[35] It is important to consider the issue of postmarriage residence from an ecological and economic perspective. For a young Campa man, the first marital unions are not necessarily of a definitive nature. There is a "trial" period of some years that begins shortly after puberty, in which the young man goes through several "marital" unions. To understand this custom, it is important to bear in mind that the ideal or preferred marriage is between cross cousins (a man marries the daughter of his mother's brother, who is also the daughter of his father's sister) or between any persons classified as cross cousins in the Campa kinship system. In his study, Bodley[36] concluded that only 1 percent of the marriages he studied were actually between cross cousins. More common, and also more culturally ideal, are marriages involving exchanges of siblings: Two or more brothers marry two or more sisters. It is obvious, however, that these ideal marriages can be achieved only in a small percentage of cases; consequently, for a young Campa man, the alternative is to begin a long pilgrimage through tribal territory in search of a companion with whom he can establish a marital relationship. During this trial period several factors may intervene to influence his decision, including but not limited to considerations regarding his wife's relatives, where to establish residence, and problems with family rivalries. Children born of these nondefinitive unions remain with the mother in case of dissolution of the union.

If we return to the question of postmarriage residence and mobility, we can understand why oftentimes what appears to be a marriage is nothing more than a trial union, in which the "son-in-law" resides and provides his services in the home of his "wife's" parents for an indefinite period. If the couple decides to make the union more permanent, the husband will look for a place, clear the land, prepare the fields for planting, and build a house. This activity takes at least a year and a half. When the cassava has grown and is ready to be harvested, the couple will move to the new house. The new residence may be neolocal, that is, equidistant from both sets of parents; virilocal if the husband's father enjoys special prestige; or uxorilocal if the new residence is near that of the wife's family. The Asháninka demonstrate great flexibility in this respect as well and make decisions based on various factors, including social prestige, security, and ecological advantage.

Many other factors determine the mobility of this society and, as we have said, all are somehow linked to economic and ecological factors. An initial category of movements can be defined as periodic; these are the long hunting expeditions carried out during the dry season; collective fishing trips with poison (*barbasco*), which local Campa groups from surrounding areas join; visits to relatives; and "trade" expeditions. In all of these movements, all family members may participate; therefore, the house and fields may be temporarily abandoned for weeks or months. The trade expeditions are eminently male activities and are generally carried out only by small groups of men.

There is a second category of more permanent moves that are due to more obviously ecological reasons as well as ideological motives. Because of the poor soil of the tropical forest, a Campa farm suffers a process of erosion and progressive exhaustion; after three or more years of cultivation, it is therefore more advantageous, in terms of "energy costs," to abandon it and start a new one. In some cases the clearing of a new lot near the home is impossible because of the topography or the poor quality of the soil, or simply because all of the good lands were already worked in previous rotations. In this case the residential unit must move to a new location, perhaps very far away. The construction of the new house and farm divides the family temporarily when the husband and older sons move to the new location to do the work. The death of a family member is another reason for abandonment of the home and later the farm. A place of residence may also be abandoned because hunting and fishing have become scarce, there are too many mosquitoes, or the area is infested with jaguars. Disputes with neighbors and fear of armed or magical attacks are sufficiently valid reasons to change residence. In some cases the proximity of Peruvian settlers is the reason for moving away.

As can be inferred from the cases of mobility that we have mentioned, the implicit cause of these movements can be found in the ecological conditions of Campa Asháninka society. The lack of good soil and resources, masked by the apparent abundance of the jungle, does not permit high demographic concentration or permanent agricultural use of one territory. Nevertheless, the current situation seems to be the product of the geographical marginalization to which this indigenous people has been subjected by Peruvian society. It is likely that before the invasions, control of the richest alluvial ecological regions had led this group's organization toward other formulas, but this is a statement that for the moment remains in the realm of hypothesis.

The minimal social unit, the nuclear family, is economically self-sufficient; this independence is reflected in the social sphere. A man feels closely linked to his primary relatives and to his secondary matrilateral relatives who are actual or potential members of his wife's family of socialization, but these relationships do not go beyond secondary relatives. The Pajonalinos (Asháninka residents of the Gran Pajonal) who can provide firm genealogical information about their bilateral tertiary relatives are few.[37] With regard to differences in generational levels, Ego cannot go back more than two ascendant generations (father's parents, etc.), and most of the time the informant (man or woman) has no knowledge of the primary collateral relatives of his or her matrilateral or patrilateral grandparents.

For these structural reasons and for economic-ecological reasons, the Asháninka rarely organize in associations larger than the ones we have mentioned as temporary expansions of the nuclear family. In some cases, especially in the northeastern part of the Gran Pajonal, there are small villages composed of the dwellings of some conjugal families residing together. These may be villages of an extensive polygynous family that, in addition to a husband and several wives, includes unmarried sons and daughters as well as married daughters with their respective husbands and children. In some cases we have confirmed that the prestige achieved by the founder of this group may result in his married sons practicing virilocal residence. The result is that a group of this nature may be composed of forty or fifty individuals, giving it the appearance of a band in which the founder enjoys a certain authority.

A special form of transitory grouping is the war or raiding party based on territorial and kinship ties or circumstantial ties with very specific interests. The Asháninka have been and still are excellent warriors, but during the four centuries of contact with whites, their war expeditions have undergone many modifications with regard to their causes, form, and frequency. Since the latter part of the nineteenth century, raids have been caused and stimulated by rubber contractors and large landowners who need slaves for their businesses. In the eighteenth century, war parties took part in the great messianic rebellion movement led by Juan Santos, and they were mainly war expeditions against viceregal troops. Before this time, the possible reasons for raids included the kidnapping of women, family revenge, and territorial defense against members of other linguistic groups or members of one's own tribe. Many of these causes continue to exist; added to them are new reasons that serve as stimuli for the aggressiveness of the Asháninka: mainly the abuses committed by settlers and by government officials.

This aggressiveness, repressed under the new circumstances, finds two escape valves: suicide and "friendly" duels or competitions between adult men. It is difficult to say with certainty if these two cultural forms, which surely belong to Campa tradition, have received new impetus as a result of the arrival of white and mestizo settlers. We can assume, nevertheless, that the causes of discontent and frustration have been increasing from the time of the first contacts in the sixteenth century to the present day, and therefore that suicides and duels must have undergone an analogous process. At present, settlers intervene in the armed conflicts[38] organized by the Asháninka and try to stop them; the result is that the Asháninka simply organize these activities in more isolated areas.

We can represent the social relationships of an adult Campa man graphically by drawing several circles, some concentric and others intersecting. The smallest one includes Ego's family of socialization. From there his social relationships immediately expand to the sphere of consanguineous matrilateral relatives and patrilateral relatives; Ego's family of procreation is included in this circle. Beyond these relationships, there is a very wide area that includes all other Asháninka of the same territorial zone and neighboring zones with whom Ego can maintain friendly relations; in some cases this circle may be broken, which, depending on the seriousness of the situation, compromises Ego, his nuclear family, or some of his relatives. Obviously in this (zonal) sphere of social relationships one can also find individuals who have kinship relationships to Ego.

There are other Asháninka as well. They live in other regions, dozens of days' journey through the jungle. Rarely does a Pajonalino go beyond the mouth of the Ene River or up to the interfluvial cordilleras east of the Pangoa. The most knowledgeable know that all of these areas are inhabited by groups that speak dialects or varia-

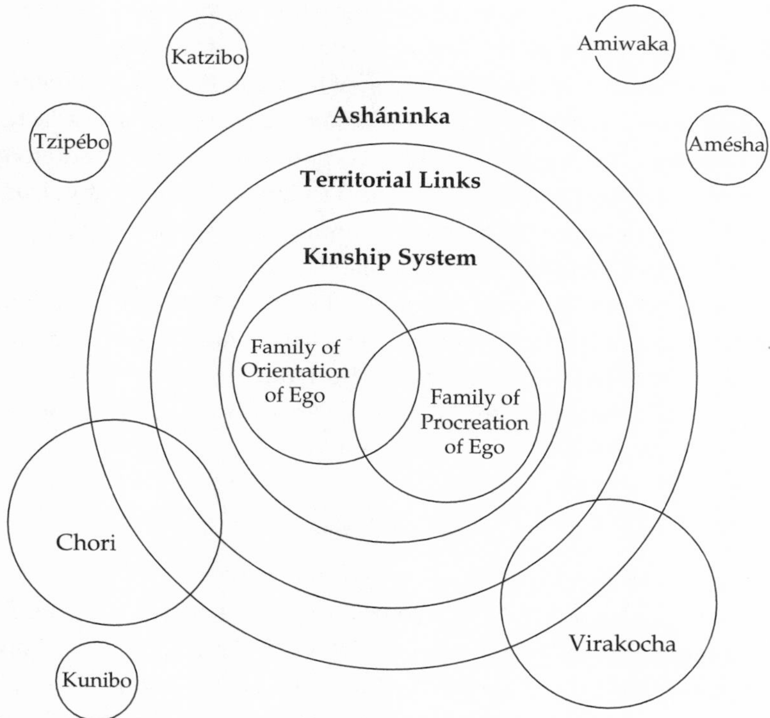

1. Tribal and ethnic names used by the Pajonal Ashéninka people.

tions of their language; others are unaware of the geographical borders of their language, but everyone considers himself or herself Ashéninka, that is, Campa, members of one cultural stock that has local varieties.

The Ashéninka—people, men par excellence, *atzíri* (human beings)—do not live alone. In their territories there are now whites: *virakocha*, with whom relations are not always peaceful. There are also Andean settlers, who occupy their territories with crops; they are the *chori*. Farther away, downriver, there are "other peoples": Kunibo, Tzipébo, and Katzibo; farther east are the Amiwaka; and toward the Andes Cordillera are the Amésha (fig. 1).[39]

Obviously this schematic representation of the social relationships of a Campa adult is ideal. Furthermore, it is based on our observations in the Oventeni region of the Gran Pajonal, and therefore reflects a partial viewpoint whose reference point is precisely the Pajonal. The diagram should not be interpreted as being ordered according to the cardinal points. The positions of the other linguistic groups, Andeans, and whites are arbitrary with regard to the places they occupy outside the kinship system; the diagram, however, does show the degree of social relationship existing between them and the Asháninka with sufficient precision. In fact, the Asháninka maintain social relations only with the chori and virakocha, for whom they may work, but there is greater impermeability with other indigenous groups.

A Flexible Model

In this section we will attempt to offer, in a very synthetic manner, the ideal model of Gran Pajonal Campa society. It is, as has been mentioned, an anthropological model we designed a posteriori on the basis of data gathered in field research. It is therefore a model that results more from our process of intellectual design than from cultural self-awareness of the informants; in this sense, very few Asháninka would express this model in the same way that we have. Anthropological work proceeds through a process of analysis and synthesis; along the way all the facts, details, fragments, and inferences are joined, combined, and processed. No informant alone could recognize all the cultural data contained in a study of his own society; similarly the anthropological model of his culture and society would seem strange to him, unless he went through the same process of analysis and synthesis. An anthropological model aspires to be a coherent synthesis in which each member of the group, although he or she may possess only some fragments of his or her culture, can recognize the totality and its essential characteristics. The extent to which the model can be universally understood by the members of the society in question is related to the researcher's capacity for understanding, analysis, and synthesis. It is clear, however, that beyond the sociological aspects of frequency of occurrence, distribution, and variation, there are cultural elements that, because of their universality within Campa Asháninka society, appeal to common experiences, ideas, and symbols shared by all members of the group.

Excluding a few modern communities that include several families in the same village and are a recent phenomenon associated with missions and haciendas, Campa Asháninka society has a settlement pattern that we can define as dispersed or nonnucleated. The most important residential unit, which is also the most permanent in nature and is economically self-sufficient, is the nuclear family, or in some cases, the extended polygynous family. Each residential unit, that is, each nuclear or extended family, has its dwellings in the center of a clearing, which, in turn, is located in the center of the fields or farm; the jungle forms a sort of protection around the farm. A river or creek must be relatively close. From the central yard a series of paths or trails, barely perceptible to the untrained eye, connects the dwellings with the river and, passing through the farm, with several points in the jungle. Some trails end a short distance away and are used by the men of the group, especially boys and young men, to reach certain places where they can hunt birds or small animals. Other paths lead to a more extensive and complex network that connects the family with its neighbors and with other Campa Asháninka families in more distant places. There are Campa trails that take many weeks to cover on foot. The distance between any two residential units varies greatly according to the region and consequently the natural resources found there. In riverbank areas, the waterway is the principal axis along which *chacras* are located; they are close enough to each other to permit voice communication. Whistles, shouts, cow horns used as trumpets, and the small drums used for dances are some of the many means used to communicate with neighbors. This ideal distance between neighbors cannot always be maintained, especially in mountainous areas. In the Gran Pajonal, a day's journey or more may separate one family group from another.

The Asháninka have no word to define the nuclear family, but they identify the kinship group with the expression *nosháninka* (my family, my people). The word is applied to bilateral kin and to individuals with whom a fictive kinship relationship has been established, as in the case of a man who includes another within his kin as a *pawachóri* (father's brother) or alternate father, a term of respect that also requires respect. A Campa adult may have nearly fifty people among his *nosháninka*, but because of the type of dispersed settlement, social and territorial "boundaries" do not coincide. Unlike other tribal societies in which there is a convergence between the social group and the space it occupies, between the "tribe" and the village, between the system of moieties or clans and the location of the houses, and between the kindred and the communal house or longhouse, in the case of the Asháninka the territorial and social boundaries are less defined and therefore more dangerous, but they are also more flexible. As a logical extension, it can be said that a Campa, upon leaving his *chacra*, confronts unknown quantities in terms of social relationships. Some of the other residential units surrounding his may be part of his consanguineous kin or his kinship by election; these are the *nosháninka*, who constitute the local group that shares a delimited but unstable territory. Beyond those limits, however, unknown social boundaries begin, especially because the extreme mobility of this ethnic group constantly modifies the social panorama and its composition. The local group can also be defined as a dispersed community in which, in some cases, one man, the *curaca*, has greater authority. The members of the various residential units of this local group may collaborate with each other for fishing, hunting, and mutual protection, but cooperation is less frequent in agricultural tasks. The monthly nocturnal feasts where they drink *masato*, sing, and dance in the central clearings are the most frequent gatherings of the members of the local group.

Some of the most salient characteristics of Asháninka society can be linked to this type of social structure. Once again we mention flexibility and adaptability in social terms. An Asháninka man is accustomed to moving frequently within the area of the local group as well as throughout the entire ethnic territory; this familiarizes him with other tribal members with whom relationships are based, not on kinship ties, but on ritual or ideological ties (see the section on "sacred trade" below). These treks, contact with strangers, and new and different experiences lead the Asháninka to make judgments that are more personal and less group oriented. The social control generally exercised in a tribal society by a constant associative life, in which daily face-to-face relationships act as permanent pressure on behavior, carries little weight with the Campa Asháninka. Campa interpersonal relationships seem to be less subject to the pressure of group opinion and depend more on personal evaluation and decision. This is clear even in the most formalized and institutionalized aspects of interpersonal relationships. Because social relationships tend to be mainly of a direct interpersonal nature without group mediation, Asháninka culture has developed two areas of extreme formalization for personal social interaction: rituals or etiquettes of greeting, which are part of the larger context of "sacred trade"; and the social and ritual architecture of the houses. Ritualization of greeting and speech and ritualization of space act as a script for appropriate social and cultural behavior because the social control exercised by the presence of the group is very minimal.

For the visitor who reaches a Campa Asháninka hamlet through the dark jungle trail and the twilight of the cassava field, the most surprising thing is the cleanliness and almost dazzling light of the clearing. Perfectly packed down, the light-colored or reddish soil is free of the plants, vines, and bushes that constitute the panorama and obsessive perception of the jungle; this space immediately suggests the contrast between "culture" and "nature." Apparently there is no rigid pattern for the organization of space. The location of the houses is not governed by a strict cardinal orientation; even size and shape have a very wide margin of variability. A certain constant is found, however, in the shape of the clearing, which tends to be rounded, and in its location in the central part of the *chacra*. Nevertheless, the Asháninka clearly classify and distinguish two types of houses. This is an architectural differentiation. *Pankotzi* is the open house with a simple roof of two slopes made of palms and a square or rectangular floor plan. This is the type of construction frequently found in the lowlands and warm regions near the rivers. *Tantótzi* is the closed house that is rectangular but complemented on one or both short sides by an apse, which gives the house the appearance of an oval. This type of construction is more common in the highlands and cold regions, such as in the Gran Pajonal, where the temperature may go as low as eight to ten degrees centigrade.

Regardless of which type of construction is used, an Asháninka family residential unit will always have two houses: the *intómoe* and the *káapa*. In this case the distinction does not refer to the architectural and physical characteristics of the construction but to its social and ritual function. The *káapa* can be defined as a house for single men and guests, or the men's house, whereas the *intómoe* is the women's house, the house where the nuclear family lives and where cooking and sleeping occur, the house par excellence. During his life cycle a Campa man, and to a lesser degree a woman, resides for varying periods of time in one or the other type of house according to his or her social age, temporary status, and role relative to the situation at the time. The presence of the *káapa* is structurally linked with the characteristics of mobility mentioned above. The man in Campa Asháninka society is mobile by definition and is so from the early years of his life.

An Asháninka boy lives in the *intómoe* until puberty; at that time he receives his G-string, which he will wear under his tunic, and goes to live in the *káapa*, the single men's house. He sleeps there and eats food prepared by his mother, which he picks up at the *intómoe*; from the *káapa* he leaves on hunting and trading trips and especially in search of a female companion. At times, he will return after a few months as a son and guest, but little by little he will begin to separate from his family of socialization and especially from his mother. The cutting of this psychological umbilical cord is fundamental to the Asháninka personality. Abandoning the *intómoe* is a traumatic experience; one young friend told us that for many nights he cried alone on the raised palm wood floor of the single men's house, surrounded by the darkness of the jungle. The myth of Tzía, the little bird that in primordial times committed incest by raping his own mother and was later killed by his father, codifies this norm, granting it sacred value by linking it to an archetypal situation.[40]

The *káapa*, however, is not just the temporary residence of the unmarried sons; it is also the house where the partners (and perhaps future husbands) of the daughters stay. Campa Asháninka travelers on trading visits also sleep in the *káapa*. On these occasions the rituals of space and speech find their most intense expression. The visitor, if he is not a *nosháninka*, must conduct himself with extreme prudence and special observance of ritual norms. He will announce his presence from a distance with the horn or with special shouts that follow very precise rules. It is not only discourteous to surprise inhabitants, but it can also be dangerous. Once in the yard, the traveler will approach to within a few meters of the *káapa* and, standing with his back to it, will wait, at times more than an hour, for the head of household to greet him from inside and invite him in. This period of silence or uncertainty has a variable duration, the causes of which have been difficult for us to determine, but it seems clear that the relative social position of both participants plays an important role. A *curaca* will take his time before inviting a guest into the *káapa*. Once inside, the men sit facing each other. The wife will bring the cassava or the *masato*, and a long ritual conversation will begin, conducted in a special tone of voice and using reiterative forms. The content of the conversation includes information about the visitor's place of origin and kinship group in an attempt to find a connection and discard all possible suspicion. Meanwhile, the owner of the house and the guest exchange the woven cotton bags, the *táato* or *sarato*, of small possessions that they carry over their shoulders; this begins an exchange of gifts. A cane box containing annatto paint, a comb, a knife, a skein of cotton thread, or a mirror might be exchanged. Then come more serious trade negotiations. If the guest decides to stay the night, he will sleep in the *káapa*; if his wife and children are traveling with him, the women will sleep in the *intómoe* and all the men will sleep in the *káapa*. This hospitality can last for days or weeks and doubtless will be repaid in the future. In this way a constant circulation of goods and ideas—that is, of culture—a continuous establishment of social ties, and a readjustment of friendships and enmities guarantees unity, cohesion, and ethnic self-identification to this society, which is fragmented into thousands of units that appear to have few ties to each other.

Attempting a schematization, the dangers of which we are aware, we can affirm that in Campa Asháninka society and culture, men and the male constitute the mobile element; they are the hunters, the travelers, the traders, the warriors, and the potential husbands, who reside temporarily in the *káapa* of other families. They are the peripheral and constantly mobile part, so to speak, of the society. With them circulate objects and information; they themselves are a mobile network through which the culture lives and circulates. The women, in contrast, are the more internal, nuclear, and stable part of Asháninka society. Because they are charged with tending the crops, the real economy of the society depends and is based on them. Because they are tied to the land, the house, the *intómoe*, and the children, their mobility is restricted. They are the catalysts, the stabilizers, and the keepers of the culture in its least variable and least dynamic aspects. They are the ones who fulfill the principal role of socializing the children, and they are the ones who primarily select which cultural elements will be transmitted from generation to generation.

The complementary opposition between male mobility and female stability seems to be an essential part of the Asháninka societal model. An understanding of the social and cultural dimensions of this model must be complemented, however, with an analysis of its ideological support, which we will examine in more detail in the last chapter of this book. Nevertheless, we can already advance the idea that the equilibrium between change and tradition, between adaptation to new external circumstances and dissolution by cultural inflexibility, is achieved through the tense relationship between female stability and male mobility that seems to color all of Campa Asháninka culture. This is an existential attitude that we define, simply by analogy, as *gnostic*. As will be seen in more detail in the final chapter of this study, in Asháninka thought, the human condition and the present order are caused by an abnormal behavior; this is an erroneous situation that, directly or indirectly, produces errors. Error, as a possibility of abnormal action, is a consequence of ignorance and the cause of *perdition* of humanity, which was primordially transformed into animals. In this regard, it is important to bear in mind that the concept of being lost has force and meaning in the present daily life of the Asháninka. The same expression used in myths to indicate the transformation of men into animals is used in daily language to indicate the possibility of becoming lost in the jungle, a very frequent eventuality. Error and ignorance of norms are causes of real and symbolic perdition. The consequence of this concept is a gnostic existential attitude: Knowledge saves; ignorance leads to being lost. Knowledge is, in essence, respect for Campa Asháninka cultural norms. This conception is offered as a nucleus of resistance in the face of potential acculturation produced by the advance of the national society.

THE SPIRITUAL WORLD

If the Asháninka's relationships with other people can be represented horizontally, their relationships with the sacred world must be symbolized on a vertical plane. The *atzíri*, or human being, is in the midst of a vertically ordered cosmos, whose limits are the upper world and the subterranean world. Man is on the earth not as the expression of a cosmic dialectic represented by superior good and inferior evil; rather he is on the surface of the earth as a traveler toward other cosmic zones, which he will reach regardless of his moral behavior. Death will put an end to this journey and open the new path. But there are other "deaths" in the life of a Campa Asháninka that permit him to ascend or descend to mysterious sacred spaces. Dreams, visions (which may or may not be assisted by hallucinogens), lived myths, and various initiation paths can give man contact, though perhaps fleeting, with these worlds of life after death. The same earthly spaces where one lives—the jungle, the small lakes, the rocks, the caves, and the open spaces of the *pajonales*—represent "openings" into these extrasensory worlds. "Nature" is not alone in offering initiation routes; "society" itself, the culture, also possesses entryways. It is the dead, not yet resigned to their present condition as members of a new society and inhabitants of a new world, who appear to the living, seeking old kinship or friendship bonds. The vision of a *peyári*, the corporeal portion of a dead person—that element that is destined to wander eternally on earth separated from its spiritual essence, which, in contrast, has access to the upper and lower worlds—causes a mystical trauma that can lead to death. Only the *shiripiári* (the shaman) can attempt to save the affected individual.

For Asháninka society the *matzíntzi*, the person (usually a woman) who practices black magic, is the main actor in a drama in which she reveals to her victim the secrets of the magical realm of the culture. Again the *shiripiári*, who is familiar with all the cosmic spheres and is an expert traveler in the universal elements, will be the only human capable of reestablishing the temporarily lost order.

This entire cosmological system is contained in myth, where it finds its best support. All that is believed and done on these planes has been and is constantly being revealed in myth, thus reactualizing a knowledge of paradigmatic acts carried out in archetypal time, *in illo tempore*.[41]

This is not the place to pause for a detailed analysis of Campa Asháninka spiritual culture, but it is appropriate to point out an aspect that, throughout four centuries of relations between the Asháninka and white invaders, has influenced the formation of a type of judgment present in nearly all writings about this indigenous people. This is the difficulty of discovering a ritual, or something that a Christian mentality in the last four centuries might interpret as such, within this spiritual world. Except for the nocturnal gatherings marking the lunar cycle, it is difficult to find other cultural forms that could have suggested to missionaries and travelers the existence of a structured religious system. Naturally there exist rites of passage, funeral rites, rites of divination, exorcism, and other rites, but their subtle nature escaped the superficial observations of white visitors. Even twentieth-century ethnologists have been insensitive to this religious message; they have gone so far as to openly deny the existence of any spiritual form among the Asháninka, even though this spirituality had been perceived, albeit imperfectly, by the first Jesuit visitors.

This attitude has indelibly marked the nature of relations between whites and indigenous people and still has an influence at present. The Campa Asháninka are truly the savages; they do not even have a religion; their conquest and submission will represent salvation for them and is a duty of the western Christian. This perspective allows for a better understanding of the complete ignorance that has surrounded a phenomenon as profoundly religious as the Juan Santos rebellion (see below). This ignorance is shared by viceregal Peru and by modern historiography.

Before we conclude these ethnographic notes, we must mention, albeit briefly, an extremely important cultural phenomenon in Asháninka society. This is barter or exchange of gifts or sacred trade, which, far from being only economic and social in interest, must be understood as an eminently religious feature. The profound meaning of the institution has been synthesized by Gustave Van Der Leeuw in the formula *do ut possis dare.*[42] *Dare, c'ést se mettre en rapport avec . . . ; participer á une deuxiéme personne au moyenne d'un objet, qui proprement n'est pas un objet mais partie, morceau, du moi. Donner, c'est apporter dans l'existence étrangére quelque chose de soi-même, en sorte qu'un lien solide se noue.* ("To give is to establish a relationship . . . ; it is to become part of another person through an object, which, strictly speaking, is not just an object but a part, a piece, of myself. To give is to put into the other's existence a piece of myself so as to establish a solid link that ties us.")[43] Marcel Mauss[44] said that for many primitive peoples, refusing to give or receive a gift is the equivalent to a declaration of war; it signifies rejection of the *communio.* This is because implicit in the offering is a mystical force that gives cohesion to the group, vitalizing it in a communion. Causing objects of value to circulate is the same as causing grace to circulate, according to Marett.[45] This is why the Asháninka do not trade or exchange (in their understanding of the term) with everyone. Whites and Andeans are excluded from this chain of credits and debits, where esteem and prestige, and consequently the individual's position within the group, are played out through generosity: "I have my chickens at my house. When someone asks me for them, I give them [because] one should not be stingy," says a Campa song. A man who does not give generously to others is not a completely "socialized" individual; he is tacitly shunned by his society. A child has to learn the rules of this game from a very tender age because not following customs and etiquette—not respecting the guest, not giving him food, or not trading generously with him—means breaking this flow that unites people; it means breaking communion, an offense against society itself. Given these considerations, we can better understand why the punishment of a child who breaks the rules is very severe. One who receives acquires something of the essence of the possessor, and this would be dangerous if there were not a corresponding gift.[46]

Ayúmpari is the word that defines the man with whom one engages in the sacred trade relationship. It is untranslatable; it does not mean customer, or trader, or friend. *Niyúmpari*, 'the one with whom I exchange gifts': He does not belong to my family or my kinship system; I might not even know him, but he speaks my language; he is an Asháninka. He knows the proper greeting, accepts my food and gifts, and repays them with others. He might come from very far away, bringing tunics, annatto[47] paste (the sacred paint that defends against visible and invisible enemies), ceramic pots made near the Perené or Tambo Rivers, gunpowder, machetes, and the precious salt, which is almost the traditional currency. Salt—from the mountains that form one of the last cordilleran ridges and that penetrate the jungle almost like an Andean offering to the forest inhabitants—has always been an extremely important element of exchange for the Asháninka, as well as for the other groups of the central jungle. It is difficult to attribute a monetary category to it because, as we have pointed out, we are not in an exclusively economic perspective; nevertheless, historically its importance stands out as compared with other elements of exchange. At present shotguns, cartridges, and knives—that is, western goods—are supplanting salt in its role as "currency," but not completely. For the Ashéninka of the Gran Pajonal, which is several days' travel from the Mountain of Salt, the arrival of an *ayúmpari* bearing a basket of salt can solve the problem of the long trip, the work of extracting the salt, and all the risks entailed in leaving home. A caneful of annatto, a skein of cotton thread, or a caneful of tree resin can be sufficient payment.

At times an *ayúmpari* may think that he has not been adequately compensated; this leaves a debt and the commitment of paying it off as soon as possible. Months or years may go by, however, and the creditor will pass up no opportunity to remind the debtor of what he owes. The spoken word must then acquire all that mysterious force and potency that determines and commands attention and respect. "One who pronounces words sets powers in motion."[48] There are powers that can increase with a rise in tone, with the appropriate rhythm, or with repetition and that lead almost to the fixing of the discourse in a formula: a litany whose success depends not so much on content but on adherence to form. Because basically this is the renewal of an oath or contract, what is sought is revitalization of the consecrated word.[49] In these *collections*, as Spanish-speaking Ashéninka call these arguments, there are insults and accusations; the two *ayúmpari* threaten each other in the most violent way: with death, with magical attacks. Again the word is charged with dangerous powers that must be countered with other words, shouted more loudly in the face of the opponent and reinforced with gestures. The arm is raised, beating the rhythm, while the foot violently stamps the ground. Suddenly the argument decreases in intensity; the two *ayúmpari* take advantage of this to catch their breath. Other people may have gathered around them. The men begin new trade negotiations; the women talk quietly in a separate group. No one seems the least bit interested in what the two *ayúmpari* are saying. Again the argument may explode violently. It will follow the same cycle as before: the same violence of words and gestures inevitably followed by calm. Afterward each of the traders will go on his way. There is no ill will, only the certainty of having wisely used the force of the spoken word. The response to ethnological curiosity is, "If I don't speak loudly, it's not right; he won't pay me. That is how it's done."

The importance of the exchange of gifts was not well understood by the explorers of past centuries. Only some seventeenth-century Franciscan missionaries realized the strategic significance of possessing the Mountain of Salt. On it depended the trade and social ties of a large part of the central jungle Asháninka. This will help us to understand the reason for the efforts of the Franciscans, and of the Spaniards in general, to achieve military control over that source of supply.

The brief sketch of Campa culture that we have set forth here has brought us closer to an aspect that is rarely appreciated in white visitors' accounts. This is the intense sacredness that pervades this society. To the Asháninka the world is a sacred totality saturated with forces, powers, positive or negative "spirits," or polyvalent beings. "Nature is not exclusively *natural* because the cosmos is a divine creation; created by the hands of the gods, the World is permeated with sacredness."[50] Everything in the world shares this numinousness, the *mysterium tremendum* that infiltrates even the most simple daily gestures and that binds all human existence in a constant interplay of powers, obliging humans to harmonize or balance with them in order to preserve their physical and spiritual integrity.

The absence of grandiose community rituals, the lack of showy forms of prayer, and the extreme discretion of the Campa Asháninka with respect to all their ideas have deceived most missionaries and explorers who have had the opportunity to live among them. This may explain, at least in part, the phenomenon of Asháninka resistance to white and mestizo cultural penetration. After four hundred years, this indigenous society remains immutable in the face of foreign advance. It withdraws from its ancient territories if the pressure is too great; it enters into contact if it so desires and withdraws again. The phenomenon of acculturation can be considered minimal for this indigenous people of the Peruvian jungle. Some foreign elements have been installed in the cultural complex, but there has never been a renunciation of Campa Asháninka tradition in favor of indiscriminate surrender to new cultural ways.

The path of growing disintegration down which many groups of the Peruvian jungle have been forced as a result of the establishment of missions has not been followed by the Asháninka.[51] Rarely have they resigned themselves to living in groups in large mission villages, which are contrary to their deepest traditions; they have never abandoned their language to learn Quechua, the lingua franca; and the most external aspects of their culture have not been substantially modified by the presence of whites. A resistance of this sort can be explained, in large part, by a strong and conscious adherence to their own spiritual world, a transcendent world that permeates all of Asháninka culture.

CHAPTER TWO

Mythical and Mystical

CHUNCHOS AND ANTIS

Around 1500 Vicente Yáñez Pinzón discovered the mouth of an enormous river on the Atlantic coast of South America, but nearly half a century would pass before a thorough exploration of the Amazon would be conducted. The account of the 1542 voyage, written by Father Gaspar de Carvajal, would be published in *Historia general y natural de Indias* by the chronicler Gonzalo Fernández de Oviedo. Thus began a long series of writings about Spanish penetration into the Amazon jungle: a cycle of chronicles, accounts, and letters referring to *entradas*, or expeditions into the jungle; a cycle whose conclusion in time is difficult to establish because it appears again well into the seventeenth century.

Sixteenth-century Spaniards used the word *entrada* (entry) with a double meaning: the action of penetrating the jungle, and the mountain pass used for that penetration. The passes generally took their names from the closest highland city; thus, to the south were the passes or "entries" of San Juan del Oro, Camata, and Cochabamba, and farther north those of Rupa Rupa and Chachapoyas. The passes, however, could also be referred to by the name of the closest jungle tribe.[1]

Spanish penetration into the jungle began immediately after the occupation of the coast and highlands of Peru and was carried out through the same mountain passes that served as normal communication channels between the Inca Empire and the eastern region. In 1535 Alonso de Alvarado and thirteen soldiers managed to reach the jungle through the natural pass of Chachapoyas. A year later he repeated the feat, crossing the Utcubamba River and the Bagua region and founding San Juan de la Frontera, which would later become the city of Chachapoyas.[2] Two years later, in 1538, Pedro de Candia used the southern pass of the Amarumayo (the present-day Madre de Dios); he crossed the Paucartambo Mountains and finally emerged near Carabaya. The exploration was continued a year later by Pedro Anzures de Campo Redondo, who in five months crossed the Beni, established contact with the Mojo Indians, and returned to the highlands in Ayaviri.[3] At the same time Alonso Mercadillo was seeking his fortune through the center of the cordillera. From the city of Jauja he proceeded to Huánuco, and from there he followed the course of the Huallaga or Chupachos River. This is the expedition to the Chupacos or Chupachos, which might be considered the first discovery of the Amazon, three years before Francisco de Orellana's expedition. According to the document discovered by Varnhagen, twenty-five of Mercadillo's men entered as far as Machifalo, a province that Carvajal's account describes as located between the mouths of the Napo and Putumayo Rivers.[4]

Some of these expeditions are described by chroniclers Pedro Pizarro, Pedro Zárate, Francisco Gómara, and Pedro Cieza de León, but they are not of interest for our purposes here. We are instead concerned with explorations of the Asháninka region.

Before the arrival of the Spaniards, there were contacts between the Inca Empire and the eastern populations. Although there is a lack of written documents, or the documents are limited to a few vague, imprecise references noted by chroniclers, there is other evidence of an ethnological nature that proves these relationships. In book 7, chapter 14 and in book 12, chapter 17 of his *Comentarios reales*, El Inca Garcilaso de la Vega discusses the Incan expeditions to the Mojo and the Chiriguano. The indigenous chronicler Juan Santa Cruz Pachacuti also deals with the imperial attempts to conquer the jungle, but our study cannot benefit from any of those data because the picture is presented with little clarity.

Based on a division proposed by Víctor Andrés Belaúnde, Raúl Porras Barrenechea[5] describes three types of Andean incursions into the jungle:

(1) Emigrations of chiefs or discontented tribes seeking refuge in the mountains. Pedro Cieza cites the example of Ancoallo, chief of the Chanca, who fled to Moyobamba and Chachapoyas. After the conquest, the Inca themselves took refuge in Vilcabamba, and Quechua-speaking populations of Andean culture were found by Franciscan missionaries along the Huallaga River in 1643.[6]
(2) Fruitless Incan expeditions into the heart of the Amazonian jungle.
(3) Successful expeditions of conquest to upper jungle regions. The expedition of Pachacutec Yupanqui, mentioned by the later chronicler Antonio Vásquez de Espinoza, can be included in this category. Pachacutec entered as far as Xauxa and "continued on to the province of Tarama and subjugated it along with other populations to the east."[7] Though not very explicit, this is a reference to an Incan military expedition to the indigenous group that concerns us here: the Asháninka.

At the time of the first references to Spanish expeditions to the jungle, a series of terms referring to the indigenous people who inhabit it also makes its appearance. These include several names with multiple meanings, which are therefore of little help in an ethnological reconstruction. Some names have survived the years and have been used for centuries; others appear only once from their resting place in the archives. Some have changed meaning to the point of losing their original significance. Perhaps the term that appears most frequently in the early writings is *Chunchos*. It is an Andean term, a somewhat derogatory term used to refer to the eastern populations. But the word *Chuncho*, which is still used, has not always been unambiguous. Although for the Andean settlers *Chuncho* meant simply "inhabitant of the jungle," for some Spaniards the term acquired a limited and specific meaning. Thus Pedro Anzures, upon setting out for the Beni, intended to reach the Chunchos, whereas the Greek Pedro de Candia, in his conquest of the province of Ambaya, makes no mention of them. At times the term indicates only the tribes of the Amarumayo (Madre de Dios) and Omapalcas (Beni) Rivers. In other cases the word *Chuncho* is applied to the jurisdiction of Larecaja in the province of La Paz. Herrera and Garcilaso de la Vega refer to the Chunchos; to the latter they are the Mussu or Mojo conquered by Túpac Yupanqui. In the sixteenth century, the Chunchos were tribes from the eastern foothills of the Andes, an indefinite area in the process of being conquered.

After the name's first specific uses, its meanings expanded beginning in the seventeenth century. The word *Chuncho,* however, seems to indicate the indigenous people east of Cuzco and Puno more than the northern populations.[8] The term was similarly used by Jesuit Father Miguel Cabello de Balboa, author of *Miscelánea austral,* when in 1595, near the age of fifty, he carried out an expedition and mission to the Chunchos in the Polobamba (Apolobamba) and Carabaya area. These Indians "are a people of the Andes, not far from Chuquiambo; all are heathens and no Spaniards have ever reached them."[9] As early as 1594 Cabello de Balboa, in a letter to Viceroy Marqués de Cañete, used the word *Chuncho* to refer to the indigenous people who occupied the Apolobamba Valley beyond Camata.[10] Almost thirty years later, Franciscan Father Gregorio de Bolivar carried out a new expedition into the jungle of Cuzco and the highlands. In a report he sent to the king of Spain in 1628,[11] he did not limit the name Chuncho to the jungle dwellers of the south but applied it to all known groups of the eastern Peruvian viceroyalty.

The history of the word *Andes* is even more curious. It is difficult now to establish the exact meaning it had in the Quechua of the empire. It is true that it indicated "east" in the quadripartite division of the Inca cosmos: the Antisuyo. The name *Andes* makes its appearance in the first writings about the jungle, but unlike its present usage, which is restricted to the mountains, its range of meaning was much broader. Of the first accounts, that of Juan Alvarez Maldonado is perhaps the only one that uses the term *Andes* to refer to the cordillera, that is, as a synonym of *sierra*.[12] About ten years later, in 1582, a description of the province of Jauja was written by royal order. Several residents of the city signed the document, including Felipe Guacra Paucar, "Ladino Indian who has been in Spain."[13] In this official document, it states that the Indians of the Xauxa territory did not suffer from illnesses; they only became ill when they went down to the hot country, "such as the sea coast and the Andes."[14] In the usage of the residents of Xauxa, the *Andes* are the jungle, the upper jungle (cloud forest) that forms the borders of their province. The magistrate of Huarochirí used the name *Andes* with exactly the same meaning some years later.[15] We refer to Diego Dávila Brizeño, who recounts an indigenous legend recorded in Yauyos, in which there is a struggle between two local gods that ends when the god Pariacaca defeats Guallallo and casts him "to the Andes, which is a jungle in the province of Xauxa."[16] Another 1586 account describes the Sángaro River and states that, after running a long way, "it joins the Xauxa River in a narrow and very hot valley, through which it flows until reaching the Andes; it is a plentiful river believed to be the main tributary of the Marañón, so renowned throughout the world."[17]

By extension, the word *Andes* came to mean the indigenous people who inhabited the eastern area of the province of Jauja. It had become not only a geographical term but also an ethnic name, an extension perhaps implicit in the name when it belonged exclusively to the Quechua linguistic context. In a memorial presented to the king in 1582, the missionary Diego de Porres referred to the Andes Indians who inhabited the Cuchoa or Marcapata Valleys and distinguished them clearly from the Chunchos, who were located farther south, some sixty leagues from the city of Cuzco.[18] Also Father Joan Font, whom we will discuss in greater detail below, often used the expression *Andes Indians* in his final statement to refer to the indigenous people of the jungle of Jauja Province.[19]

Within approximately forty years, the ethnic-name meaning became definitively rooted in usage. *Andes Indians* were the inhabitants of the jungle region located in eastern Jauja Province; the name began to be limited to certain Indians, and its usage was very different from that of the word *Chuncho*. In 1643 the *teniente* (lieutenant) of Tarma, Juan Fernández Darana, wrote a letter recounting his efforts to find Father Illescas and his companions, from whom nothing had been heard since 1641. This Spanish colonial authority reported having traveled more than fifty leagues from Huancabamba to the lands of the Ipillo and the Abitica, all among the "Andes nation."[20] The area explored by Juan Fernández is Asháninka and Amuesha territory. In Father Diego de Córdova Salinas's chronicle, the expression *Andes Indians* appears constantly, alternating with *Indians of the Andes*.

By the mid-seventeenth century, the term *Andes* included two meanings: the geographic one and the ethnic one. In the first meaning, *Andes* is the forested area east of the mountainous country of Jauja, Andamarca, and Huancavelica, especially the upper jungle;[21] in the second, the *Andes* are the indigenous people who live in these areas, not all of the jungle inhabitants, who are generally called by the more generic name *Chunchos*. The ethnic meaning of *Andes* survived until this century, although in the bibliography of the last thirty years it has fallen into disuse. The geographic acceptation has had the opposite fate, expanding to include the cordillera, not only the Peruvian part but also the entire range of the South American continent.[22]

THE PILCOÇONES

Two means of jungle exploration were used in the sixteenth and seventeenth centuries: two types of expeditions with distinct purposes that may have had the same mind-set. Mythical and mystical individuals succeeded one another in the zealous search for earthly fortune or the Kingdom of God in the Peruvian jungle. The same inspiration and faith sustained both in a race in which the existence of the Indian was important only as a useful means to reach their goal.

They searched for the Paititi or El Dorado, myths that had traveled with the conquistadors from Spain, or heaven, or both. Faith in the Paititi slowly declined and was practically nonexistent when the missionary, the mystic, appeared in the eighteenth century. Nevertheless, in the sources left by these two types of expeditions, a certain difference in interests is evident. There are always extremely scant data regarding the indigenous people and virtually no descriptions of human types or information of ethnological value; the missionary, however, invariably offers more reports about the indigenous people and their numbers. The missionaries' writings are generally directed to their superiors in the order, who wish to know the number of Indians seen; these documents are therefore often true censuses. The legacy of the travelers of mythical mentality is smaller. The name of an immense river, the Amazon, is owed to Carvajal, according to whom women like those of Homeric tradition clashed with Orellana's expedition at the mouth of the Río Negro. We also have the fables of the Ewaipanoma, who "have eyes in their back and their mouth between their breasts": the ancient story of Pliny carried in the cultural baggage of some conquistador. These old legends are tenacious; they survive to our century, when they reappear disguised as scientific interest, as explorations carried out in the name of progress for the jungle regions.

The Franciscans arrived early during the viceroyalty of Peru. They were in Quito in 1533, but not until 1546, during the height of the civil war, did Father Francisco de Santa Ana found the first monastery in Lima. There are indications that they had already established themselves in the nearby Pachacamac Valley. The Jesuits—the new order born in the same years as the conquest of Peru—did not arrive until 1569 and had to be temporarily housed in the Dominicans' monastery, where a relatively recent antagonism was soon rekindled.[23] Despite its late appearance on the Peruvian scene, the Society of Jesus was the order that began and developed the most vigorous mission activity in the jungle.

In fact, in 1582, when Martín Hurtado de Arbieto organized the conquest of the Manarí, Pilcoçon, and Mamorí Indians, he was accompanied by two priests and one brother, all Jesuits, whose names are unknown[24] but who presumably are the same ones who would appear a dozen years later, again working with the Pilcoçones. In 1575 Viceroy Don Francisco de Toledo[25] issued a document granting Hurtado de Arbieto conquistador's privileges in the area of Huánuco and "in the provinces of the Manarí and Pilcoçones and Mamorí, all residents of said province of Bilcabamba."[26] The only surviving document from this expedition is a brief declaration made to the magistrate of San Juan de Lúcum in Vilcabamba by a witness, one Toribio Bustamante. The 1592 declaration states that Hurtado de Arbieto and the three Jesuits were accompanied by sixty-five soldiers because the Pilcoçones were at war. The account continues as follows:

> And it was a public and widely known thing . . . that having reached said Pilcoçones Indians, they welcomed him in peace, and he founded and populated the city of Jesus, where they lived for many days, until said Indians rose up and killed some soldiers . . . and burning the houses . . . with flaming arrows that they shot at said houses. For this reason they were forced to leave said land, and they came to the city of Guamanga.[27]

It has yet to be established which area and which Indians Hurtado de Arbieto and the Jesuits visited. There is information about the Pilcoçones starting in 1571, when Hurtado de Arbieto was appointed by Captain General Viceroy Toledo to fight Incas Titu Cusi Yupanqui and his brother Túpac Amaru, rebels in Vilcabamba. With the death of Titu Cusi, the new Inca Túpac Amaru was pursued by Spanish troops under the command of Martín García de Loyola. There are extant official documents regarding this Spanish expedition into the Cuzco jungle. In an official report by Francisco Valenzuela, it states that he, together with Martín García de Loyola, pursued the fugitive Inca to "a large river referred to as of the Pilcoçones, where they built rafts, which they boarded, and they traveled downriver . . . until they reached the town of the warring Manerí Indians. . . . [There] they caught him and brought him to said city of Cuzco."[28] The document is vague with regard to where the Pilcoçon Indians were located, but this tribe was likely in the upper jungle because it was the first group that the expedition encountered after leaving the eastern mountainous region of Cuzco.

Presently in all the jungle area surrounding Cuzco on the east, there is an Arawak-speaking tribe that is linguistically and culturally related to the Asháninka: the Machiguenga group. Its area of greatest concentration is the Urubamba River and its tributaries. There is no reason to think that the Machiguenga are recent arrivals in this part of the jungle, and it can be accepted with substantial certainty that their establishment east of Cuzco dates from pre-Columbian times.

Don Francisco de Toledo provides further information regarding the Pilcoçones. After executing Túpac Amaru in the imperial city, the viceroy headed for Lake Titicaca, La Paz, and Potosí. He participated in the expedition against the Chiriguana and, probably upon returning from this mission, wrote a document that is useful for defining the location of the Pilcoçones. The document bears the date 20 March 1573, but the place where it was written does not appear. It is a letter to the king of Spain regarding matters of war.[29] It states in the pertinent part,

> Following the cordillera south, through Tarama (Tarma) and Bombón and the Xauxa Valley, which are all Christian Indians, is the province of Mama and the Pilcoçones at the Mayomarca River; they are heathens and warlike; those of Mama live on the border, and the Pilcoçones live more in the interior in the Vilcabamba area of governorship, conquered by Martín Hurtado de Arbieto by order of his Excellency Don Francisco de Toledo, viceroy of these kingdoms. Martín Hurtado de Arbieto is now governor of those provinces.[30]

Further on, the document names some groups found south of Cuzco and east of La Paz. These include the Opatari, the Arabano, and the Chunchos, tribes that Toledo includes in the governorship given by Castro to Juan Alvarez Maldonado.[31]

While Hurtado de Arbieto was conquering the area east of the Urubamba River and perhaps reaching the headwaters of the Amarumayo (Madre de Dios) River beyond the Pantiacollo Range, Juan Alvarez Maldonado was devoting his attention to a more southern zone. The latter's expedition occurred fifteen years before that of Hurtado de Arbieto. Fortunately we have received a description of the journey and discoveries of Alvarez Maldonado;[32] from these documents it is clear that the Pilcoçones were located, at that time, along the Urubamba River and even farther north. Alvarez Maldonado provides a list of tribes, in which the name *Pilcoçones* does not appear, and the groups mentioned are all indigenous groups found east of La Paz, probably belonging to the Chapacuara[33] linguistic group.

The Pilcoçon Indians thus become a little more defined, and their geographical situation becomes clearer to us. We know positively that the conquistadors did not use this term to indicate the jungle populations east of the highlands and Charcas, and that they preferred it to designate the Indians of the Urubamba River and the Vilcabamba and Huamanga areas; it is significant, however, that this term is related to the Quechua language. A possible hypothesis is that some Andeans might have used this term to refer to the upper jungle populations. The word is Quechua and not Aymará; that is, it was picked up by the Spaniards from their Quechua guides from Cuzco, Vilcabamba, and perhaps Huancavelica.

We have paused to consider the issue raised by the name *Pilcoçones* because the term can certainly be considered a synonym of *Machiguenga*—whose appearance in the bibliography is more recent—and of *Campa*, which first appears in the documents from the second half of the seventeenth century.

THE JESUIT FONT

The most interesting expedition into the central jungle of Peru is, without a doubt, that of Font and Mastrillo. Jesuit Father Joan Font and Brother Nicolás Durán (or Nicolás Mastrillo) began exploring the jungle east of Jauja and Andamarca in November 1595, and it appears that they did so without the complete authorization of their superiors. The account that exists is very simple. It consists of two letters. The first was written by Font on 5 November 1595 to Provincial Father Joan Sebastián from the Inopay Valley; the second was written to the same authority a few days later by Nicolás Mastrillo.[34] The Jesuits continued exploring, but there is no existing documentation of these later expeditions. Nevertheless, the expedition had an interesting duration and an interesting end, about which some documents do exist.

The letters of Font and Mastrillo constitute the first somewhat detailed account of the Asháninka. All previous sources contain only vague references or simple mentions of the Pilcoçones or the "heathens of the Andes"—approximate data that simply tell us that there were contacts, but nothing more. The aforementioned exploration, however, is very important because it initiated the Spaniards' expeditions into this area of the jungle. The two Jesuits preceded by forty years the arrival of the Franciscan missionaries, who would visit the Campa in 1635. None of the Franciscan mission histories that we consulted provides this information, perhaps because the name *Pilcoçones* does not suggest to historians a specific relationship to the present-day Asháninka.

The residents of Jauja and Andamarca maintained relations with the inhabitants of the nearby jungle, as is evident in the aforementioned document, "Descripción," by Guacra Paucar.[35] These trade agreements and good neighbor relationships are confirmed by information cited by Font and Mastrillo, who found a native of Andamarca who had been living with the Pilcoçones (Campa) for fifteen years in the middle of the jungle.[36] Although among the indigenous peoples of the mountains and jungle there were agreements, based perhaps on ancient Inca penetration and on mutual respect, the situation was not the same with regard to the Spaniards. Font's words describe the situation with substantial precision:

> The Indians, frightened and fearful of the Spaniards' treatment of them, have become strong there [in the jungle], and no one

> has been able to reach them, although it has been attempted many times by many routes, although the Indians have often come out peacefully to search for, buy, or, as they say, rescue some things . . . , and [they have] come out many times to ask the priests to teach and baptize them; they have not only made this request of the magistrate of Xauxa but have also come to Lima to ask the Viceroy to send them only priests, because in no way do they want any other Spaniards to enter there.[37]

It is not easy to judge these statements objectively. Font may slightly exaggerate the Pilcoçones' desire to receive visits from missionary priests in his eagerness to justify to the ecclesiastical and civilian authorities his evangelization plans, but the other statements can be considered substantially truthful. In fact, while the members of the expedition were approaching the first Asháninka hamlets, they were observed and watched by the jungle dwellers, who feared the arrival of Spanish troops. This was in spite of the fact that an Indian had been sent from Andamarca to let the Campa know of the expedition of the Jesuits, who were accompanied only by Spanish guide Juan Vélez, a friend of the Pilcoçones, and by some bearers from the mountains. Later, once Font and Mastrillo were lodged in the home of a Campa named Veliunti, they had to dispel doubts about their true intentions. The Asháninka were not convinced of the true identity of the priests. They thought they were Spaniards, soldiers. Their guide Vélez had to clarify that the priests were not seeking gold or silver, nor did they wish to enslave the people. The most skeptical Indian was convinced: "[N]ow I believe that they are priests because they eat what we give them."[38] This was an extraordinarily strong argument that convinced the Indians of the good faith of this visit. The Campa knew how to respond generously. Font points out that Veliunti's son, "of beautiful face, lively and joyful . . . , wanted to talk to us and show his joy and did not know how; he demonstrated it with much laughter from time to time and by cutting some branches that blocked the road."[39]

The Font and Mastrillo expedition stayed a few days at Veliunti's home. The Indians built a chapel there, "like their houses," with wooden columns, a palm branch roof, and cane walls.[40] The Asháninka hospitality was perfect. Each Indian who approached the two priests offered them honey, or a monkey, or birds "and other little things." These rules of Asháninka etiquette and hospitality, which few other travelers would understand even in our own century, are noted with precision by Font:

> [A]fter the caciques sat down, Mangote placed before Veliunti the gift that he had brought for him, which was a cage containing a turtledove, and he began to speak, and he spoke for more than a quarter hour without anyone interrupting him. Then Veliunti began to speak, thanking him, and his speech lasted another quarter hour. Then the other cacique took over and told him to open his gift, and Veliunti thanked him with a speech as long as the other one.[41]

Font and Mastrillo continued their journey of exploration. They crossed plains as green as "one can desire in the most populous areas of Spain";[42] they crossed three rivers with water up to their waists and traversed one on a raft. Font noted, "[W]e were guided very lovingly by Cacique Mangote, who accompanied us. He of the Pilcoçones, who is also called Chiquiti, twice sent us meals on the trail, and in his home he welcomed us with harmonious flutes."[43] This is how the Asháninka greeted their first European visitors in 1595.

Naturally Father Font and Brother Mastrillo are not very generous with ethnological data: They are men of the sixteenth century. Nevertheless, their two letters contain some data of cultural value apart from the information useful for historical reconstruction: testimonies that further confirm the ethnic filiation of the Indians they visited. "The Indians . . . are taller and more lively than those of the Pirú; their dress is only a long red shirt; their faces are well proportioned and would look better if they did not paint them red."[44] Obviously these are general observations that allow us only to deduce that these indigenous people belong to the great "pre-Andean" ethnic area;[45] it is not possible to reach more specific conclusions. The possibilities, however, can be narrowed down with other information provided by the Jesuits. The Indians live "divided and spread out, without any type of town, throughout all these plains and forests."[46] Because of the geographical area visited, there are only two alternatives: Asháninka group or Amuesha group. Of course, in order to accept this conclusion, one must also accept the relatively static ethnic situation of the area at least over the last four hundred years, but an opposing viewpoint is absolutely unsustainable with ethnological arguments. To choose between the two alternatives presented, we can turn once again to the letters of Font and Mastrillo: "All these subjects speak one language, which is not difficult to pronounce but is more difficult to learn because our interpreter does not know it very well."[47] The Amuesha language cannot suggest such an observation to a Spanish speaker. Amuesha is extremely difficult to pronounce, whereas for a Spanish speaker the Asháninka language is phonetically quite easy.[48]

No more could be asked of sources written in the late sixteenth century. Some brief reports on the spiritual life of the Pilcoçones must be viewed with caution. It was necessary to make a favorable impression on the provincial priest in order to obtain concessions, and therefore, there were crosses in all the Indians' houses.[49] Font and Mastrillo, however, thought that these indigenous people were very close to the gospel, easy to convert to Christianity, and morally superior to many Europeans: "They have only one wife; there is no stealing among them, nor do they generally get drunk; in fact, they even consider it a disgrace, especially in public."[50] But the two Jesuits were mistaken about the weakness of traditional convictions among the Asháninka. Their account continues: "[A]s far as I have been able to tell to date, they have no idolatry";[51] from this, Brother Mastrillo deduced that the Pilcoçones were godless, an erroneous judgment that would eventually reach modern ethnologists through all the other sources.

In the final part of Mastrillo's letter, there is one last recognition of the generosity and hospitality of the Asháninka.[52] Few other travelers would know how to accept this courtesy, or they would take it as a right.

As has been said, the two Jesuits continued their exploration, but we have no other account of the trip's conclusion. They probably wrote no more letters, or perhaps those that existed were lost. What is certain is that Father Joan Font was greatly interested in the expedition because a short time later, during the government of Viceroy Luis de Velasco, he repeated it. He again went through Andamarca, but this time in the company of another Jesuit, Brother Navarro. Still not satisfied, Font entered the Andes three more times through Cintiguailas (Sintihuailas or Cintihuailas), that is, by way of the present-day Mantaro River before it joins the Apurímac.[53]

These explorations along the Mantaro must have been carried out before April 1601 because around September of that year, Font arrived at the court in Valladolid with two Indians, a map of the discovered country, and a letter for the confessor of the king. In it Joan Font recounted his first expedition and described and exaggerated the Pilcoçones' fear of the Spanish soldiers, adding, "[T]hey asked me not to abandon them and to beg Your Majesty to accept them as subjects."[54] All this enthusiasm, however, was not purely apostolic. In fact, before leaving Peru, the Jesuit left the one thousand leagues of the newly discovered territory in the hands of Captain Manuel Zurita Nogueral. The latter, according to Viceroy Velasco's decision, settled with two companions "in the land of the heathen Indians of the Marañón River, precisely in the Ancomayo Valley, that is, where the Mantaro River joins the Apurímac."[55]

Font's letter continues with greater strength of conviction. There is a short summary of the prior expeditions that is somewhat confusing but certainly effective, in which the new lands are described as "very populated" and "full of great things." As an extreme recourse of his dialectic he resorts to the old, almost always infallible, exotic argument: "I brought these two Indians with me for this purpose, so that returning there, they may encourage them and tell them how they come for your cause and what Your Majesty orders because they will believe them."[56]

Jesuit Joan Font soon achieved what he desired. Font asked that the marquis of Zea, eldest son of the duke of Lerma, be named protector of the newly conquered lands. This explained why the province was called Nueva Lerma. The missionary methods of the Jesuits inspired Font's plan of action. He requested the founding of a town of five hundred Indians in the Ancomayo Valley along the Cintihuailas River. There, in a seminary or "college," he would educate Indian children, who would also serve as hostages. "In the name of the Indians, I request that the task of teaching this people and running the seminary be given to the Priests of the Society. . . . It is not advisable for the bishops to get involved in matters of this town, nor to visit it, nor to charge tithes until his Holiness orders what must be done."[57] These were dangerous ideas of independence that would compromise the success of the entire project, but that must have been part of the agreement reached with the "Captain of said frontier and land of War,"[58] Don Manuel Zurita. For Zurita, Font's request established a large part of the products obtained with the work of the Indians, who would be given land, tools, and a hospital. The remainder of the products would be for the viceroy, and finally, a small portion would be allocated to decorate the church and to buy trade objects for the heathen Indians.[59]

In late November 1601, Father Font left Spain. He had a royal letter authorizing him to conquer and convert the Pilcoçones and the Nueva Lerma Indians. But the Jesuit wanted to ensure the results of his arrangement. Before arriving in Lima, he contacted the viceroy and requested a secret interview without the knowledge of the rector of San Pablo College. In March 1602 Viceroy Velasco and Father Font met and agreed that the latter should "immediately make his mission and expedition to the heathen Indians who live in the Andes and land of war, frontier of the city and province of Guamanga and the Sángaro Valley." In addition, lands extending from Abancay and Azángaro to Jauja were granted to Captain Zurita. In other words, as Marcos Jiménez de la Espada points out, "a scandalous and arbitrary jurisdiction."[60]

Despite all the precautions taken to keep the secret, the matter fell into the hands of Jesuit Rector José Teruel and even of the Dominicans. There was strong opposition: The rector wrote a letter to the viceroy, reminding him of the peaceful conversion system in use among the Jesuits and expressing his strong disapproval of Font's project. He cited the very small number of Indians who would be converted, and furthermore, he added, they were stupid, cruel, and murderous barbarians; it was not prudent to take risks nor was it possible to protect the Spaniards. The viceroy did not desist. From Aranjuez came a royal letter dated May 1602, in which the king categorically forbade Font to carry out his plans. Meanwhile, however, the enthusiastic Jesuit returned disillusioned from a new expedition to Huamanga. The geographic difficulties, lack of food, and sparse Indian population had diminished his original fervor.[61]

The entire matter came to a conclusion when Joan Font was forced to give a sworn statement under threat of excommunication. Naturally these final statements by the priest must be considered in light of the circumstances. They are pessimistic: There are very few Indians and very scattered; the most ever found in one place is twenty-four, and they may disperse at any moment. The climate is very harsh; moving from one place to another is a difficult task. He concludes, "[A]fter having considered them for many years and truly pondered, I judge and say . . . that even if I were a free cleric, there is no benefit among them, first of all because there are so few of them and they are not subjugated, with no leadership or authorities."[62] Other Jesuits also made unfavorable statements about the project. Finally, in January 1602, Father Joan Font swore *in verba sacerdotis* that the mission was not worth the effort; he also promised to remain in Lima and not attempt any new plans.[63]

Thus ended the first attempt to establish missions among the Campa. The failure should be attributed more to the Jesuits' internal disagreements than to difficulties presented by the Indians themselves. For the Asháninka, the best protection, the most effective barrier, was their own culture. They do not live grouped in towns; they are somewhat nomadic, although this characteristic is diluted in periods of two to several years; they hold firm beliefs in their traditional ideas, although these are not expressed openly or celebrated in ceremonial activities—all of these elements and the very cultural essence of this population form their best defense against "civilization" or westernization. This explains, at least in part, why the Asháninka—despite having been among the first jungle populations to have contact with the Spaniards, and despite being the group closest to the Andes and therefore the one most susceptible to colonizing influences—have kept their traditional culture nearly intact to the present day.

THE FRANCISCAN EXPEDITIONS OF THE SEVENTEENTH CENTURY

The right of conquest of the Pilcoçones was not requested by any other Spaniard after Father Font's attempts, although beginning in 1598 Lorenzo Maldonado, Hurtado de Arbieto's successor, managed to obtain a royal permit over the Campa province.[64] Maldonado's successor, Pedro de Leagui, was not concerned with the Pilcoçones area. A memoir written by his field master mentions only the Chunchos located along the Beni River.[65] Conquest and colonization were suspended in 1650; in 1681 the author of *Recopilación de Indias,* unaware of all the previous events and documents, stated that those regions were neither discovered nor conquered.

In other sources written around the same time, there is no reference to the Pilcoçones or the Campa. In a 1597 description of Peru, there is only a brief explanation about the *andes,* or jungle, stating that it was for all practical purposes unexplored.[66] The Jesuit representative of the province of Peru published an account that is very interesting from an ethnographic point of view. This document, written in Rome in 1603,[67] contains accounts of indigenous traditions in the highlands and valuable data about the Diaguita, the Chiriguano, and the Yuracare, but there is no information about the Indians of the central Peruvian jungle.

Although there are no historical data regarding conquest attempts conducted against the Pilcoçones, it is known that forty years after

Font's first expedition, the Franciscans took the initiative of evangelizing the populations east of Jauja. This time they went through the entryway much farther north.

For years, residents of the present-day mountain city of Cerro de Pasco had had contact with the "heathens." Some Andeans had planted fields in the jungle; there they traded with the jungle dwellers, who in turn risked going to the mountains. Huancabamba was founded as a result of these relationships, and the new town was turned over with parish title to the Franciscans. In 1635 Franciscan Brother Gerónimo Jiménez entered through the Huachón heights, followed the course of the Huancabamba River, and turning south, reached the Cerro de la Sal (Mountain of Salt). On the banks of the Chanchamayo River, he founded a town with a chapel, which he called by its Asháninka name: Quimirí (the present-day town of La Merced). In December 1637 Gerónimo Jiménez and Brother Cristóbal Larios attempted to explore the Perené River, but Jiménez died at the hands of the Indians.[68] The only remaining documentation of these Franciscan expeditions is the reference made in Córdova Salinas's chronicle. Brother Jiménez must not have kept a diary of the expedition.

The Franciscan attempts at exploration were repeated. In 1641 Father Illescas left Huancabamba with the intention of traveling down the Perené River. He was accompanied by two priests from Quito. There was no further news of this group until 1686, when it was discovered that they had been killed by the Shipibo of the Ucayali River.[69] Earlier, in 1643, the *teniente* of Tarma, Juan Fernández Darana, had carried out several expeditions to try to find Father Illescas. In one of his letters there is information regarding the regions explored and the Indians seen there. These were always Andes Indians of the Perené region, who did not offer significant resistance to Fernández's soldiers, although they hampered the search to prevent, according to the *teniente* of Tarma, the arrival of more Spaniards to their lands.[70]

Not everyone who ventured into the Chanchamayo jungle did so with evangelizing zeal. The first open clash between the Asháninka and the Spaniards must be attributed to a conquistador of mythical mentality. Around 1645 word spread that at the Mountain of Salt there was also gold. The news immediately brought several Spaniards to the area, who were joined by two priests more interested in gold than in the conversion of souls. The Indians welcomed the expedition peacefully, but a few days later at the Salt (Perené) River, the expedition was attacked. Two Spaniards survived and assimilated rapidly into Campa culture, so much so that one of them married a Campa woman, and the other organized the indigenous defense against a new Spanish expedition in pursuit of gold.

Francisco Bohórquez and forty-six Spaniards headed to Quimirí (La Merced) after having taken over three mountain towns near Tarma. Upon trying to cross the Chanchamayo River, Bohórquez was detained by the Asháninka, led by the Spaniard Villanueva. The two Spaniards, however, reached an agreement. After a few months, together and allied, they attacked the mountain town of Vitoc, stealing cattle, food, and women. There was no trace of the gold they had been seeking at the beginning of their adventure. This situation could not last long, however. Viceroy Conde de Salvatierra sent troops under the command of Juan López León, who in a short time defeated and captured the rebel Spaniards. Bohórquez and Villanueva were sent to Valdivia prison in Chile.[71]

In 1651 the first chronicle of the Franciscans in Peru was printed in Lima. This is the aforementioned work by Córdova Salinas.[72] It is interesting to observe that, at this time, knowledge of the Asháninka was still extremely limited. The Franciscan chronicle represents the extent of official information about the residents of the jungle missions. Córdova Salinas based his data on information received by the Franciscan missionaries who explored the jungle from Quito in 1634. There is mention of the Amazon, its sources, and the Indians living along its banks, but all the names that appear, even that of the river, seem to be of Omagua origin, that is, in the Tupi-Guaraní language.[73]

In the same year that Córdova Salinas's chronicle was published, one of the most recent conquistadors of the Peruvian jungle presented the king of Spain with a report on newly discovered and conquered lands. This is Fernando Contreras's "Representación" regarding Los Minarvas Province.[74] For our purposes it is interesting to establish to which part of the jungle that report refers. Contreras mentions an area that he refers to as "of the Minarva Indians," natives of the province of Aucaya or América Oriental, located east of the Huancavelica mines. The region occupied by the Minarva Indians was such fertile jungle that, according to Contreras, the Minarvas "live at leisure, hunting and gathering . . . [in] families [that] appear like those described in Genesis."[75] The conquistador can only be referring to the Huanta jungle, the watershed of the Apurímac shortly before it meets the Mantaro. In fact, the data he presents next support this hypothesis. This would be, then, a new exploration of the region already visited by Father Font more than half a century earlier. The distance between the newly discovered lands and Guamanga is forty leagues.[76]

Fernando Contreras's report provides interesting details. It is easy to deduce that the Indians visited by his expedition are of the Campa Asháninka family. This deduction is based on information of an ethnographic nature as well as on geographical considerations. Each family lives far from others in an arroyo or small valley; their fields are close to home. Periodically they visit each other to drink and dance. They are not warlike, although they have bows and arrows that they use to hunt and fish.

> The people are pleasant and of good size and faces; they are Spanish-like and cheerful and kind, very docile and easily subjugated, not at all like Jews . . . , but generous and giving; like Negroes, they believe very easily; they do not know how to lie; they are very trusting and do not know how to steal; . . . each man has many women, but all the women serve one, and the rest are like concubines.[77]

The conquistador adds that they do not worship the sun, the moon, or idols, but that they believe in a Lord who is in the heavens, and that there are "hell and a devil, whom they call Camagari."[78]

This is the first appearance of this Campa-language name, quite accurately transcribed and interpreted.

Without a doubt, one of the most curious and intriguing pieces of data in this entire "Representación" is the reference to the tribute that the Minarvas were to pay the *pobate*: "[E]very two years they would send tributes of beautiful feathers, honey, and aromatic vanilla to the Pobate, who is farther inland and referred to in this manner by the Minarvas, because in their language this means something like 'King.'"[79] This is an astonishing revelation that motivates Contreras on further explorations toward the east. The *pobate* lived in the Yuchiquerín Valley at the foot of a great snow-covered mountain range (perhaps the Vilcabamba Range), but the expedition turned north before managing to locate the mysterious mountain king. Contreras traveled down a river until he reached a place where three great rivers meet. It is very difficult to establish with certainty the place referred to in this part of his account. As a hypothesis this could be considered the meeting of the Ene River and the Perené, already joined by the Pangoa. What is certain is that in this place the conquistador found

> three more castes of Indians of different languages and Lords of larger and more populated provinces than the Minarvas's province; they are called Nocanganis, Canparites, Opanegis, people who were very happy to see us . . . , and I learned from them . . . much information about the many peoples there are on both sides of the river, downriver, before and after the great meeting of the two major branches of the great Marañón River.[80]

In this case the ethnological conclusion is even more difficult to reach than the geographical one. The word *Noñanganis* (*Nosangani*) can be considered as belonging to the Arawak language. No further conclusions can be drawn, however; therefore it is difficult to specify whether this is a Campa group or a Piro group because these two are neighboring tribes. With regard to the name *Opanegis*, we do not even venture a guess.

Where Fernando Contreras's "Representación" truly constitutes a contribution is in the use of the ethnic name *Canparites*. Of all the documents reviewed, this is the first one that uses the term that later would become well known and exclusive. On the basis of the scant data provided by Contreras, it is practically impossible to establish the origin of the root word *canpa(rite)*. This subject will be discussed at length below; here it is important to note its appearance in this written document.[81]

Contreras's account adds a few vague pieces of information regarding these Indians he discovered and concludes with an interesting reference to the exchange of fish from the river for salt from the western mountains. This is an allusion to the important intertribal trade that linked several tribes of the central jungle with the Asháninka of the Mountain of Salt and that was later used by the Franciscans as a means of communication and domination.

BIEDMA AND HUERTA: EXPLORERS OF THE TAMBO RIVER

After the events involving Bohórquez, the missions in the area of Chanchamayo and the Mountain of Salt were abandoned by the Franciscans, who opted instead to focus their efforts on the jungle of the upper and lower Huallaga River. Here easy successes stimulated the evangelical daring that, in the person of Father Manuel de Biedma, became a mission among the Setebo and the feared Cailliseca (Shipibo).

Biedma entered the lands of these lower Ucayali River tribes at the mission of the Panatahua (Huallaga) across the Cushabatay River, which has its source very near the lower Huallaga and flows into the Ucayali north of the present-day city of Contamana. It was 1663, and Biedma remained among the Setebo until 1665. This background information regarding Father Biedma is important because it will be evident in his missionary work years later with the Campa and in his use of words of Setebo, Shipibo, or Panatahua origin.[82] It is possible that Biedma may have spoken some of the Pano languages with considerable fluency after living in the Ucayali region.

Not until 1671 did Biedma receive permission to conduct a new expedition into the region of the Mountain of Salt. The viceroy of Peru, the count of Lemos, supported the initiative with four hundred pesos. In 1673 Quimirí was newly founded, and Father Biedma, now assigned to these missions, erected the town of Santa Cruz de Sonomoro.[83] The texts that mention this event coincide in providing a list of names of indigenous groups who welcomed Father Biedma. The name *Campa* does not appear on this list, although José Amich's *Compendio histórico*, the oldest source, inserts it. We will see below how Biedma himself began to use the term later. The "tribes" mentioned by Amich, and by Manuel de Sobreviela and Bernardino Izaguirre after him, are Asháninka groups referred to by different names according to their place of origin.

> Those who live at the foot of the mountain slopes are called *Andes*. Those who first came to give obedience were the Pangoa, the Menearo, the Anapati, and the Pilcosumi . . . , the Satipo, the Copiri, the Cobaro, the Pisiatiri . . . , the Cuyentimari, the Sangireni, the Zagoreni, [and] the Quintimiri.[84]

It is curious to note how, after more than seventy years, the name *Pilcosumi*, the old term used by the Jesuit Font, reappears.

In the years that Biedma dedicated to the new missions of the upper Perené, he studied the Asháninka language. Together with Father Izquierdo he compiled vocabulary lists and manuals for confession and translated hymns and prayers.[85]

Earlier we noted that all biographical information on Biedma interests us, especially because the diffusion and definitive adoption of the name *Campa* in all documents written after 1686 can almost surely be attributed to him. In fact, it is only after 1686 that this ethnic name is used with a previously unknown deliberateness and constancy. In the following pages we will attempt to reconstruct the process that led to this conclusion.

Father Manuel de Biedma was a great explorer of the Peruvian jungle and fortunately had the foresight to write about his journeys down the rivers,[86] which his companions did as well. In 1676 the Franciscan traveled the Mantaro, Apurímac, Tambo, and Ucayali Rivers to the point where they flow into the Pachitea.[87] We have been unable to find the report of this exploration, if in fact one exists.

Some time later, Biedma was still interested in exploring the Tambo and the Ucayali. He had heard reports of the presence of many Indians there and even of an empire, the Enim, which years earlier had sought the banishment and imprisonment of Francisco Bohórquez. Additionally, the Indian traders who came to the Mountain of Salt told Biedma about some priests who dressed like Franciscans and preached. Biedma believed they might be Father Illescas and his companions, from whom there had been no word since 1641. Encouraged by this information, Biedma told his superiors and the viceroy, the duke of La Palata, of his desire to explore that region. The viceroy supported the idea and ordered the magistrate of Jauja to help the missionary with supplies and men.[88] After several setbacks, Biedma managed to reach the Perené River only a few leagues before it meets the Ene; he christened this place Puerto San Luis de Perené (located approximately in the area of the present-day Puerto Ocopa mission). From there he sent three lay brothers, who traveled down the Perené to where it joins the Pachitea, where they found a large Cunibo town, which they named San Miguel. This occurred on 29 September 1685. After a few days, the three envoys returned to San Buenaventura de Savini, where they rejoined Biedma. There is no known account of this trip in existence.[89]

The positive reports of the expedition encouraged Biedma to carry out another expedition soon; but it was not until a year later, in late August 1686, that the Franciscans managed to carry out the project. The Lima government provided assistance in the form of a dozen soldiers and two black slaves under the command of Captain Don Francisco de Rojas y Guzmán. In early September the expedition reached the Cunibo town of San Miguel, where they were surprised to find that the Jesuit priests had gotten there first, built a chapel, and baptized about fifty Indians, "without any prior catechism or decree," as Franciscan historian Amich points out. The

Jesuits had also named authorities and left two Omagua interpreters and doctrinarians there.[90]

The unfolding of subsequent events is not relevant here in all its detail, but two facts must be pointed out: in the first place, the decision to rush Father Francisco de Huerta to Lima with news of the Jesuits' appearance on the scene; and in the second place, the return trip by Father Biedma and the rest of the group to San Luis de Perené.[91] Both Huerta and Biedma wrote accounts of these trips; in these documents, therefore, we possess the first sources of information about the indigenous peoples of the Perené, the Tambo, and part of the Ucayali.

The importance of these two sources from an ethnological perspective is obvious. Although Biedma's diary is quoted by Amich, Sobreviela,[92] Raimondi, and contemporary Franciscan historians, one must suspect that, except for Amich, none of them saw or directly consulted the document in question. Amich himself transcribed it only summarily.[93] Our searches in national archives and libraries have not yielded positive results. It is possible that Biedma's writings are now in the General Archives of the Franciscan Order in Rome.[94] Unfortunately we have been unable to obtain a copy of the text and have had to resign ourselves to working with Amich's summary. In contrast, we have had better luck with the writings of Huerta and Biedma's other companions.[95]

We will pause now for a discussion of some of the data that can be obtained from an analysis of Amich's transcription. In early October 1686, Biedma received word from some Cunibos that the Jesuits at the northern missions wanted to return to San Miguel, cross the river, and punish the Taraba (Tambo River) Indians for the death of Jesuit Brother Herrera a few months earlier. Biedma and the others resolved to return to San Luis de Perené because

> it was not advisable to wait in that town for the Jesuits or their people to arrive, because there was fear of an argument and quarrel between the soldiers of both factions, which would be a great scandal for those barbarians [the Cunibo]. That staying

> there did not imply more right of possession over those who had already been taken so many times.

In addition, Father Huerta, now in Lima, had in all likelihood explained the conflict between the two religious orders to the ecclesiastical and civilian authorities.[96]

The return expedition was organized. Chief Cayampay, baptized with the name Don Felipe, was charged with accompanying and guiding the Spaniards. The Cunibo was easily convinced to participate in the expedition with the incentive of a raid on the Piro to punish them for the death of the Jesuit brother, "and as the Cunibo were enemies of the Piro, they quickly agreed to the expedition."[97] The Spaniards were accompanied by 180 Cunibo warriors in thirty canoes.

We owe all the information, data, and names of the rivers and tribes that the expedition encountered on its trip back to the Pangoa region to Cayampay, or Don Felipe, who was "very knowledgeable about all those places because he traveled throughout the area constantly."[98] Naturally the names that the scrupulous Biedma carefully wrote in his notes are all of Cunibo origin, that is, in a Pano language; thus appear, for the first time in written documents, names of rivers never before recorded by Spaniards. The Taguanigua, Erereca, Cheopcari, Chinipú, Guanini, etc., are all rivers that have different names for an Asháninka or Piro. Obviously the tribal names follow the same rule as the place names. At the small Sampoya River, the expedition encountered Amaguaca (Amahuaca) Indians. Farther south, upriver on the eastern side in the Taguanigua tributary, lived the Pichabo and the Soboybo. Even farther away, between the Guanini (the Unini or Oveni of the Campa?) and the Guanué, lived the Mochobo. All of these are tribes of the great western Pano linguistic family,[99] but when the expedition penetrated farther and farther along the Tambo River, the guide Don Felipe Cayampay no longer named Pano groups but began to speak of other Indians: the Campa and the Piro. The Campa tribal name, practically unknown before this date, appears to be linked to a Cunibo speaker, that is, to one of the Pano languages.[100]

Does the term *Campa* never appear before this moment? To answer this question, it is worthwhile to go back a few months to the moment when the Franciscan expedition was preparing to travel downriver to the Cunibo. It was the month of June 1686. In the group was Father Francisco de Huerta, who was in charge of keeping a detailed diary of the exploration.[101] Among the first revealing data that we find in Huerta's notes, the following must be pointed out: Of all the people participating in the venture, only one was indigenous, "the Indian interpreter from the Panatahua"; there were also two blacks. Not one Asháninka or Andean took part in the expedition.[102] According to Izaguirre, the interpreter accompanying the Spaniards was a Setevo (Setebo) Indian convert from the Panatahua missions in the Huallaga River basin. It is difficult to establish on what data Izaguirre bases this statement because this information does not appear in the documents consulted; they mention, only and always, a "Panatahua Indian." The interesting thing, however, is that whether the interpreter was Panatahua or Setebo, we are dealing with the Pano linguistic group.[103] Again the information supplied to Huerta for his diary was of Pano origin. The Panatahua guide and interpreter Alonso knew the Cunibo language and demonstrated this in the first encounter with this indigenous group. All the information about the Asháninka that Huerta noted during the trip to and from San Miguel can be attributed to Alonso.[104]

The other documents from the General Archives of the Franciscan Order mentioned above confirm this supposition. For example, in Father Antonio Vital's letter,[105] the name *Campa* appears only once: in a list of tribes based (as he himself states) on information he received from a Cunibo woman from San Miguel. A similar case exists with the account of Captain Francisco de la Fuente, dated 18 September 1686 in San Miguel de los Cunibos.[106] De la Fuente also notes "information that has been acquired from the nearby people inhabiting these lands,"[107] that is, data obtained again from Cunibo informants. Among the several named tribes, Campa appears again. Finally, Captain Bartolomé de Veraun wrote an account dated 23 October 1686 in San Buenaventura de Savini after the trip.[108] Once again the term *Campa*, whose origin can be attributed to the Panatahua interpreter, is present.

The term *Campa* also appears in letters written by Manuel de Biedma to the general commissioner about mission problems in November 1685 and March 1686, that is, before the trip to San Miguel de los Cunibos. This information, which seemingly contradicts that which is set forth above, must be considered in light of Biedma's personal history. It is useful to recall his previous stay with the Ucayali River Setebo and his possible familiarity with the Pano languages. Furthermore, we must not forget that Father Biedma by this time could speak the Andes or Campa language,[109] and therefore a hypothesis regarding the endogenic origin of the ethnic name *Campa* is not completely valid. In fact, as mentioned above, the word *Campa* has no meaning for the Indians themselves, possessing only a clear derogatory connotation that is not inconsistent with our hypothesis regarding its exogenous (Pano) origin.[110]

Another hypothesis that should be noted and that suggests interesting connections is the one that relates the word *Campa* to the Tupi-Guaraní language.[111] This language was and still is widely spoken in South America, and during the centuries of the colony, it was one of the most common linguas francas in the tropical jungle. Its extensive scope can be attributed both to the intense ethnic movements of its speakers and to the work of the missionaries, who intentionally propagated it to facilitate contact with the indigenous people. Many words of Tupi-Guaraní origin became rooted in the Portuguese and Spanish of some regions of South America. In fact the term *Camba* is used in a large part of Bolivia to indicate, in a general sense, all the people of the jungle areas. *Camba* means "black" or "little black person" in Tupi-Guaraní and, by extension, is applied to jungle dwellers in Bolivian Spanish. In the seventeenth- and eighteenth-century writings, the spelling of the word *Campa* is still undefined; sometimes the *p* is replaced with a *b*.[112] It is therefore not unreasonable to think that the name of this Peruvian jungle tribe may be related to the Tupi-Guaraní language, especially because other words of this lingua franca were commonly used by some of the seventeenth-century missionaries and travelers.[113]

It is true that the adoption of the name *Campa* began slowly but surely, starting in 1685 and 1686, and that it is doubtless related to the Franciscan writings we have cited. The word *Campa* makes its appearance for the first time in subsequent official documents.[114]

ETHNOGRAPHIC CONTRIBUTIONS OF THE 1686 DOCUMENTS

We have yet to analyze the ethnographic value of the information contained in the documents related to the Franciscan expedition of 1686. From the transcript of Father Biedma's diary we can deduce a series of valuable data regarding the location of the tribes of the upper Ucayali, the Urubamba, the Tambo, and the Ene.[115]

Through a slow and often fruitless geographical reconstruction, we have been able to plot on the map some of the indigenous groups mentioned by the missionaries. The results, though scant, are of interest for the ethnology of the region. The intrusion of Pano groups into the Asháninka area appears clear from the outset (fig. 2). The Pano doubtless belonged to a more recent cultural stratum of northern origin; they possessed a technology superior to that of the pre-Andean Arawaks and managed to occupy vast areas that were previously Asháninka. Small Asháninka groups, isolated from their center, are mentioned by Huerta at the Tahuania River, an eastern tributary of the Ucayali. In 1930 Günter Tessmann mentioned Campa Indians along the upper Sheshea, also an eastern tributary of the Ucayali.[116] The Cunibo who occupied the Ucayali then formed a long appendage, a wedge intruding into the center of Asháninka territory, dividing it into two parts, the most compact of which was found pressed against the cordillera, whereas the other part was surrounded by Pano groups. A notable intrusion of Pano groups[117] into the present area of Asháninka and Piro concentration can be confirmed throughout the 1686 writings.

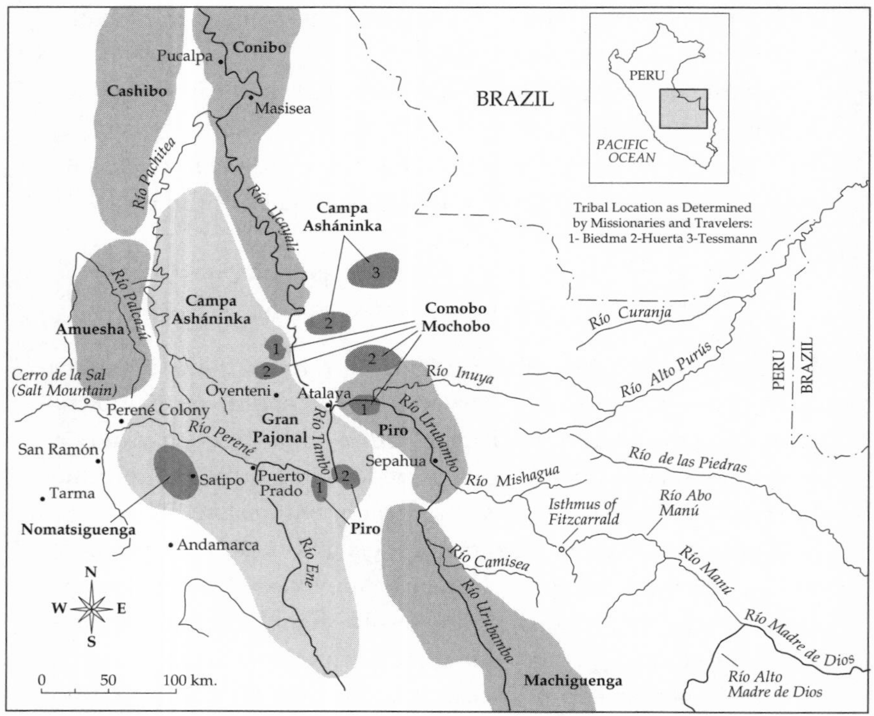

2. Ethnolinguistic areas of the central jungle of Peru.

Our statement that it was the Pano groups who were intruding into the Campa (or pre-Andean Arawak) area and not vice versa is supported by two types of evidence: ethnological and historical. From an ethnological perspective, the higher degree of technological development of the Pano populations as compared to the pre-Andean Arawaks is clearly demonstrable. Even the Pano type of social organization, though limited in some cases to a mere union of extended families, permitted better and more effective organization for war expeditions. The role of dominant group, in this case, is played by the Pano. The historical data provided by the 1686 expedition confirm this hypothesis. The Cunibo living in San Miguel and helping the Franciscan missionaries are described as pirates who were little given to craftsmanship: "[T]hey are great privateers and live by stealing and killing other nations . . . ; therefore they do not make any clothing for their wardrobe."[118] So great was the fame of the Cunibo as warrior-sailors that Father Antonio Vital advised the Franciscan general commissioner that these Indians be used for the conquest and domination of other tribes.[119] The Cunibo who accompanied first Huerta and then Biedma back to the Perené clearly confirmed their tradition of piracy. Father Huerta tells us, "The second day of the expedition of our Ene [present-day Tambo], we went ashore to rest from the hot sun, and the [Cunibo] Indians followed some tracks of people a short distance to some Campa homes and, surrounding them, they plundered their homes, capturing the women and children and stealing everything they had."[120] The Indians accompanying Huerta continued pillaging on both sides of the river until they had filled their canoes with more than forty prisoners and many objects of booty. Huerta knew how to take advantage of these abilities of the Cunibo because, upon arriving in San Buenaventura (Pangoa), he sent two Cunibo men and the Panatahua guide Alonso to the Asháninka hamlet of Sabini to get all of the inhabitants.[121]

Information of more concrete ethnographic value is scanty in these documents. The very few descriptions of indigenous people refer mainly to the Cunibo of San Miguel, the objective of the expedition. Nevertheless, the Campa are frequently mentioned as being associated with the Mochovo (Mochobo) Indians, and in some cases, with the Piro. This mingling of diverse linguistic groups must be taken into account in any ethnological analysis of the area. The phenomena of borrowing and transculturation must be examined in accordance with these suppositions.

The evangelical results of the expedition to San Miguel de los Cunibos were not destined to bear subsequent fruit. Not only were there difficulties with the environment and the Indians, but also an old controversy between the Franciscans and the Jesuits was renewed. The territorial limits of their respective areas of missionary action were not yet set in 1686. The encounter of the two orders in San Miguel led to a true accord being reached in 1687, which defined the Jesuits' district from Maynas up to and including San Miguel, and the Franciscans' district from Andamarca up to but not including San Miguel.[122] Thus the Franciscans lost the opportunity to count on the "military" support of the Cunibo for the conquest of the Campa and the Piro of the Tambo and Ene Rivers.

In July 1687, Father Manuel de Biedma traveled down the Tambo River in search of an appropriate place to found a new mission. Shortly after the confluence with the Ene, he was attacked and killed by the Piro. These were the same Piro who the previous year had been the object of a raid by the Cunibo who accompanied Biedma back to the Pangoa.[123] From that moment on, the Tambo River became closed territory for the white man, whether missionary or explorer. Every attempt at penetration was rejected by the Piro, the Asháninka, and the Mochovo, who defended the integrity of their territory for almost two and a half centuries. It was really only from 1918 on that one could travel the Tambo River with any degree of security.[124]

Only a very tenacious armed resistance by the Asháninka can explain why their conquest was always understood by the missionaries in military terms. As early as 1685, before the expedition to San Miguel, Biedma advised military occupation of the Mountain of Salt to more easily dominate all the tribes that depended on that product.[125] The project contemplated the possibility of establishing a military post on the Mountain of Salt or turning it over as part of an *encomienda* to a Spaniard, who would run the salt mines and give salt only to those Indians carrying a written permit from the missionaries. Fortunately for the Indians of the central Peruvian jungle, this project was never carried out.

The Asháninka put up strong opposition to missionary penetration. Nearly one hundred years had passed since the first expeditions, and the evangelical results were practically nil. The Indians not only refused to cooperate, but they also defended their territorial integrity with weapons. It was concluded, therefore, that only a military campaign could be successful against them.[126] The Asháninka had good reason to distrust the Franciscan missionaries, whom they associated and almost identified with their traditional enemies: the Cunibo. Obviously relations between the Asháninka and the missionaries were not facilitated by the piratical attacks carried out by the missionaries' Cunibo and Panatahua guides and companions.

On 30 August 1686 the Franciscan expedition to San Miguel was traveling down the Tambo River. Some Cunibo canoes accompanied the Spaniards. Suddenly two Indians, a Mochovo and a Campa, appeared from an inlet. The missionaries approached them, offering them needles and little bells, but the Indians rejected the gifts. In response to Biedma's doctrinal insinuations, the Campa answered "with heretical pertinence, saying that we worshipped a stick [the cross] and that their God gave them farms and food; and turning to the Conibos, he told them to watch out, that we were tricking them in order to enslave them."[127] The wise Campa theologian was right, as the sequence of later events proved. The Cunibo, willing to give in to the white advance in exchange for the new metal tools, would soon find themselves involved in forced recruitment to fight the Jívaro rebels in 1691. A few years later, tired of Spanish abuse, the Cunibo would follow the example of other tribes and manage to regain their freedom and traditional way of life through an armed uprising. The price paid to the white man, however, would never be recovered. Little by little the new diseases brought by the Europeans would decimate this group, which in the mid-nineteenth century, understanding the cause of its disappearance, completely isolated itself from the whites and their cities and began to avoid exogamic marriages. An ancient tradition was reborn among them, giving them hope for a future of new greatness and dignity, a future, however, that had been irremediably lost since 1686.

A different fate awaited the Asháninka of the central Peruvian jungle. The eighteenth century appeared on the horizon full of an ancient energy that lay hidden and dormant in almost all of the indigenous peoples of America: a messianic faith in the restoration of their own ethnic dignity.

Young Asháninka hunter, Gran Pajonal, 1964.

Poshano, the *shiripiári* (shaman) from Tzirompiani, Gran Pajonal, 1964.

Intómoe (longhouse) of a *shanchosi* (chief) from the Shumawani region, Gran Pajonal, 1964.

Young Asháninka men making drums, Shumawani, 1964.

Asháninka woman, Gran Pajonal, 1967.

Young Asháninka woman, Gran Pajonal, 1967.

Asháninka musical bow at the Franciscan mission of Oventeni, Gran Pajonal, 1964.

Young Juancito wearing his new *kushma* (tunic), Gran Pajonal, 1963.

Pashúka and Irene, mother and daughter, Gran Pajonal, 1964.

Asháninka men from the Gran Pajonal, circa mid-1960s.

CHAPTER THREE

Century of Rebellion

In the history of the central Peruvian jungle, the eighteenth century is characterized by two types of events that are different yet closely related. The first thirty years of the century represent the prolongation and end of the attempts at exploration and conversion to Christianity, which were initiated in 1595 by the Jesuit Father Font and were continued, with an inconsistent rhythm, by Franciscan missionaries throughout the 1600s. The early part of the eighteenth century marked the discovery of the Gran Pajonal, a vast area of which there had been vague information from Indian sources. During the rest of the century, however, the indigenous response to missionary attempts and Spanish penetration was expressed violently.

Practically from the first expeditions through Jauja or Huancabamba until the last great expedition on the Tambo River by Franciscans Biedma and Huerta in 1686, evangelical results had been limited. Few Asháninka groups had been incorporated definitively into the Spanish world. Although from a strictly geographical viewpoint many lands and rivers had been explored, the human aspect of the missionary situation could not be considered as thriving. In 1713, in a report to King Philip V, the Franciscans expressed discontent and pessimism with respect to the Asháninka; the converts sent in 1699 from Quimirí to form new towns were unsuccessful "because of the natural evil of the Andes Indians."[1] For these reasons, perhaps, the old Franciscan plan to occupy the Mountain of Salt militarily reemerged in 1716, when Father Francisco de San Joseph wrote to the general commissioner about the status of the "pagan" missions.[2] If the mountain were occupied, all the neighboring "nations" could be conquered and subjugated because many Indians who came from great distances on foot or by river depended on the supply of salt. Nevertheless, added Francisco de San Joseph, the task would be difficult because the chiefs had ordered all the Indians to refuse to show the trails to the missionaries, to refuse to help them, to deny them salt, and to deny them entry into the interior. The indigenous resistance was not exclusively passive. In March 1724 several Franciscans, fourteen Spaniards, and twenty Christian Indians were killed near Jesús María (the old Puerto San Luis at the confluence of the Ene and Perené Rivers). The attackers were Piro and Mochobo Indians.[3]

During these years, however, the Franciscans founded many mission centers in an attempt to counteract indigenous rebellion. Jesús María was founded at Puerto San Luis, where Biedma's 1686 expedition went ashore. Catalipango was founded a few miles to the south, on the western bank of the Ene. San Tadeo de los Antis was founded on the eastern bank of the Perené, and Nijandaris was established between Quimirí and the Mountain of Salt. Metraro and Eneno were founded even farther north, beyond the Mountain of Salt.[4] In general, these were small groups of houses that were inhabited only seasonally by some Andean settlers or Indian converts; a small chapel completed the village. According to reports written at that time, there were more than a thousand Campa Indian converts in the only two missions in the central jungle: Jauja and Tarma.[5]

Because evangelizing could not be exercised in depth, since the Asháninka were resistant to any and all foreign elements, the Franciscans decided to extend their radius of action into new territories. To the north, toward the Ucayali, their boundary was imposed by the presence of the Jesuits; to the south the terrain was rough and the distances too great; the natural area for expansion was the highland between the Tambo, Perené, and Pichis Rivers. There had been a few vague reports of the Gran Pajonal only since the early years of

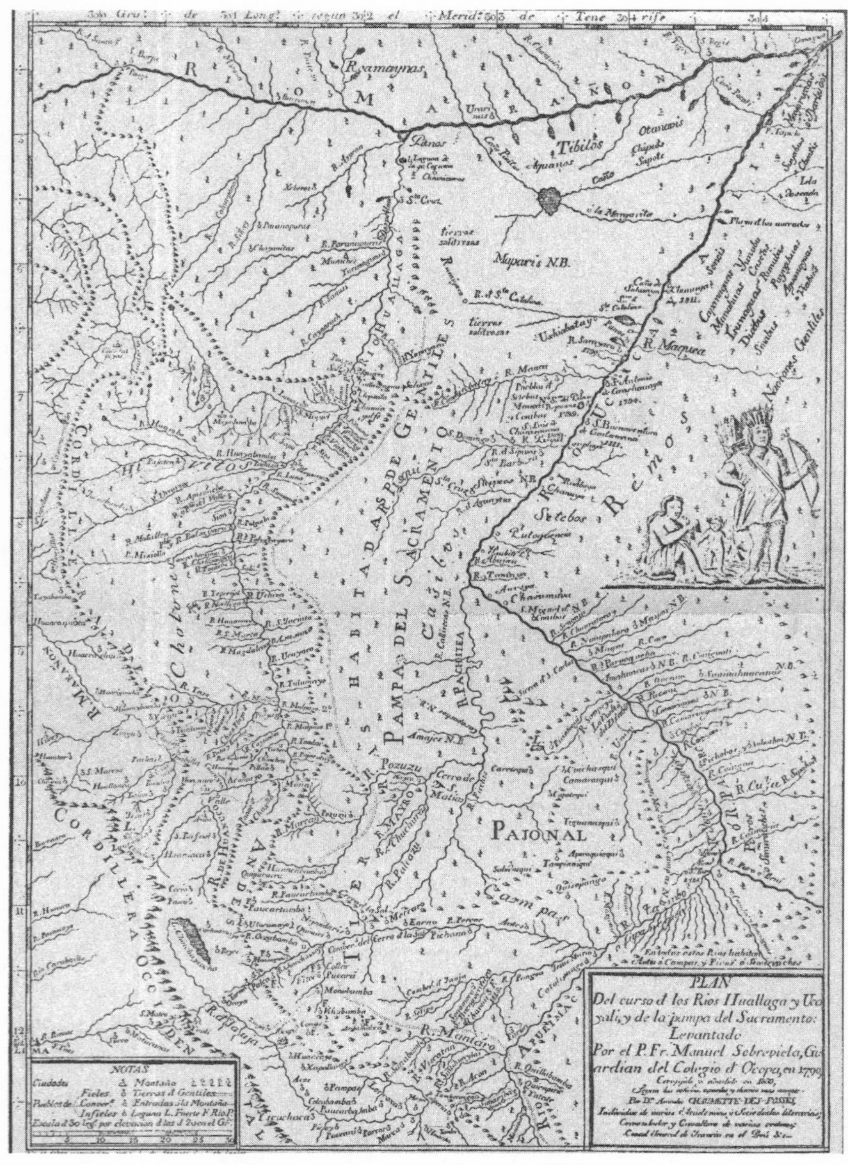

3. Map of the central jungle by Father Manuel de Sobreviela, 1793.

the eighteenth century. Its altitude above the rivers that surround it and its difficult access, scarcity of waterways, and ethnic isolation were likely the reasons it remained virgin territory until this time (fig. 3).[6]

Discovery of the Pajonal, through a strange twist of fate, was reserved for the Frenchman Juan Bautista de La Marca, who had come to Peru as an engineer. A few years after his arrival, La Marca joined the Franciscan order. He became a priest in 1726. He was immediately sent to Sonomoro (Pangoa), where he learned the Asháninka language and wrote a grammar, dictionary, and some doctrinal texts.[7] In 1733 he explored the Gran Pajonal.

La Marca's discovery opened the Pajonal to Franciscan missionary action. In 1735 three priests and a lay brother organized an expedition in Sonomoro. They were accompanied by some Asháninka from the Perené under the command of "Cacique" Mateo de Assia. For more than forty days the missionaries traveled the highlands, baptizing children and adding saints' names to the indigenous toponymies.[8] This sort of topo-hagiography, so common at that time and slightly confusing to geographic reality, was continued a year later by Father Alonso del Espíritu Santo. This Franciscan left Catalipango (Ene) to make an expedition into the area inhabited by the Piro and Cunibo, who had been left isolated since the death of Father Biedma in 1686. Once he reached the place along the Ucayali where San Miguel de los Cunibos had been established, Father Alonso decided to return to the Ene by way of the Gran Pajonal. He crossed the Chipanique (Chipani, Chipanaqui) and arrived near Pirintoqui Lake. Little by little he traveled through a large area of the Pajonal without encountering resistance from the Indians.[9]

In 1736 the census of Indians of the Gran Pajonal revealed a relatively prosperous situation; in 1739 ten villages were recorded by the Franciscans.[10] The conquest of the Pajonal, though barely begun, was considered a conclusive fact. Some Europeans and criollos began making plans to colonize the new lands and presented a petition of conquest.[11] There was nothing to indicate that a different fate awaited the indigenous populations of the central jungle.

YEARS OF WAITING

The Juan Santos rebellion, perhaps one of the most important by indigenous populations of the South American jungle, reflects a state of saturation reached by the native communities who were mistreated and offended in their deepest traditions. The indigenous peoples' clear awareness that the growing advance and ever greater intrusion by whites and mestizos into their territories was the principal cause of their cultural decline and slow physical agony found its expression in a messianic hope embodied in the figure of Juan Santos.[12]

The movement of 1742 was nothing new for the missionaries. Since late in the sixteenth century, there had been many uprisings by several tribes. During the first years of expeditions and conquest, the Jívaro Indians of the northern jungle had caused problems, destroying the Spanish installations founded by Juan de Salinas. From that date (1599) until well into the eighteenth century, the area north of the Marañón had put up strong armed resistance, and its colonization had been impossible.[13] The case of the Maina (Záparo) Indians of the Pastaza and Morona Rivers is more tragic. After having resisted the conquest until 1619, they surrendered to Pedro Baca de Vega, who took four thousand of them to the Borja mission. Their mistreatment at the mission resulted in a general rebellion in 1640, which soon failed. Some years later only one of every ten Maina Indians distributed among twenty-one *encomiendas* had survived captivity. The Shipibo (then called Calliseca) had also rebelled from the time of the first contacts. In 1660, together with the Cocama, they attacked the missions on the lower Huallaga. Ten years later they attacked the Panatahua missions, and in 1698 they were free from all white domination.[14] These are just a few of the cases of a dramatic history, as yet unfinished. If the central jungle had remained relatively calm, this was simply because of the delay in Spanish penetration of that area.

Nevertheless, by 1687, a few years after the effective start of missionary activity among the Asháninka, there had already been an outbreak of rebellion. According to Father Manuel de Biedma,[15] one hundred Asháninka from San Joseph de Savini had rebelled, leaving the mission, going off into the jungle, and rejecting any contact with whites. The rebels had taken refuge with the Ene River Indians and there, fearing a raid by the whites, had hidden the women and children in "safe houses, where they leave the women and children when they go to fight, something never before seen here."[16]

A more direct antecedent of the events of 1742, although bearing no causal relationship, is the Ignacio Torote uprising. In 1737 this Campa Indian from Catalipango met with twenty other Indians and, after having killed a lay brother and his assistants, headed for the Sonomoro mission and killed the priests there. A witness, who survived by hiding, later stated that Torote had gone to this extreme to defend his freedom because "you and your companions are killing us every day . . . , taking away our freedom."[17] All of Torote's companions were captured, sentenced to death, and executed; he escaped and disappeared forever into the jungle.[18]

JUAN SANTOS THE MESSIAH

The scant historiography that exists regarding Juan Santos Atahualpa fluctuates between two equally passionate extremes that make the task of reconstruction extremely delicate. The difficulty does not lie so much in establishing the greater or lesser degree of truth of the sources (one must consider that there are no indigenous sources from the time of the events); rather the challenge is to avoid the polarization of the later historiography, whose extremes are the Franciscan chroniclers and contemporary Republican official historiography on the one hand, and the *indigenismo* of the 1930s on the other hand.

Nevertheless, when the few official documents that are contemporaneous with the events insist on portraying Juan Santos as only a lying, power-hungry, fugitive criminal, the suspicion naturally arises that the information is slanted. Ethnological knowledge demonstrates that a single individual cannot control, as he pleases, several hundred Indians from diverse linguistic groups (*tribes* in a loose sense) by basing his authority upon deceit. The political unity of nearly all of the Indians of the central Peruvian jungle, a unique and unprecedented panindigenous phenomenon, presumes conscious loyalty to a messianic ideal of liberation. It is this success of Santos's message, more than his personal background, that is significant. It is this positive reaction of the Indians of the jungle and part of the mountains to the call of a messiah that cannot be hidden by the ethnocentric, scholarly, *histoire-historisante* that official Peruvian historiography has almost always practiced. We cannot, however, rely on only strictly historical interpretations that do not perceive in millenarian forms the expression of ideas of the regeneration and resulting spiritual salvation that are implicit in all religious practice.[19]

In late May 1742, when the rainy season was ending and the savannas were their most intense green, a mountain Indian of about thirty years of age with short hair, wearing a red *kushma* (sleeveless cotton tunic), arrived at the upper Shimaqui (Shimá) River of the Gran Pajonal. In this place called Quisopango lived Santabangori, the same Campa who in 1733 had welcomed and provided lodging for Father La Marca.[20] In this same town in 1736, several Campa families taken from another Gran Pajonal area had been forcibly resettled.[21] It was therefore not coincidental that Juan Santos chose this place to issue his call to all Indians of the central jungle. Many families forced by the missionaries into a new situation were gathered there; in addition, Quisopango was quite far from the mission centers of the Perené and the Chanchamayo, and it took several days to reach the area over small and very difficult trails. Quisopango, in the heart of the Gran Pajonal, was practically impregnable. The only nearby river, the Shimá, was extremely rough and impossible to navigate, even at its outlet into the Tambo.

This Quechua Indian had come from Cuzco, traveling by river in the company of a Piro called Bisabequí. There in the imperial city he had left three brothers: one older and two younger. According to Franciscan historiography, Juan Santos was a fugitive from justice "for having killed his master, who was a member of the Society of Jesus."[22] This information has never been confirmed and, as Francisco Loayza states, is based on the statements of six biased witnesses (five Spaniards and one Indian), taken three years after the beginning of the rebellion. Many other Franciscan sources—most of them also biased—do not mention the alleged murder at all. In June 1742, a month after Santos's arrival at the Pajonal, Brother Domingo García wrote a long report about recent events, in which he says nothing about the alleged crime.[23] The information regarding Juan Santos's crime is mentioned in these terms: Witness José Bermúdez stated that an Indian named Basilio Huamán informed him that an Indian named Juan Cosco had told him that Juan Santos Atahualpa was a fugitive from Cuzco, where he had killed a Jesuit priest. Obviously the information is not firsthand; additionally it must be noted that the Jesuits issued no denouncement, nor did they record this information in their chronicles or documents.[24]

Little is known of the early life of Juan Santos. It appears that he was educated by the Jesuits in Cuzco; it is even said that the priests of the Society were aware of the nobility of his heritage.

> They say that he was in the Indian school run by the priests of the Society, and on one occasion when he was resting on a bench or platform, a priest of the Society walked past, accompanied by another, and they say that he said, "Look here who belongs to the Kingdom of Peru; as there is no one else closer to the Inca of Peru, this one is on the verge of rising up with the Kingdom someday."[25]

Juan Santos had even traveled to Europe as an attendant of a Jesuit priest. He repeated several times in his speeches to the Franciscans who went to visit him that he had been in Europe and Angola.[26] It seems that Santos had contemplated rebellion for a long time. A 1744 document[27] states that, between 1729 and 1730, the rebel traveled through the mountains from Cuzco to Cajamarca, asking the Indian chiefs and Indian governors for all the support and help they could give him when he would enter the jungle and proclaim his rights of Inca lineage. It is difficult to determine the accuracy of this information. In 1730 Santos would have been approximately eighteen to twenty years old; this means that his revolutionary decision would have been made in his youth at the Cuzco school, even before his trip to Europe.

Let us return to the Gran Pajonal plains. We possess no direct sources regarding what Santos proclaimed in Quisopango. Izaguirre[28] imagines a full declaration, a sort of revolutionary manifesto, containing the basic principles and justification for the rebellion. It is difficult to imagine hundreds of Asháninka excited by a statement of social and political vindication: "He then took on the attitude of a sociologist, adding that he would order and balance . . . his empire, that there would no longer be sweatshops, bakeries, or other difficult occupations, much less slavery."[29] Let us think rather of a tacit understanding between Juan Santos and the Asháninka inhabitants of the upper Shimá, based on their common condition as persons subjected to an order totally alien to their own will and cultural tradition. Juan Santos had no need to resort to the social arguments that so concern contemporary western historiography. If Santos chose the central jungle—where there were no mines or sweatshops—as the center of his movement, he had no reason to focus it on practically nonexistent socioeconomic causes.

We do not know the content of the declaration of this Andean messiah brought down from the mountains via the river, as the Asháninka myth of the Kesha divinity prescribes.[30] Santos, however, acted in accordance with the strictest Asháninka spiritual tradition. Dance, that ceremony that pleases the divinity, had its preferred place with Santos. He drank *masato*, and regarding coca, "he says that it is the plant of God and not of witches, as the Virakochas [Spaniards] say."[31] Perhaps he announced in the Asháninka language, which he spoke,[32] the same thing that he would later say to the priests: "[H]e had wanted to reveal himself for a long time, but . . . God had not authorized him to do so until that moment."[33] With regard to his Inca title, it is possible that Santos referred to it, although this prerogative would have carried more weight with Andeans and Spaniards than with highland Indians.[34]

A few days after Santos's arrival at the Gran Pajonal, the Perené, Mountain of Salt, Chanchamayo, and Ene missions were abandoned by all of the Indians. Santos sent emissaries with the order to meet at the Pajonal. They all responded to the call, not only the Asháninka but also the Amuesha, the Piro, the Simirinche, the Cunibo, the Shipibo,[35] and the Mochobo. Indians came from the Ucayali, the Pampa del Sacramento, and the Pachitea, and farther south from the Urubamba. The entire central jungle came, as if the signal had been silently awaited for years, as if the waiting had been transmitted from father to son along with other traditions. The subjugated Asháninka in Sonomoro sent word to Santos that they could not move because there were too many blacks who would stop them. Santos responded that he had "feet to travel to go get them."[36]

It was Father Santiago Vásquez de Caicedo, the converter of San Tadeo, who took the initiative to go visit this strange man who was attracting all the Indians from the missions to the Gran Pajonal with a mysterious magnetism. One afternoon in June 1742, the Franciscan arrived at the upper Shimá. In front of Santos's hut, the Indians formed a semicircle that soon closed around the missionary. Santos came out, said some prayers in Spanish and the creed in Latin, and then sent for food for the guest. A short time later the messiah explained his ideas. He had come to organize his kingdom with the help of his children: the Indians, the mestizos, and the blacks purchased with their money. He told the viceroy not to try to stop him "with four Spaniards . . . because . . . he would wring his and his son's necks like chickens."[37] In addition, he added, the viceroy should find an escape route because "his relative the Englishman" was arriving by sea.

When Father Santiago Vásquez returned to San Tadeo and Sonomoro with more precise information about the events at the Pajonal, two Asháninka converts and the mayor of Sonomoro were sent to conduct another interview with the rebel. They would return a few days later with the same firm response: Juan Santos Atahualpa was Apu Inca and had a right to his kingdom. He was a Christian, prayed every day, read the doctrine in a book, and preached to the Indians as the priests did. He wore a silver crucifix on his chest and had nothing against the priests or the law of Christ, but he wanted the blacks and *virakochas* (Spaniards) to leave his land. The mayor of Sonomoro became ill while in Quisopango and thus stayed there longer before returning; he had a chance to observe that many Indians, some from very far away, swore obedience to Santos.[38]

Blacks came down frightened from the Pajonal with this news: Santos himself had made them promise before a crucifix that "they would tell the truth and not add or take away from those that he said."[39] The blacks were frightened because all of the Indians wanted to kill them, although Santos opposed all violence. From the account of Fathers García and Del Santo—based exclusively on the reports from the blacks who fled the Gran Pajonal—a seemingly confused and contradictory image of the rebel is obtained. This contradiction is apparent only because it does not correspond to the typification of Franciscan historiography, to that figure of the bloodthirsty, ignorant renegade guilty of having brought chaos where only peace and order had reigned.

Throughout the rebellion, Santos's attitudes are portrayed as those of a moderate man who did not allow himself to be carried away by the illusion of success or to give in to excesses. One perceives in him a mystical inspiration that rose above the level of concrete operative action and oriented his acts toward levels that, in a way, share in the mythical conception of time and action. His worldly actions, which are concretely historical, cannot be reduced to terms that can be analyzed with the same rule as, for example, events of an economic nature. Like all promoters of nativist messianic movements, Santos based the rebellion against the whites upon eminently religious reasons. His ideas (possibly his doctrine), which represent the inevitable syncretism of two centuries of Christian presence alongside primordial indigenous religious thought, are those of a religious renewer rather than those of a social revolutionary in search of worldly power.

It is in these terms that one can understand why, when Santos discovered that in Sabirosqui, not far from Quisopango where he was, some Indians had tied up some blacks and intended to kill them, he rushed there from his general headquarters to help the prisoners.[40] After freeing them he admonished the Indians: "[I]n talking to them about that he reprimands them . . . that he is opposed to all that."[41] In Sabirosqui itself, a mission center of substantial importance on the Gran Pajonal, the rebellion was carried out peacefully. The black guards were captured with their weapons and advised to leave the Gran Pajonal. The firearms were retained, "and he says that he will return them to the priests . . . , even three knives that I [Father Domingo García] had given to a black so he would buy me three *cusmas*; he took them away from him, but he will return them to me."[42]

Santos had no intention of frightening the Spaniards with bloody acts, and it was surely not fear that held him back, nor the impossibility of carrying them out. There was in him a clear desire to obtain what he was asking through conversations with the priests. In early June 1742, a month after his arrival in Quisopango, he asked that Father Manuel del Santo visit him. This interview never occurred because of the fear and distrust of the missionaries. Only when the rebellion had become an open war would the Spaniards try to remedy these initial errors by sending a mission of Jesuit priests to meet with the rebel.[43]

The first blood spilled by the Indian messiah was, to the great astonishment of the Spaniards, pig blood. Santos sent for the cows from the Sabirosqui mission, looked at them, said they were good cattle, and added that he himself would bring sheep in the future, "but not pigs, as they are bad livestock, and he ordered I don't know how many pigs of the town killed."[44] In the sworn statements of six witnesses taken in 1745 by the governor of Tarma, one of them stated that Santos had the pigs killed, "saying that they were animals harmful to health."[45] This was a sensible measure, though inconceivable to an eighteenth-century European peasant mentality.[46]

But what exactly did this man of Incan lineage, sent by God, "whose wisdom is comparable to Solomon's," this strange man "who can make the mountains crumble" at his will, want? We will never know exactly. What remains are the few broken phrases of Francisco and El Congo, two frightened blacks bearing the message from Santos, which was later transcribed by Fathers García and Del Santo.[47] The rebel demanded his kingdom, which had been taken from him by Pizarro and the rest of the Spaniards, because he "has not gone to take anyone else's kingdom . . . , and the Spaniards' time has run out and his has come. . . . Nor did he want blacks because they were thieves just like the Spaniards, and besides, they had their kingdom in Africa, the Congo, and Angola, where he himself had been and seen them . . . with long beards saying Mass, and . . . although they may not be white like the Spaniards, they can certainly be priests."[48] Santos stated that in the future the priests would go alone to the jungle to teach their Indians, and that if they did not wish to go without blacks or Spaniards to accompany them, he would bring the bishop of Cuzco to ordain his children, the Indians, as priests.

The Juan Santos rebellion was essentially indigenous; blacks were excluded from it. To understand the rebel's attitude toward blacks, one must consider the function that blacks served in the conquered jungle. The only ones who possessed firearms, aside from the few Spaniards installed in the most important centers, were their black assistants. Each mission had these armed slaves who were charged with keeping watch and defending the missionaries. We do not have sufficient data to induce a general judgment about relations between the jungle Indians of the missions and the blacks, but the indigenous attitude throughout the rebellion leads us to believe that these black guards, due to their function, were hated. Although the first time, Santos limited his actions to threatening them and forcing them to leave the jungle, the rebel Indians wanted to kill them. Nevertheless, the neutral position of the blacks—indifferent and detached from the interests of either of the two sides—later suggests to Juan Santos the possibility of using them as mercenaries. The black slave did not have much to lose in a fight in which he did not believe and for an ideal of freedom that had not been his for a long time. One of the most effective assistants of the revolt was Antonio Gatica, a former black slave from the Anti mission of San Tadeo.[49] The rebel himself had declared it: The movement can count on the support of some blacks purchased with their money.[50] The blacks, aware of their exclusive military support function, had no illusions about their future in the new Indian kingdom of Juan Santos Atahualpa.

Regarding the highland Indians, Santos was sure he could count on their help; he stated this to Fathers García and Del Santo through the blacks Francisco and El Congo: "[A]fter he finishes gathering these people, he'll go up with them to Quimirí, where he will call the highlanders, his subjects, so that they will accompany him in his enterprise."[51] Although this statement might have seemed a little illusory to the Spaniards, they would soon recognize it as based on a situation of which they were completely unaware. Many years earlier, the viceroy, the duke of La Palata, had contributed to misrepresenting an ethnic reality, which had, in contrast, been clear to the first conquistadors of the eastern Andes. The Andeans and the upper jungle Indians were in contact. Most of the inhabitants of the eastern Andes had commercial dealings with jungle groups and often had coca or cotton farms in the warm jungle valleys. In 1685, when the viceroy, the duke of La Palata, had to explain the exodus of the Indians who were leaving mines and forced labor camps, he contradicted the common opinion that they were fleeing to the land of the heathens; he did not believe that was so because "for them, being Indian is not a privilege because they kill them and treat them like enemies only because they are others."[52] The viceroy was wrong. Many fugitive Indians settled in the jungle and disappeared forever in the eyes of the Spanish crown.[53]

By 1743 the rebellion had the support of "many highlanders, who have joined . . . those miserable savages."[54] That same year the expedition of the governor of Tarma captured a highland resident of that city, Pedro José Pulipunche. A short time later, in late October 1743 near Quimirí, the Spaniards captured another highland Indian, Bartolomé López, who stated that more than fifty highland Indians and several Campa were lying in wait to attack the expedition. The Andeans' support of the rebellion had begun some months earlier, in August 1743. Santos had won the trust of the hesitant Quechuas of the neighboring highlands when he set free two highlanders captured by his Campa (a Franciscan lay brother and the mayor of Quimirí, who had been sent by Father Lorenzo Núñez as spies from Chanchamayo to the rebel camp). Word had spread that the new Inca wanted the Quechuas and was calling them to his side: "[O]n this occasion he had been joined by one hundred Indians from the highlands."[55] A few years later military measures would be taken to prevent the desertion of the highland Indians. In 1746 two forts would be constructed: one in Chanchamayo and the other in Ocsabamba (Oxapampa), "so that in this way the heathens' audacity would be contained, and the highland Indians would be prevented from entering the jungle."[56]

"AND THE SPANIARDS' TIME RAN OUT"

The external history of the Juan Santos Atahualpa rebellion is long and full of military incidents. One can distinguish two major periods in the revolutionary movement. The first ten years (1742–52) are characterized by bellicose actions: clashes between indigenous detachments and Spanish troops sent from the capital. The second period begins with the withdrawal of the rebel Indians from the highland town of Andamarca in 1752 and does not end on an exact date, but is prolonged into well into the last third of the eighteenth century. In the first ten-year period, the rebellion is established through a series of military successes that guarantee the rebel Indians an autonomy and isolation that will last for the remainder of the century. The second period, the result of the first decade of struggle, is peaceful; during it the Asháninka and a large portion of the central jungle groups enjoy an independence unknown since before the conquest. We will see below how the true victory of Santos's uprising consists of having caused colonial Peru's marginalization of the entire vast area of the central jungle. For almost a century the reconquest of the Asháninka, Piro, Amuesha, Mochobo, and part of the Cunibo would be a practically impossible task.[57]

Let us return to September 1742. Don Benito Troncoso, governor of the frontiers of Tarma, managed to gather an army numbering just under one hundred and decided to confront the rebel Indians. He encountered no rebels in Sonomoro and therefore decided to penetrate to the very heart of rebel territory: the Gran Pajonal. Santos, however, was not there, nor were the bulk of his followers. A few Pajonal Asháninka were defending the houses of the old Quisopango mission. Santabangori died in this battle; he was the old Campa whom La Marca knew, the same one who, a few months earlier, had sent a message to the priests "that the things of the world were coming and going and that the Spaniards should not come . . . and . . . attack him too."[58] Troncoso's expedition retraced its steps and withdrew to the highlands, while another Spanish group managed to penetrate as far as the town of Quimirí, which it found deserted.[59]

Between October and November 1742, Troncoso's troops carried out two more expeditions to the Mountain of Salt—to Eneno and Nijandaris—in an attempt to locate Santos and the Asháninka who were responsible for the deaths of Father Domingo García and two other priests, which had occurred around that time on the Perené. Father Domingo García, according to a document written in 1745 by Viceroy Villagarcía,[60] must have been the immediate cause of the violence unleashed by the Asháninka under Santos's command. In fact, the Franciscan had whipped one of the main Indians of his mission "with indiscreet immoderation."

In Lima the elderly Viceroy Villagarcía was concerned about the events in the jungle and expressed this in three letters he wrote to the Franciscan commissioner and in one addressed to the king.[61] In 1745, when he was replaced by the new viceroy, José Manso de Velasco, he tried to downplay the importance of the rebellion, stating that the jungle and its inhabitants should be conquered with friendship and not with weapons.[62] The solution came too late and was certainly not put into practice by his successor.

The first months of 1743 passed without incident. The rains prevented the Spaniards from entering the jungle. Around June, however, the rebels began to approach the town of Quimirí, and Santos warned

Father Lorenzo Núñez to leave the mission and retreat to the highlands. It was on this occasion that the two highland spies captured by the rebels were freed and returned to the Spaniards with messages for the mountain Indians: Santos did not want to harm the Quechua Indians or anyone else; he only wanted what rightfully belonged to him.[63] The news was celebrated in Tarma with song and dance; the Indians announced that they would drink *chicha* in the skulls of the priest and the governor.[64] In early August 1743, the Chanchamayo River was filled with Campa, Piro, Amuesha, and Mochobo Indians. Father Núñez hurriedly fled but was caught by a group of rebel Indians carrying a message from Santos: If the Spaniards wished to see him, they should wait for him in Tarma.

Santos Atahualpa's messages were not given their proper importance. They were considered to be the ramblings of an arrogant Indian who had not yet felt the force of Spanish weapons. His generosity with prisoners was interpreted as weakness and fear. Two companies of troops arrived from Lima with eight pieces of artillery (four cannons and four mortars) and a large quantity of gunpowder. Two hundred soldiers gathered in Tarma. In October the troops reached Quimirí, but naturally there was no trace of the rebel; at that time the small town of Huancabamba, farther north of the Perené, was receiving a visit from the rebels. The Spaniards decided to build a fort in Quimirí that would serve to contain the advances of the rebels as well as the numerous desertions of the highland Indians. The fortification, armed with the eight pieces of artillery, was put under the command of Captain Fabricio Bártoli and his company of eighty men from Callao. Most of the army withdrew to Tarma. Four days later the rebel Indians appeared and surrounded the fort. On this occasion Juan Santos obtained one of his greatest military victories. There are several versions of the events, but all agree on one thing: During a one-month period, Santos offered Captain Bártoli two fifteen-day truces, as well as numerous opportunities to surrender and retreat safely to the sierra.[65] Bártoli did not wish to abandon the fort; he had hopes that the reinforcements he had requested via messengers would arrive from Tarma. When the last truce ended, the Spaniards decided to flee under cover of darkness, but they were intercepted by the rebels. Not one man was spared. It was not until January that three hundred soldiers under Troncoso's command reached Quimirí. From the other side of the river, they could see that the fort was occupied by the Asháninka rebels.

Only after the sacrifice of Bártoli and his eighty men did the authorities resolve to seek direct contact with the rebel leader. It had been more than a year since Juan Santos's entry into the jungle, and the Spaniards had been defeated on the battlefield as well as morally. Most of the neighboring highland Indians supported the movement; many had deserted to join the rebel forces. The central jungle was impenetrable to all whites. There were attempts to negotiate by the Franciscans. Father Núñez and Commissioner Brother Manuel Albarrán received authorization from Santos to meet to discuss the terms of a truce. That meeting was never held, however, because the authorities in Spain had other plans. In late 1744, King Philip V's secretary, the marquis of Ensenada, wrote to the highest authority in Buenos Aires, naming the lieutenant general of the Royal Armies and president of the High Court of Chile, Don José Manso de Velasco, the viceroy of Peru. He also recommended to Manso de Velasco that several soldiers from Buenos Aires and Chile be dispatched under his orders to fight the "Rebel Indian" of Peru.[66] The crown's decision to name a new viceroy eloquently revealed the importance that the revolutionary movement had acquired in the eyes of the mother country.

Shortly before being replaced by his successor, Viceroy Villagarcía believed he could resolve the situation through the Jesuits. Father Irusta, who knew the area and was acquainted with some Asháninka, especially Mateo de Assia, was charged with entering into negotiations with the rebel.

> Father Irusta entered the jungle with another priest in the summer of 1745, and they took many tools. Father Irusta spoke with the chiefs and leaders whom he knew. What he was able to arrange with them, they did not tell anyone; but by the

> effects that were seen later, it was clear that he had not achieved anything.[67]

Little is known about this mysterious Jesuit mission beyond what the puzzled Franciscan historian Amich managed to deduce. When the Jesuits returned to Lima, José Manso de Velasco was the new viceroy. We do not know the Jesuit priests' impressions of the rebel, but they must have been amazed at the indigenous support for the movement. Years later, Viceroy Manso de Velasco would include in his memoirs vague phrases in which a clear fear of the tenacious rebellion is evident.[68]

The immediate result of the Jesuits' mission was the naming of General Don José de Llamas, marquis of Mena-Hermoza,[69] as chief of operations; by January 1746, the new general had managed to gather a force of approximately one thousand men. Despite the difficulties of the rainy season, in March five hundred men under the command of the marquis of Mena-Hermoza entered rebel territory at Huancabamba and headed immediately for the Mountain of Salt. To the south, nearly four hundred men commanded by Troncoso were to meet with the first group, passing through Quimirí and Ocsabamba. The forced marches, the rains, and the difficulties in obtaining provisions wreaked havoc among the Spanish troops. General José de Llamas had to turn back after leaving fourteen men dead of exhaustion in the jungle. Throughout the entire expedition, they had not seen even one rebel. The Spaniards had crossed Amuesha and Asháninka territory but had been unable to join battle even once; it was as if there were no Indians or rebels in those places.

Troncoso met a different fate. At the edge of the Chanchamayo Valley, in Nijandaris, some Asháninka attacked him; the soldiers fled back toward the highlands. The results of the two expeditions were disastrous; they lost men, animals, provisions, weapons, and most important, confidence in their military abilities. Juan Santos Atahualpa had mysteriously disappeared, thus defeating the Spanish troops without any military intervention. José de Llamas believed that he could attribute this failure to deceit by the Jesuits; according to him, the Jesuits had assured him that as soon as he and his troops reached the Mountain of Salt, Mateo de Assia would turn the rebel over to them.[70] Whether it was deceit by Mateo de Assia or Father Irusta, or an illusion of General Llamas, one thing was certain: Juan Santos would never be betrayed.

The defeat suffered by the Spanish expeditions convinced Viceroy Manso de Velasco to suspend this type of military action:

> These expeditions of excessive cost and little effect are an intolerable burden on the provinces, and in the inevitable loss of the beasts of burden necessary for transportation of supplies . . . , [the expeditions] suffer the irreparable harm that they do not receive from the Barbarians . . . , [who] never show their faces. . . . [N]ature fights on their side with the shelter it offers them. . . . [T]hey hide easily . . . , swimming across even the deepest rivers. . . . [E]ven the Incas did not concern themselves with bringing these subjects into their Empire.[71]

It is believed that Santos had an army of five hundred warriors. In reality these calculations reflect complete ignorance of the true extent of the rebellion. Juan Santos had at his disposal the support of all of the Indians in the central jungle and in a large part of the border highlands, but he did not have them gathered into a regular army; all or some of them would simply come when the rebel needed them for an action. This is what happened in mid-1746, when a group of Simirinche (Piro) carried out an incursion through the Tulumayo River valley and arrived in Monobamba. Among the captives whom the Piro took to Quimirí was the town priest. The Indian messiah welcomed him and, after giving him some letters for the viceroy and the Franciscan commissioner, as well as a message for General Llamas, set him free to return to the mountains. A group of rebel Indians escorted the priest through insurgent territory.[72]

Given the minimal success of aggressive military actions, the viceroy decided to follow a defensive policy of containment. In August 1746 a decision was made to build two forts, in Chanchamayo and Ocsabamba,

> and that several groups of people take up residence in their shelter. And that when circumstances permit, the rebels be attacked and punished, not allowing them any assurance or calm with easy battles, until they are annihilated.[73]

In other words, they were planning to adopt the strategy of Juan Santos, thus recognizing four years of mistakes and failures.

The Franciscans could not accept the idea that in a few years they had lost all of the missions established during nearly a century of work. In early 1747 there were two attempts at peaceful recovery of some of the former missions. In February Father Manuel Albarrán thought he could enter the Pangoa jungle from the south, through the old Acón River pass, and then travel down the Ene to where it meets the Perené. The relative calm of the Asháninka of the Huanta jungle led him to believe that the rebellion had not spread to that region. When the expedition reached the Mantaro River, however, it was abandoned without warning by its highland Indian porters, and a short time later it was attacked. Three priests and ten Spanish soldiers lost their lives in the Huanta jungle. An eyewitness would later state that the attack had been planned by some fugitive black slaves and renegade Guamanguino Indians, who were also fugitives from justice.[74] Nevertheless, this incident demonstrated that this means of access to the jungle was also closed and that the movement begun by Santos was more widespread than had been believed.

The second attempt at a peaceful expedition was also unsuccessful, but at least it did not have a tragic ending. In May 1747 the new Franciscan commissioner, Lorenzo Núñez, decided to send three priests to meet with Juan Santos. Again the rebel showed generous conduct, which was puzzling in the eyes of the viceregal authorities. After discussing matters and failing to reach an agreement, two of the Franciscans returned to Ocopa, whereas the third, Father Otazuo, remained in rebel territory and received permission from Santos to travel freely throughout the area. Otazuo did not pass up the opportunity to try to regain the trust of the Asháninka and other Indians, but he was unsuccessful. Three months later, Commissioner

Núñez, concerned about the fate of Father Otazuo, arrived in Quimirí. Santos freed both priests and, as was his custom, had rebels accompany them until they crossed the Chanchamayo River.[75]

Three years of relative calm followed Father Otazuo's efforts to achieve peace. In his final conversations with the Franciscan, Santos had stated that it was impossible to enter into an agreement without first consulting with the Quechua chiefs, who were also committed to the rebellion.[76] This had seemed to be a dilatory argument, but in 1750 the authorities discovered three Indian conspiracies in Huarochirí, Canta, and Lambayeque. In Huarochirí the Indians managed to organize an uprising but were defeated and captured a short time later; in Canta and in the north the conspirators were discovered immediately. Many Indians were taken to Lima and publicly executed. Some of the chiefs involved in the rebellions managed to take refuge with Juan Santos.[77] Viceroy Manso de Velasco, recently named the count of Superunda, confronted the growing rebellion with the by now traditional repressive measures, making examples of the rebels by beheading them and displaying the heads in the Lima town square, and establishing five companies of soldiers in Jauja and Tarma. It was not until thirty years later, with Túpac Amaru, that the executioner's scaffold was replaced by greater respect for the Laws of the Indies.

Perhaps enthused by the success achieved with the Quechua conspirators, the viceroy decided to attempt another expedition against the jungle rebels. José de Llamas organized two groups of soldiers. The first, under the command of Llamas himself, entered the jungle through Chorobamba; the second entered through Tarma. The troops were constantly harassed by small bands of Asháninka; bridges were destroyed, and along the trails pit traps with spears made the advance insufferable. It was said that Santos had withdrawn to Eneno on the west bank of the Perené. This Spanish expedition also had to withdraw to the cordillera without achieving victory.

Not everyone, however, felt that the solution to the Apu Inca Santos uprising should be sought through military means. In July 1750, Franciscan missionary Joseph de San Antonio sent a request to King

Ferdinand VI,[78] asking that sixty missionaries be sent to Peru, that forts be constructed in the Mountain of Salt region, that the hospice of Ocopa's status be raised from *propaganda fide* to *colegio*, and above all, that the causes of the rebellion be eradicated, that is, the bad example of the Spaniards. The Franciscan openly accused the authorities of responsibility for the uprising. Peru, he said, was

> in the most unfortunate state and in danger of being lost due to the excessive and wicked greed, tyranny, cruelty, and scandals, which are increasing daily, and the terrible consequences that follow from them against the poor Indians, mestizos, and many Spaniards; and the same thing in the sweatshops, mines, mills, and sugarcane plantations, where horrors are carried out against the unfortunate poor, who . . . for the sake of being free of so many tyrannies, taxes, extremely heavy public burdens, accompanied by cruel violence, many flee into the jungle, choosing the company of the heathens as better or less evil.[79]

This was the situation in the provinces of Peru, with the aggravating circumstance that

> idolatry . . . is very severe, and the Faith very adulterated . . . because, as the Indians see that what many Spaniards are doing to them is against the Law of God, and . . . they are kept in this unfortunate condition for many years, they doubt or disbelieve the doctrines that we Missionaries and their priests in the Missions and Provinces preach to them; and as a result the Supplicant [Father Joseph de San Antonio] was forced . . . not only to preach against the idolatries but also to publicly burn the idols that reached his hands, outside of confession, in the Missions of the aforementioned Provinces.[80]

In the opinion of Father Joseph de San Antonio, the solution could almost certainly be found through a pacifist attitude by the missionaries. Perhaps by forgiving the rebels and accepting them back into the fortified missions that would be built in Chanchamayo, Mountain of Salt, and Ocsabamba, they could convince some converts to turn over the rebel Santos. Again the only hope was a betrayal that would not take place. The missionary added that in this way the danger of a larger rebellion would be avoided because "if this [Santos] . . . headed for Lima with 200 Indian archers, one could fear . . . a generalized rebellion among all the Indians in the provinces of the Kingdom."[81] The Franciscan's fears were not unreasonable. In 1751, a year after these warnings, numerous groups of Campa and Piro rebels headed up the Sonomoro River. The rebels advanced slowly, not in a violent action of military invasion but in a retaking of territory. It was like an ethnic movement, a return to primitive emigrations, a search for their former lost territories. It took the Indians a year to recover the entire area of Sonomoro, Mazamari, the Pangoa, and Satipo. The Sonomoro fort and farms were abandoned by the few Indians who were faithful to the missionaries. Amich states that these Indians would die a short time later on the desolate punas of Andamarca, where they had gone to seek refuge.[82]

By 1752 the former Campa, Amuesha, and Piro territory had been totally retaken by its inhabitants. Not one mission, not one Spanish establishment, had withstood the slow but tenacious reestablishment action of the rebel tribes. In that same year Juan Santos wished to give the Spaniards one more demonstration of his power, or perhaps he still had faith in a general rebellion of the highland Indians. He conducted a great expedition to the cordillera. In August 1752 numerous Asháninka under his command entered the town of Andamarca, subdued it, and captured the parish priest and another priest. The rebels took supplies and a few head of cattle and after three days withdrew again to the jungle from which they had come. The Spanish soldiers hastily sent from San Gerónimo, Palca, Matahuasi, Comas, Jauja, Huancayo, Ocopa, and Tarma arrived only in time to hear the story of the two priests and to capture two of Santos's guides, who naturally were immediately hung in Jauja.[83] Once more Santos had avoided taking lives among the highland inhabitants and priests.

The first period of the Santos Atahualpa rebellion, that is, the ten-year period that we have characterized by its military actions, ended with the rebel attack on the town of Andamarca. From 1752 on, the rebellion took a different route; it was not active but instead peacefully enjoyed the military successes it had achieved during its first ten years. The uprising was generally considered over in 1756, when Brigadier Pablo Saez de Bustamante conducted an expedition to Quimirí and returned to Tarma without having been attacked. This was an accidental occurrence, however, having no specific meaning; certainly it cannot be considered the end of the Asháninka insurrection. As has been noted, the results of the movement begun by Santos Atahualpa continued from 1752 through the rest of the century and beyond, into the nineteenth century. The assumption that Santos died between 1755 and 1756 would also be an insufficient reason to consider this date the end of the rebellion. The rebellion and its consequences went on for a long time, preventing subsequent missionary and colonization attempts and giving back to the indigenous groups of the central jungle an independence and an autonomy that they had lost early in the seventeenth century.

"HIS BODY DISAPPEARED IN A CLOUD OF SMOKE"

The mysterious silence surrounding the rebel after his appearance in Andamarca was not broken with Pablo Saez's expedition to Quimirí in 1756. The Spanish brigadier was only able to confirm that the rebels had erected a cross on a huge rock in the middle of the plaza. The church that José de Llamas had encountered in 1750, "well swept and decorated . . . , with lighted candles on the statues of the saints,"[84] had not been rebuilt by the Asháninka. Llamas himself had set fire to it and the rest of the town during his 1750 expedition.

In August 1756 Viceroy Manso de Velasco wrote that lately the rebel "has not made his presence felt . . . , but this has not been cause for lack of care, and the troops are maintained."[85] These few words of the viceroy sum up the attitude of the authorities and missionaries with respect to the entire central jungle; an appearance by rebel Campa was expected at any moment, and penetration into former Franciscan territory was not attempted. Attention was directed instead to the Huallaga River region, from where the plan was, for the second time, to proceed to the Ucayali. In fact, in 1766 Franciscan Father Salcedo reached the old Cunibo mission of San Miguel on the upper Ucayali; among the Indians there he met two Campa followers of Santos, who stated that some time earlier, in Metraro, the messiah had disappeared in a cloud of smoke.[86] In that same year, however, a new general rebellion begun by the Setebo Runcato involved all the Ucayali River groups. Besides the Setebo, the Shipibo and the Cunibo also participated, as well as the Campa and Piro groups of the Tambo. The entire central jungle was definitively lost to colonization; Santos's rebellion had given the jungle Indians a previously unknown unity and had awakened in them an ancient taste for freedom and independence.

In the decade of the 1770s, geographer Cosme Bueno wrote, regarding Tarma Province, that it was not usable because of the insurrection and that the only possible course of action was the maintenance of border forts to contain the rebels.[87] The situation was no better in the eyes of the missionaries. We have some reports[88] from Father Francisco Alvarez de Villanueva, from which we can glean that between 1773 and 1775, it was still believed that Santos was alive and ready to renew hostilities at any moment. Brother Bernardo Peón y Baldés signed a letter on 25 March 1773, in which he advised dealing with the Ucayali missions and then, with the help of the Shipibo,

> reconquering the Campa nation and the towns of the Mountain of Salt, where *a rebellion occurred and* the false Inca *continues* [emphasis added] frightening Peru; as to what the Court should do and causing large expenditures by the Royal Treasury with the troops that form the Tarma cordon . . . , the false Inca rebel can only be defeated in two ways: through Tarma, which is the border, or through the area of Ucayale.[89]

Through Tarma, the letter continues, it is nearly impossible; through the Ucayali, however, it could be attempted by obtaining the help of the Shipibo and the Cunibo. Two years later, in July 1776, Father Manuel Gil wrote to the general commissioner, advising that the soldiers stationed in the city of Huánuco not be withdrawn because an "appearance by the rebel" was suspected; the rebel knew that there were troops in Tarma and therefore surely preferred the Huánuco region for an attack. In this letter the missionary went on to accuse the military of not wishing to take action against Santos because "as long as there are rebels there will be troops, and as long as there are troops, they'll have someone to give them money." Father Gil concludes, "[T]here is the rebel with four barbaric Indians . . . : enough to instill terror, not only in the orderly troops that Your Majesty supports, but also in the militiamen, who are many."[90]

Nearly fifteen more years passed before the Franciscans dared to penetrate the territory of the Asháninka rebels. It was not until 1788 that Manuel de Sobreviela carried out a short exploratory expedition into the Vitoc (Chanchamayo) Valley to see if it could be repopulated by settlers. Forty-six years had passed since the moment when Juan Santos withdrew to the Gran Pajonal and proclaimed his rebellion.[91] In 1789 two forts were built—one in Uchubamba and the other in Vitoc—in the hope of protecting the new attempts to conquer the Asháninka groups. For eighty years more, however, until the founding of the city of La Merced in 1868, a large portion of the Chanchamayo region was impenetrable to whites. The same thing occurred with the Pichis, the Pachitea, the Gran Pajonal, the Perené, the Tambo, and the Pangoa.[92] Only in the south, in the region of the upper Apurímac and the Mantaro, did the Franciscan missions manage to regain some territory; this occurred between 1782 and 1790.[93]

The curious prophesy of a humble lay brother of Charcas Province had come true.[94] Santos's uprising began in 1742, and during a long rebellion he managed to carry out his promises, at least in part. Former tribal territories, free of Spaniards and blacks, had returned to their legitimate owners. The entire viceroyalty had been shaken by a strange and unforeseeable force; a new dimension of the Indian had replaced the capital's frivolous and superficial prejudices. Santos's messianic call, though unable to reach its culmination, had forever created an informed and aware indigenous people, who were prepared at any moment to protect their freedom and independence. Juan Santos had triumphed from the moment he was not betrayed, from the moment his "children, the Indians," those "heathens who live a brutal life, with no law and no king,"[95] had pledged themselves to the undertaking and followed him for many years, firmly believing in his principles, continuing the rebellion even after his death, and then keeping his memory alive, forever incorporated into their mythical world. Whether Juan Santos was still living in 1775, as Father Manuel Gil's letter maintains,[96] or whether that information does not correspond to reality is an issue whose importance is relative. It is not impossible: Santos would have been between sixty and sixty-five years old. There is no documentary evidence, however, that demonstrates with a certainty that the rebel's death occurred between 1755 and 1756,[97] as Franciscan historiography would have it.

The date of the physical death of Juan Santos might interest biographers, but in the eyes of Asháninka tradition, this fact is of little importance. For those Indians who preserve the memory of the great rebellion, Santos has never died: "[H]is body disappeared in a cloud of smoke."[98] The image of the Indian messiah bearing a message and a promise of sovereignty blends into the memory of the Asháninka and is lost, perhaps like his physical body in the smoke. His teachings and the spirit of his rebellion endure among his "children, the Indians," although the only tangible thing that persists is a small pile of rocks, silent remains resting against the Mountain of Salt, the sole witness to an ancient tomb that faced east.[99]

CHAPTER FOUR

The Walls Close In

Asháninka territory, closed to white penetration since 1742, was shrouded little by little in an impenetrable cloak that denied missionaries and travelers any knowledge of the region. Thus in the final years of the eighteenth century, the dismal reputation of the Campa was invented: fearsome warriors completely lacking in humanitarian behavior, knowing no filial mercy, who do not "heed their mothers' teachings."[1] This century, which saw in Europe the origin of the "noble savage," witnessed in Peru, in stark contrast, the birth of a "black legend," whose basis was the acrimony born of defeat and wounded pride. This black legend continues to the present day despite the isolated efforts of nineteenth-century Romanticism to redeem the jungle Indian. We do not find the immoral, brutish, and cruel Campa before the eighteenth century, but only after, when a long rebellion of bows and arrows had triumphed, revealing unforeseen indigenous traits. The nineteenth-century sources inherited and prolonged this vision of the "savage" Indian and conveyed rancor and fear toward the free, rebel Asháninka who had regained his independence.

Early nineteenth-century viceregal Peru still made some attempts to regain the lands of the central jungle. A timid missionary expedition ventured along the Ene and Tambo Rivers in 1807, hoping to assess the rebel territory; all it managed to do was to confirm that the area was lost to the crown and the church. The missionaries nostalgically recorded the presence of the ruins of former Spanish installations.[2] A year later a report was presented to Viceroy Abascal. This was the last official document of the colony that showed interest in the central jungle. The document is interesting[3] because it criticizes the central government's policy and recommends reconquest of the jungle by "new methods": granting tools to the peaceful Asháninka and using weapons against the rebels.[4] In those days, however, official Peru did not have time to devote to the *Chunchos*, as they called those whom they considered savage jungle Indians. The authorities were instead occupied with verbal and occasionally military disputes regarding the best form of government; in this way many years went by without the central jungle populations having to suffer the usual attempts at colonization.

Nevertheless, at the beginning of the independence period, two political events had an indirect influence on the jungle and, as a consequence, on the Asháninka. In 1823, after the battle of Ayacucho, the Franciscan school at Ocopa was abandoned by many members of that community. Some fled to Cuzco; a few stayed and were later taken to Callao by the Republican troops to join General Rodil's Spanish troops, who were stationed there. Just thirteen years later, in 1836, President Luis José de Orbegoso reopened the monastery to the Franciscan community, again summoning priests from Spain. During this time the monastery had been used as a teaching school, and the Franciscan missions in the jungle had been abandoned or turned over to a few priests of the secular clergy. This event notably reduced missionary influence and penetration in the central jungle or substituted the presence of a missionary with undeniable experience and a central administration and policy with that of a new, inexperienced missionary, who was often more interested in the worldly benefits that he could obtain from this new situation than in his evangelizing mission. In many cases, a new sort of *encomendero* replaced a missionary organization of long tradition; in other cases, the process of Christianization and white penetration simply came to a halt.

The second event that had indirect repercussions on the life of Asháninka society was Simón Bolivar's 1824 decree, which declared the highland Indians to be owners of their lands, thus clearing the way for the dissolution of the Indian community. In fact, community members sold their new possessions, thus being left after a few years without lands or money and, worst of all, without a clear or defined social position. Many of these members of a new dispossessed class were forced to seek a different situation and other lands in the Amazonian region of the country. It was during this time that farms were started by border highland Indians and mestizo cultural elements penetrated the upper jungle populations.

The nineteenth century began late for the Asháninka. Despite being the century of travelers, especially of foreigners, the latter did not risk entering Campa lands until well into the century. Alcydes D'Orbigny, Eduard Friedrich Poeppig, Smith, and Lowe never made contact with the rebel Indians, and Francis de Castelnau passed through their territory very quickly. From the Indians' point of view, the 150 years from the beginning of the nineteenth century to the present can be outlined as follows:

(1) an initial period of approximately forty years, during which there was no official attempt at reconquest and even European travelers, like later ethnologists, avoided their territories;
(2) a period of approximately sixty years that witnessed alternating "civil" and "missionary" expeditions, which in reality, save rare exception, can be classified as intimidatory military missions resulting in a white incursion that typifies the third stage;
(3) the rubber era, which covers the first fifteen years of the twentieth century.

After the 1920s there were occasional visits by ethnologists, as well as highway engineers, settlers, and new types of missionaries. We will attempt to summarize the history of these modern *entradas*, or expeditions, which can explain much of Asháninka society's present attitude toward ours.

GUNS FOR THE CHUNCHOS

In 1845 Don Ramón Castilla assumed the presidency of the republic. What the history books especially remember about this president of Peru is his abolition of Indian tribute paying and black slavery. In 1849, a few years before taking this measure, Castilla had authorized the immigration of Chinese workers to serve as manual labor in coastal agriculture. This decision has an interesting precedent for our story: In 1848 Castilla's government believed that the Campa were the solution to the labor shortage on the coast. Franciscan priests Cimini and Rossi were charged with delivering to the authorities the hardly evangelical evaluation of the "human resources" of the central jungle. The plan was to capture a substantial number of *Chunchos* from the Chanchamayo jungle, where this "breed" abounded, to aid in agricultural production on the coast. The Perené River Indians, however, stopped the Franciscan expedition and forced it back to a place called San Ramón at the confluence of the Tulumayo and Chanchamayo Rivers, where, from 1842 on, two companies of troops were stationed with two cannons "of small caliber, the kind that cause great confusion, hurling bullets at the Indians."[5]

It can be said that interest in the jungle, especially the Chanchamayo area, began for republican Peru with Castilla's first term of office. Mariano Eduardo de Rivero, prefect of the Department of Junín, was in charge of recovering the territory lost to the Juan Santos rebellion. This was not a peaceful recovery; this era was marked by the construction of forts, the use of weapons, and the stealing of Asháninka women and youth, initiating a violent conquest that would reach its most extreme expression during the rubber era in the early twentieth century. At the same time, the state facilitated the immigration of foreign settlers who wanted to take up residence in these areas; they would be guaranteed ownership of the lands (which were really tribal lands, but that issue was never even raised) and given certain privileges.[6] Years later a government minister would say that "these settlers, who were mainly corrupt adventurers, dispersed, taking with them the instruments and provisions that they had received."[7]

A new conquest of the jungle had begun; the entrepreneur was now independent Peru, which had entered an age of modernization—the same Peru that built the first railroad in South America and that allowed itself the luxury of sending a Navy ship to California to provide security to a few Peruvian adventurers in search of gold. Whereas in colonial times there was interest in winning converts for the religious faith, what now mattered was conquering territory for the establishment of haciendas, which were being formed on the coast and in the sierra at the expense of the ancient Indian communities destroyed by Bolivar, and in the jungle thanks to the efficiency of the carbine. Regarding the use of violence as a system for "civilizing" the jungle, nearly everyone was in agreement. We must not forget that the country was experiencing an era of militarism; the presidents of the republic, those who collaborated with them, and those who opposed them were all military men. So too were the members of foreign missions invited to provide technical reports on matters of regional or national development. In 1851 U.S. Navy officer Lewis Herndon traveled through the central jungle; his opinion had been requested regarding the possibility of navigating the most important rivers in the region. Herndon went as far as the fort of San Ramón; there he had the opportunity to gather information on the state of relations between the Indians and the settlers. The soldiers of the garrison were in a continuous state of war with the Asháninka who, although they had abandoned any ideas of regaining their lost territories, were making any attempt at white advance beyond the Chanchamayo River impossible.[8] The captain of the fort told Herndon how two years earlier a general and his officers who were visiting the installations were struck by Asháninka arrows, which were a constant threat to the lives of the settlers and their wooden homes. Concern was so great that some settlers decided to build adobe houses with strong doors and windows in order to withstand attacks carried out with flaming arrows.[9] For the soldiers and settlers it was risky to bathe in the river, and it was not uncommon for such an action to be met by a shower of arrows from the other side. The fort was armed with four cannons and had fifty soldiers on duty; nevertheless, its function was limited to simply protecting the farmers of the area.[10]

Herndon did not have much respect for the Indians—"here, as in other places, they are lazy drunks"[11]—and it was his opinion that North American Indians would have destroyed the fort's crops in just a few attacks.[12] After he was given some Asháninka arrows, which had fallen on the bank as some soldiers were washing their clothes, and following the advice of the San Ramón soldiers, several Tarma settlers, and a missionary, Herndon decided to change course and abandon exploration of the Perené River. We would find him months later along the Ucayali, attempting to organize an expedition upriver toward the Chanchamayo, but this attempt would also fail because no guide was willing to accompany him into Asháninka territory.[13]

There were some who disagreed with the official policy of aggression in the jungle:

> The Campa who inhabit the Chanchamayo jungle are very hostile, and one cannot enter into a friendly relationship with them. It is amazing, nevertheless, that the heathens of the same nation that inhabit the Santa Ana Valley . . . are quite friendly. I myself was welcomed and given lodging with them during a trip I took in 1858 . . . ; this depends on the means that have been employed in attempting to conquer them. Certainly the cannon and the gun that have been used in Chanchamayo are not the best methods.[14]

Antonio Raimondi, however, was an isolated voice that fell on deaf ears.

The expeditions continued at intervals of several years, and the method was always the same: They trusted only in the gun. In 1868 a military expedition entering the area with weapons was stopped at the Perené and had to return to the sierra;[15] the following year a colonel organized another exploration.[16] The recommendations on how to achieve domination of the Asháninka sound anachronistic: occupy the Mountain of Salt with a company of two hundred soldiers.

That idea was two hundred years old but had never been successful; it would reappear on other occasions until it finally disappeared from government concerns when the Mountain of Salt was definitively occupied by settlers. The official reports of the two expeditions do not allow us to glean any information regarding what really happened as they passed through Indian territory, but John Nystrom, a foreign engineer working for the Peruvian government and stationed in the region, has left us some extremely interesting pages. According to Nystrom, the 1868 expedition left a horrible toll in its wake. The soldiers stole or destroyed everything they found. Near Quimirí they destroyed a Campa blacksmith shop, stealing bellows, anvils, and tools as booty, which, upon their return to Lima, they abandoned and never used. The following year's expedition under the command of Colonel Pereira continued the tradition, stealing everything it found in its path. The soldiers returned to "civilized" lands with the following trophies, which had been left behind by the Asháninka in their huts: one hundred arrows, ten bows, fourteen baskets, one drum, two flutes, one loom, some spindles, twelve packets of bean and orange seeds, some *mate* (gourd) vessels, and four pounds of salt.[17] The list is pathetic in its poverty. "Civilization" advanced and could not pause for sentimentalism; one was either for it or against it. Now the business of conquest was in civilian and military hands, and there was no reason not to conduct it like any other war or invasion. Why speak hypocritically of Christianization? The foundations of the black legend of the *Chunchos* had been laid decades earlier by the missionaries themselves. Were these not, after all, rebel savages who had destroyed all traces of civilization with Santos's rebellion?

During these same years, all of Europe embarked upon the colonialist race toward Africa, and there was no shortage of attempts to regain the old American possessions. These were the years when the new "crusades" were preached and launched to "break through the darkness that envelops entire populations," as King Leopold of Belgium said, referring to Africa. And who better to "break through the darkness" than armed soldiers, the new heralds of progress? The

Indians, like the Africans and Asians, needed the white man's salvation because they were "extremely backward . . . ; they cannot make any advancements nor perfect any of their works."[18] It was unnecessary to prepare the spirits of the new conquistadors against the Indians; it was sufficient to reaffirm a few old and repeated prejudices:

> [T]hey wear a sort of wide coat, sleeveless, not so much out of decency and modesty . . . because . . . little does it matter to them . . . to disrobe even in front of someone they don't know. . . . They have very broad faces and flat noses, which gives them a very unpleasant appearance. . . . Their food is disgusting.[19]

It is curious how relations between Indians and whites had deteriorated and become much tenser in the mid-nineteenth century than they had been at the beginning of the colony. The accounts of the Jesuit Font (1595) or the first conquistadors offer us an idyllic atmosphere of peace and friendship; even the music the Asháninka offered to their visitors was characterized as "well arranged."[20] To what can this change be attributed? Why had the Spaniards' first impressions been so different? They had found among these populations strange customs and interesting beliefs, but nothing so very different from what they could find in their homeland, nothing mysterious or despicable. Although the Asháninka believed in spirits that lived in the forest or rivers or that helped them win a battle, the same or nearly the same situation occurred with the Spanish soldiers, for whom seeing an angel or Santiago in the sky was not an exceptional event. These relations, however, began to deteriorate in the early years of the seventeenth century, reaching the point of a complete break in the mid-eighteenth century, when the Juan Santos rebellion broke out. It was the West whose attitude and interests were changing with respect to the indigenous peoples of the world, and this historical phenomenon is perfectly observable in the central jungle of Peru. The years of the great Campa rebellion are years of hatred, in which the worst prejudices against the jungle Indians take shape, and it is very unlikely that a man of Castilla's era would have believed any part of the accounts of the first missionaries. It all seems to have been forgotten in this era, when a questionable nationalist theory attempted to invade and militarily occupy Indian lands as colonization zones. The time had come for the Asháninka to pay the price for the white man's progress, but it was a high price: not only the salt of the jungle and their lands, but also the spirit of their traditions, of life itself. For the Asháninka, as for all the other jungle Indians, there lay ahead terrible years of struggles and defeats, but also of victories.

On 15 May 1869 the official courier left San Ramón for Tarma. It was composed of an officer, five soldiers, and some Chinese laborers. At Pampa del Carmen the Asháninka attacked and killed two soldiers; the rest of the group managed to escape and take refuge near some settlers at Nijandaris. Some months later, a military expedition would take revenge, robbing and burning the Indians' huts "without mercy." Nystrom, who witnessed these events, exclaimed,

> What living creature, from the lowest animal to the most civilized man, could endure such abuses as those that have been committed against the Chuncho Indians, without their attempting revenge or defense of the homes where they were born and raised?[21]

In 1873 the Manuel Pardo government passed a law that facilitated the immigration of European colonists, who were assured more benefits than President Ramón Castilla had granted years earlier. A short time later three thousand immigrants arrived and were sent to Chanchamayo, contrary to the original plan, which specified that they would be granted coastal land. The military expeditions of 1868 and 1869 and another to the Pichis River in 1870 were related to these governmental projects. A large portion of the immigrants who settled in the newly conquered area of La Merced (the former mission center of Quimirí) were Italian; the government promised them assistance and armed protection. But a few years later two Italian officials who visited the colony heard the settlers' fears and complaints. The settlers were requesting modern weapons, automatic

Winchesters, and shoes in order to continue the raids against the Asháninka; in addition, they asked that more forts be built to protect the farmers while they worked their lands.[22] The report by the Italian mission was heeded, and in 1876 a new official expedition was organized; it was led by Arturo Wertheman, the same man who in 1873 had failed in his attempt to navigate the Perené. On this occasion he had twenty armed men and the promise of support from the "Zepita" battalion, which had been called away at the last minute to an opportune revolution in the southern part of the country, but a shipwreck during the first days of the trip brought the mission to an end.[23]

The new expedition now had the support of soldiers, at least for the first days of navigation. A few days after they left the fort at San Ramón, when they were still on the Chanchamayo River, the Asháninka attacked from the shore. The expeditionaries fired and went ashore, where they managed to recover more than sixty arrows. Before fleeing, the Indians set fire to their blacksmith shop, showing a strange attachment to this symbol of the long years of missionary presence. The journey continued despite constant sabotage by the Indians, who on one occasion attempted to steal the rafts. When the soldiers separated from Wertheman and headed for the Mountain of Salt and San Ramón by land, they took with them twenty-two Asháninka prisoners. The documents tell us nothing about the fate of these men, but we can assume that in the best-case scenario, they would have been parceled out as servants among the settlers. Wertheman and his men continued their voyage, going ashore to steal food and other items from the Asháninka homes; at times they encountered resistance, but in most cases they found the homes abandoned. Finally the explorers managed to navigate the Tambo and reach the Ucayali. For the second time in the span of a few years, the myth of the Tambo as a river forbidden to whites since the late seventeenth century had been shattered. A few years before Wertheman, a missionary had reached the Tambo from Cuzco by way of the Ene.[24] From this moment on, the route of the Perené and Tambo was open to reconquest, but it was not an easy route; the Asháninka would consistently fight the intruders for it.

Now traveling more calmly down the Tambo, Wertheman was able to gather information about the high mountain range that rose to the west, separating the Gran Pajonal from the Ucayali River basin. The Tambo and upper Ucayali Campa would travel up to the Pajonal via the Unini River and in about ten days reach the Mountain of Salt, where they could obtain several months' supply. What most astonished the explorer, and what in our opinion has explanatory significance, is this information: Every year the Indians (which ones and how many?) gathered at the Pajonal to celebrate a ritual in memory of Juan Santos, during which his sword was taken out and carried in a procession.[25] The memory of the messiah was alive, and his return was probably expected at any moment. The Gran Pajonal, which had been the center and heart of the rebellion, was now the keeper of the memories and the leader of the tradition. Throughout the year small bands of Asháninka traders traveled its paths to obtain salt, carrying with them tunics or ceramics to exchange for other items and for hospitality. With them traveled their traditions, their hopes, and the information of interest to their society. The Pajonal, the vast center of Campa territory not yet invaded by whites, appears to have been the center of culture and tradition through which the Indians journeyed, like a constant flow of life through their very society.

THE VOICE OF A HUMANIST

Although the foreign travelers during the first half of the nineteenth century had avoided or passed very quickly through Campa lands, the new wave of travelers who reached Peru toward the end of that century focused their attention and curiosity upon these Indians. These were the brave heirs of Juan Santos's rebellion; they were cannibals and descendants of the Incas;[26] they had all the necessary attributes for attracting the interest of these pilgrims of fantasy, whose curiosity at times slid to the periphery of science. Then, in the name of scientific inquiry, aberrations occurred that can only be explained as the fruit of an era in western history in which aggressiveness had become the standard rule of behavior. There was nothing abnormal, therefore, about the macabre operation conducted by Charles Wiener, who beheaded two Machiguenga cadavers that had been ritually abandoned in the river. Wiener saw nothing wrong with this decapitation: *J'ajoutai à mon bagage ces deux spécimens anthropologiques unique en Europe des races du haut Ucayali* ("I was adding to my baggage these two rare anthropological specimens of upper Ucayali races").[27] Some years earlier a Spanish scientific expedition had carried out similar operations, perhaps better planned from a methodological point of view but equally lugubrious and in bad taste.[28] It is amazing that one does not find in these travelers even a minimal reflection of what occupied the minds of their intellectual contemporaries in Europe. Wiener was from France, the land where the spiritual legacy of Lafitau had been adopted by the generation of the Romantics, where Chateaubriand was singing nostalgic praises of the American Indians, and where a scholar wrote, "I confess that I am surprised to see how many limit themselves to the simple enumeration of their customs, without penetrating their hidden meaning, without seeking the causes, without trying to go back to their origins."[29] In 1871 *Primitive Culture* had been published in England; its author, Edward B. Taylor, outlined the goals of ethnology and folklore, related disciplines whose reason for existence lay in a certain sympathy for the "noble savage," whether Australian or American, Aranda or Asháninka.

Some of this new folkloric humanism that had taken shape in Europe also reached Peru. It arrived in the person of the French vice consul in Callao: Olivier Ordinaire, who would remain in Peru for several years, drawn by its geography and its people.

In this humanistic traveler, the Asháninka found an understanding visitor who was willing to learn and who approached them without weapons, as Antonio Raimondi had done earlier. Ordinaire maintained that the dark portrayal of the Campa that he had been given during his three years on the coast was totally false and was caused by the writings of missionaries and explorers who had been attacked by Indians who were simply defending their lands and homes. He, Raimondi, and José Samanés had had no problems with the Asháninka; Wertheman, however, had been attacked because he had approached the Asháninka like an armed conquistador. Ordinaire added that the attitude of the jungle Indians should be judged in accordance with what had been done to them: the stealing of their women and children, their exploitation as laborers, and armed attacks against them. The Asháninka welcomed the first missionary who visited them, but with him came the road and the whites who had been expelled by their own society; the indigenous reaction could be none other than rejection.[30] It was the settlers who had caused revenge attacks through their constant aggression or ignorant behavior. Ordinaire cites the case of five whites who were killed or wounded by the Campa in Quillazú. They had apparently committed no abuse, and the crime was described as completely unjustified, but Ordinaire was not satisfied with this explanation; he wanted to know the truth and he discovered it. The five whites, who were confused with Chileans (one in fact was, and during this time many deserters had taken refuge in the jungle and devoted themselves to banditry), had disobeyed one of the most important Asháninka rules. They had entered Asháninka homes without first shouting or whistling to alert the residents of their presence; they had touched objects in the homes, behaving exactly like enemies who plan to attack.[31] Ordinaire found proof that a wise and enlightened administrative policy can produce magnificent results with the Campa. For years rubber dealer Guillermo Franzen had lived in the midst of sixty Asháninka families, who worked for him and took care of his family when he traveled to Iquitos to sell the rubber and was often away for several months at a time: *Ne sont donc pas aussi féroces q'on le croit* ("They are not as fierce as they are believed to be").[32]

Accustomed as we are to a complete lack of understanding of religious phenomena by all previous visitors to the Asháninka, Ordinaire strikes us as a true ethnologist, the only one before our time who tried to penetrate beyond appearances, seeking the "hidden meaning" of indigenous customs.[33] He was the first to observe some of the rules of reciprocity among members of Ashéninka society and the first to see, very keenly, a relationship between the system of reciprocity of services and the religious sphere. Ordinaire thought that this was a custom established by Juan Santos based on the Christian model of charity and collaboration, and he believed that certain litanies that were repeated in the nocturnal festivals by adult Ashéninka were of missionary derivation or could be attributed to Santos. Whether his hypothesis was correct or mistaken, what is interesting to note is the traveler's observation. Ordinaire wrote down some litanies, verses of songs, and beliefs about solar and lunar rituals and about the annual gatherings at the Gran Pajonal. We only regret that he did not live fifty years later, when he would have had available to him more refined instruments with which to approach these questions, because he was certainly not lacking in willingness.[34]

RAIDS AND THE GOOD LIFE

Men like Ordinaire rarely visited the central jungle, and rarer still were rubber dealers like Franzen. The last quarter of the nineteenth century witnessed the sudden and unexpected rise of a new fever that would transform the Peruvian jungle into a hell for most of its inhabitants and into a paradise for a few. Europe had begun to utilize rubber in industry early in the century, but the demand increased steadily after the discovery of the vulcanization process in 1844 and the appearance of new factories and new applications. Since the early days of the conquest of America, the largest amount of rubber had come from the Amazon jungle. In 1876 the English took some *Hevea brasiliensis* plants to Ceylon, Borneo, and India, but full production would not be reached for fifteen to twenty years. After 1910, Asian rubber would effectively compete with American and African rubber. Before that date, in the South American jungles, a mad race would take place for supremacy in rubber production. Nevertheless, in the latter part of the nineteenth century in the Peruvian jungle, there was no serious attempt to cultivate *shiringa* trees; it was exclusively an industry of extraction or harvesting. This matter is very important for understanding what happened to the native populations during the years of rubber fever.

It is generally considered that between 350 and 500 trees can be planted on one hectare; about 250 of these will end up being partially productive after the fifth or seventh year, reaching their maximum productivity after their fifteenth year of life. A crop of this type does not require more than a limited number of laborers. In the Peruvian jungle, however, rubber was not planted but harvested by searching plant by plant in the virgin jungle. This method required a great deal of manual labor as well as "skilled" workers who could search the jungle without becoming lost, who were familiar with the areas of greatest concentration of *shiringa* trees, who could live on a handful of cassava flour or a few cassava roots per day, and who could survive week after week in complete solitude. No settler was able to endure this lifestyle; the natives, however, were at the disposal of the most enterprising rubber dealers, of whom there was no shortage.

Carlos Fermín Fitzcarrald accepted the challenge of the times and situation. When he was still young, he entered the jungle while being pursued as a Chilean spy or, according to some, as a fugitive from justice for having had problems and a serious injury related to a gambling argument. It is known that at age twenty-six he had already achieved a position in Iquitos as a trader and rubber dealer; a short time later people would begin to call him the "Rubber King." He would send his children to study in Paris and would become the owner of a substantial number of natives of various groups, reinstating the old *encomienda* and tribute payment system, this time under the guise of rubber. It is difficult to follow Fitzcarrald's peregrinations through the jungle. He changed work areas periodically: the Pachitea, the upper Ucayali (where he built his main house, a luxurious home surrounded by delicate gardens tended by Chinese gardeners), the Tambo, the Apurímac, the Urubamba, the Madre de Dios, and the Purús. To allow quick movement through his vast "empire," Fitzcarrald and his two partners organized a flotilla of boats and a steamboat that could sail most of the rivers of the central jungle. On that ship one could drink the best French wine and relax in comfortable cabins; "it was all so clean, neat, and elegant," wrote a missionary,

> that we had no reason to envy the best European steamboats. . . . [A] half hour before dinner we would be offered a cocktail, and sitting down at the table, after the second ring of the bell, we were all impressed and enjoying ourselves greatly, due to the luxury as well as the excellent service and variety of exquisite food and drink.[35]

Outside the steamboat Bermúdez, the situation was quite different; there the settlers "were raffling an [Indian] girl" or paying their debts "with a shapely girl."[36] Outside the boat were the Indians' jungle and their homes; each time the travelers went ashore, all the sailors and "third class crew" were jumping like "a plague of locusts, searching all the homes and destroying everything . . . , and the passengers, jumping down the cables [would go ashore] like ants to grab plantains, cassavas, papayas, and other things, ignoring the owner of the farm, who was watching them."[37]

The rubber dealer worked with two systems, according to the type of laborer he had. With the mestizo worker he used the *enganche* (debt system), which is still very common today; it tied the laborer to the boss through an eternal debt that the worker would never be able to repay.

> Before going into the jungle, they receive as an advance provisions, work tools, and a sum of money and commodities, all at excessive prices. But this advance becomes an oppressive bond that enslaves workers indefinitely and places them at the mercy of their bosses' greed. . . . [T]he treatment to which the indigenous laborers are subjected consists of a series of inconceivable abuses, mistreatment, and calamities that would be extremely unpleasant and difficult to describe in detail.[38]

The second system and the most widely used was the one applied with native laborers. It consisted of simply enslaving a substantial number of young Indian men and women (mature or elderly individuals were eliminated, not so much because their productivity was lower, but because they did not adapt easily to the new circumstances and therefore were disruptive elements) and moving them from their place of origin to another place. The rubber dealer had understood perfectly that the secret to having calm, submissive slaves lay in distancing them from their native land. Thus separated from their familiar places, from their world, from the palpable signs of their transcendent universe, the Indians lost all interest in life, in their society, and in tradition and surrendered, defeated in spirit, to their new, sad existence, brightened only by the hope of some savior hero's return.

Even more artful was the practice effectively disseminated and institutionalized by Fitzcarrald, who with true "ethnological knowledge" of the jungle, had been able to utilize the traditional rivalries of the various tribal groups. A similar attempt had been made in the seventeenth century,[39] when the Franciscans used the Cunibo as support troops against the Asháninka. But Fitzcarrald and other rubber dealers after him obtained truly noteworthy results. The method was simple: Winchester rifles were given to the Cunibo in exchange for Campa slaves; later, Winchesters were given to the Campa, and they in turn had to pay with Cunibo or Amuesha slaves; and so on in a chain of tragic raids that tainted nearly forty years of Peruvian jungle history with sadness and horror and whose consequences are still being felt. It was at this time that the term *civilized Indian* was coined to refer to those who, armed and in the service of the whites, were charged with the sad task of dealing in human lives. The "civilized" Campa, Cunibo, and Piro would go to the groups in the interior, where they would procure payment for their debts.[40] It was common for missionaries to meet these human-hunting expeditions. When Father Gabriel Sala explored the Gran Pajonal in 1897, he met four Campa from the Tambo armed with Winchesters, who were heading to the highlands for a raid; they were to "catch laborers" for Fitzcarrald's and Suárez's Manú River rubber operations.[41]

Of the twenty-eight thousand workers in the Loreto jungle in 1913, twenty-two thousand were involved in rubber operations, and most of these workers were natives.[42] Statistical data from the other rubber harvest areas are lacking, but one must consider that the upper jungle adjacent to the cordillera did not produce *shiringa* trees; it supplied the rest of the east with manual labor that was obtained through violent means. Native populations along the larger rivers had been decimated beginning in the sixteenth century, and the Putumayo area groups were soon destroyed by the rubber dealers. In the first decade of the twentieth century alone, it is estimated that forty thousand Witoto—80 percent of the entire indigenous population of the area[43]—were exterminated in forced labor, concentration camps, and massacres.[44] These losses had to be recovered, and the upper jungle offered the best conditions as a supplier of laborers; all that was lacking were individuals with initiative and a little bravery, individuals like "Fitzcarrald, [who], scorning them and killing along the way some who opposed him, has established himself in the center of his dominion,"[45] as a court chronicler of the time proclaimed in praise.

These were the opinions and the conduct of the rubber dealers chosen by circumstance to advance the conquest of the jungle in the late nineteenth century. The opinions guiding the actions of the missionaries and authorities were not very different, although some rare exceptions risked public anathema with their favorable opinions of the Indians. The missionary explorer, who was candidly ignorant and therefore free of all prudence in his evaluations, guaranteed white aggression the nearly official support of the church:

> Chuncho means the same as a false man, a traitor, an ingrate, lazy, drunkard, vengeful, and fickle. And what will we do with such beings? What is done throughout the world: [I]nasmuch as they do not wish to live like men, but rather like animals, treat them as such, and shoot them when they unjustly oppose the life and welfare of others.[46]

With regard to the identity of the "others," it is obvious that this term does not refer to the members of other indigenous groups; for these the missionary advised several systems of domination: "Through terror and moderate punishment they will find themselves forced to appeal to the mercy of the Missionary Priest, who will then be able, with great charity and prudence, to exercise his divine ministry over those unfortunate creatures."[47] At other times the Franciscan preferred the collaboration of the settlers: "Once the rubber dealer has subjugated the savage Cachivo at gunpoint, it is the opportune time for the missionary priest to immediately enter to offer the services and consolations of our Holy Religion."[48] This collaboration was nearly always indispensable because white aggression seemed to be the best door of access for the so-called Christianization: "[C]olonizing their lands, they are surrounded and absorbed, obliging them almost forcibly, at least out of shame, to follow the customs of civilized people."[49] The force thus employed acquired an evangelical nature because

> what happens in China and Japan, first convincing their minds so they then surrender willingly, should not be a model or obstacle to us. With our Indians, both those of the sierra and those of the jungle, we must do exactly the opposite; that is, cause their will to bend, even by beating them, so that sooner or later their minds become enlightened and open.[50]

All of this had the force of dogma, as it had worked in colonial times: "[I]t was done this way in the Viceroy's time and has continued until the present in some places along the Ucayali."[51]

A few priests and explorers, however, disagreed with these viewpoints. In the opinions of José Samanéz Ocampo, Redemptorist Father Mauricio Touchaux, and some engineers, the Asháninka and other jungle Indians had no alternative other than to fight or to flee into the jungle: "[I]t is sad to see that those who have dealings with them [the 'civilized'] have become evil, whereas those who have never met them are good."[52]

Meanwhile, the Asháninka were attempting to resist the advance of the whites, using every means at their disposal, both human and divine. In 1896, before attacking a Pangoa River settlement, the shaman advised his warriors to blow hard against the white men's bullets in order to change them into leaves[53] because this use of the breath is a divine action, an archetypal act. A few years earlier the Asháninka of the Pichis River headwaters had managed to retake part of their lands. Fourteen settlers died in the attacks; the rest fled, abandoning the area to the rebel Indians.[54] In these cases the prevailing opinion among the settlers was that the guilty Indians would escape to the Gran Pajonal, where they could live without being pursued because the highlands continued to be an impregnable refuge. In fact, except for an occasional and very daring white rubber dealer,[55] no one ventured into those territories, whose reputation had not changed since the days of Juan Santos.

SALT AND BLACKSMITH SHOPS

In September 1895 Don Nicolás de Piérola took office as president of Peru with the goal of "making a handful of disorderly people, who are spread over an immense territory, the powerful people who will live on this blessed piece of the globe."[56] There was good reason for the people to be disorderly. In just two days, Piérola's revolution against Andrés Avelino Cáceres had resulted in more than one thousand dead and two thousand wounded in Lima.[57] It was a pointless revolution, "the most recent in a series of popular uprisings."[58] The disorderliness, however, was not just among a handful of people, as Piérola thought; it included all the Peruvian Indians who, from time to time, were "caught with ropes on the high Andean plateaus, pushed with the points of bayonets, and thrown against each other, like a wild beast attacks another, a locomotive against a locomotive."[59] That same disorderliness had led Pedro Pablo Atusparia and the Indians of Huaraz to an armed rebellion, which was later continued by Uchcu Pedro and the other Indians of the Andes in Azángaro, Huancané, Huanta, Ayacucho, and Puno. The popular uprisings were these: Indian rebellions against tributes or forced labor, not the rebellions organized from government halls or military barracks, which relied on strategies designed at the expense of the indigenous masses.

But we cannot demand anything of history. Neither Piérola nor the later civilian governments could afford to be sensitive to the indigenous problems, much less to the problems of a few jungle dwellers. Rubber was booming. In 1896 the European markets valued it at two pounds sterling per arroba; a year later it would account for almost 10 percent of total Peruvian exports. Its importance would continue growing until 1912, when it could no longer compete with the English and Dutch colonies. The jungle, so generous in *shiringa*, was part of this "blessed piece of the globe" to which Piérola referred, and it was time for the Peruvian state to share in its generosity. Piérola, like Castilla, believed in the jungle and saw in it a solution for Peru. Communication with the Amazon region was practically nonexistent, however, and the rubber trade was geared toward Brazil and was completely outside the control of the capital; a large portion of the benefits that the state would have obtained could not overcome the barrier of the cordillera. What was necessary was to link the coast with the jungle by means of a railroad, which would cross the Gran Pajonal and reach a navigable point on the Ucayali River. An admirer of the Franciscans, Piérola personally charged Father Gabriel Sala with exploration of the Pajonal.

Between November 1896 and March 1897, Father Sala explored the Pichis, Pachitea, and upper Ucayali and all the vast and "beautiful region of the Pajonal, [which] is a uniform high plateau 1,500 meters above sea level and surrounded on all sides by a chain of very rugged peaks measuring 2,000 to 2,500 meters in elevation."[60] The missionary entered the Pajonal from the Chicosa River, a tributary of the upper Ucayali; he was accompanied by another missionary and several Asháninka river guides. A German settler would later join the expedition. All were armed, but at least they were not accompanied by the army. Naturally Sala shared the common prejudices of the time, to the degree that his opinions are extremely crude. The Gran Pajonal Asháninka who opposed the white expedition "conducted themselves at all times as noble savages, defending their lands, their families, their freedom, and their persons."[61] Sala's prejudices caused him to see enemies everywhere. A river Asháninka who advised him not to enter the Pajonal because of the many armed Indians there who were ready to stop him, was judged to be a "skilled and savage man . . . with evil plans," whom the members of the expedition were prepared "to stab repeatedly and break his arrows,"[62] obviously with very little missionary spirit. The Franciscan imagined this to be a threat, misinterpreted the indigenous welcome ceremony at the home, and considered it normal that all the Asháninka would offer food and lodging to the expedition.[63] From the beginning of the trip, there was a long series of errors and misunderstandings, which at times nearly compromised the success of the expedition, a success that Sala constantly endangered with his attitude. For example, it seemed fine to him to practice target shooting in front of the Campa guides: "[O]ur steadiness is not bad; and if it became necessary to have to aim at some savage, we would attempt to fix our gaze on the center to at least hit the head or feet."[64]

After twelve days' march from the Ucayali, the expedition reached the first Gran Pajonal hamlet, which consisted of "eight or ten little houses, very well made and enclosed, with their little doors made of *camona*. These houses were deserted at the moment, inasmuch as their inhabitants had fled out of fear of the whites."[65] This phenomenon would be repeated many times before the missionaries crossed the entire highlands: "[O]n the Pajonal there are many little houses grouped together, but most of them are empty and others are burned; there are also many roads in all directions, which denotes that many people travel through there, but we have seen hardly anyone."[66] The missionary was surprised at the welcome they received from the Pajonalinos: "[I]t happened that the first savages who might have murdered us offered us food, drink, and cheerful hospitality,"[67] but this surprise did not change Sala's opinion of the *Chunchos*. Whenever any Pajonalino put up a little resistance—verbal, of course—to the group, the Franciscan noted, "because reason was unable to triumph, [the Indians] had to surrender at gunpoint."[68] In reality Father Sala, despite being a missionary experienced in the jungle, had no knowledge of native customs. He was astonished at the welcome ceremony each time he entered a hamlet, and it seemed to him a contradiction that the same individual who had argued against the expedition was later a perfect host, generous with food and drink. "That fierce man . . . , who at first behaved with such ferocity, from that moment played the role of clown, trying in every possible way to serve and entertain us, whether by making music, dancing, or inventing a thousand other lovely things."[69]

During his long journey across the Pajonal, Father Sala had little direct contact with the Indians. Each time he approached a hamlet, he found it deserted. The fires were lit, the food was ready, and the *masato* was fermented, but the inhabitants had fled, hurriedly abandoning everything. Their fear of the white man and of raids was constant. When the missionaries would call to a Campa whom they saw in the distance, they rarely received a response, only the sensation of having caused terror. The few Asháninka who dared to speak with Sala anxiously asked the reasons for his presence: "Why have you come to this land? Are you bringing a disease? . . . Doubtless you are carrying colds or measles."[70] Others, more daring or perhaps more frightened, tried to halt the white men's advance with long sharp palm stakes stuck into the ground.[71]

As the missionaries were approaching the south, near the area of Chanchamayo and the Perené, they began to hear news of clashes between settlers and Indians. They were fighting over salt. The Campa of the Pangoa, Negro, and Perené River areas had rebelled against the whites and against the English of the Peruvian company, who were preventing them from taking salt from the mountain. The Asháninka and the Amuesha had heard the call of the "false God Amachegua,"[72] who had declared himself the brother of God and had come down from heaven to help the Indians in combat. The entire region was suffering violent disturbances. The English farms were abandoned or burned; in the camps through which the expedition passed, they found tools, cooking pots, and other traces of the defeated colonists. Father Sala came to sympathize, if not with the rebels, at least with their causes:

> The government has decided that the salt from Chanchamayo, or the Mountain of Salt, should be tax free and that everyone can take advantage of it. Why, then, do the poor *Chunchos* have

> to be attacked when they come 20 days' difficult journey to get a little piece of salt that lasts them a whole year and is the only condiment of their foods?[73]

The government, however, had other intentions. A few months later it would send a special visitor to the Mountain of Salt to perform an inspection, declare the area the property of the State Salt Monopoly, and thus be able to work it as an industry. With the Asháninka salt, the government planned to create a fund to buy back the cities of Tacna and Arica, which had been lost in the war with Chile.[74]

The Asháninka had to capitulate to this state intervention. Little by little, whites began to occupy the Mountain of Salt region ever more steadily; they established more farms and built roads, invading Indian territory and pushing its inhabitants into the interior toward the heights of the Pajonal, where the Asháninka "are almost entirely without salt and are almost ceasing to use it because of the great difficulties and obstacles in bringing it from Chanchamayo, especially after San Luis de Shuaro and Perené were colonized."[75]

The Asháninka society's salt was being taken away, just as the blacksmith shops that had been preserved and used for centuries had been destroyed earlier. Deprived of these two cultural elements (the first traditional and with an eminently social and economic function, the second acquired and with a mainly technological function), this native society could have expected either a quicker death or an accelerated integration into white and mestizo society, but none of this happened. Asháninka culture, crippled in the technique of the use of iron, stripped of the only mine that produced this metal (in the Perené) and the Mountain of Salt, managed to recover and reestablish its lost equilibrium. Trade[76] would play a bigger role; what could not be manufactured in the blacksmith shops would be obtained by trading with other groups or with settlers; salt too would be obtained through trade. We can conclude that these new stimuli of the already traditional trade network also strengthened the Asháninka's intertribal bonds and thus increased their cultural unity.

The report of Father Sala's exploration would reach President Piérola's hands and begin a governmental action geared toward the opening of the "central route" or road to the Pichis, a longtime desire of the Pierolist national unity policy. Other explorations and other reports would follow that were equally optimistic or even more optimistic than Sala's, but political circumstances would distract state attention from the Gran Pajonal. In 1904 José Pardo's government would send a new mission to the Pajonal with instructions to verify Sala's data and study the route between Chanchamayo and a navigable point on the Ucayali. The "Unini Commission," under the command of engineer César Cipriani, would confirm Sala's information that the distance between San Luis de Shuaro and the Ucayali was two hundred kilometers in a straight line, representing four hundred kilometers of highway and an enormous expenditure for the state.[77] Cipriani was an enthusiastic defender of the plan for a railroad that would run from Oroya to the Ucayali, crossing the Perené and the Pajonal. Perhaps for this reason his opinions of the Asháninka were so optimistic: "[T]hey are honest people, hardworking, and active; if you treat them right, you can profit from them."[78] The engineer, like the Franciscan, found desolation and terror all along the way:

> The rubber dealers personally conduct frequent incursions into the Pajonal, and wherever they go they leave behind evidence of arson, pillage, and desolation; such is what we have observed on our journey, often finding burned homes, abandoned farms, Indians who have fled, and others who have taken shelter in deep and hidden ravines, where they still live in fear of being attacked.[79]

The missionary Father Alemany would encounter the same situation months later: the trafficking in human flesh encouraged and practiced by the Ucayali River rubber dealers.[80]

At the beginning of the twentieth century, interest in conquest of the jungle was still very much alive. These were the years of the great explorations, of the creation of the Riverways Board, and of the parliamentary debate over a loan of three million pounds sterling for the construction of the railroad to the east.[81] These were years in which rubber production increased at a rapid rate, in 1910 totaling 18 percent of Peruvian exports. As has been mentioned, two years later competition from the English and Dutch colonies would unexpectedly put an end to the Amazonian rubber industry, causing a halt in all private and state activities in the Peruvian jungle. Just as suddenly as it had begun, rubber fever disappeared without warning. A calm unknown in forty years returned to the rivers and jungle of Peru. A generation of Indians had contributed to the material prosperity of the western world. For some indigenous groups the cost of this tribute had been high; it had almost meant their disappearance. The Asháninka were able to survive thanks to favorable (external) historical and (internal) cultural circumstances. In 1914 Campa rebellion made itself felt once again. Settlers and rubber dealers on the Pichis River were expelled from their territory; the Franciscan missionaries suffered the same fate. The government responded to these attacks by sending repressive military missions,[82] but these were demonstrations of sovereignty and authority more than a true interest in retaking the lost rich rubber lands. The country was now looking to the new coastal industries: sugar, cotton, and petroleum. Only some missionaries and European scientists were interested in the jungle.

A FEW ETHNOGRAPHERS . . .

Arnald Van Gennep is the first ethnologist whose name appears in relation to the Asháninka. The same "attentive, scrupulous, pleasant" Van Gennep, author of the already classic work *Les rites de passage* and *Mythes et légendes d'Australie*,[83] who "can be considered one of the most representative figures of European folkloric science," in 1919 published an article devoted to a Chanchamayo Asháninka loom. It is a short, detailed document written from a European museum that reflects the focus on material culture typical of the ethnology of the early twentieth century.[84] Van Gennep had never seen an Indian up close, nor did he have any interest in doing so; ethnology was basically a type of history that used a special source, which could be "indirect." Scientific interest in the Asháninka, especially in Europe, began with this short document by Van Gennep. Naturally from the indigenous point of view, this interest was barely perceptible. A few ethnographer explorers would pass through Campa lands or travel down the rivers asking questions, purchasing objects, seeking causes, and tirelessly drawing or photographing objects, always objects. These were the years when "material culture" was the privileged child of anthropology. Long lists were drawn up of cultural characteristics and subcharacteristics, analyzing their presence or absence or modification in the populations in question, and catalogs were prepared containing thousands of terms.[85] The gathering of material, in the early days left to travelers and missionaries, was now conducted on site. At times direct observation was impossible because of the trauma caused by the conquest and colonization of the indigenous populations; in this case a survey using a questionnaire would be substituted, directed at the elderly people who remembered their traditional way of life.[86] This method was used frequently until the 1930s in North American and European ethnology; some examples of this ethnology reached the central Peruvian jungle.

Chronologically speaking, the first traveler with an ethnological interest to make contact with the Asháninka was Otto Nordenskjold. A geographer and the brother of an anthropologist, he was in South America to carry out a study of the Andes, but he took time to spend a couple of months in Chanchamayo. He was traveling under the auspices of the Leguía government and the Geographic Society of Lima. Nordenskjold was an attentive observer who patiently described native objects, which he later compared with others from different areas. Naturally he was interested much more in the form and structure of a room than in its inhabitants, but that was what the occasion demanded. Nevertheless, in Nordenskjold the Asháninka found a new kind of traveler, who was willing to drink *masato*, sleep on the *tarimas*, or palm wood platforms, and respect their way of life. Nordenskjold perceived the effects of the rubber era, revealed in the scant Asháninka population along the large rivers and in the presence of observation towers on some posts in strategic places. These were used by the Indians to observe the Ene and Tambo Rivers, from where the rubber dealers' raids would be launched without warning. The Swedish geographer sympathized with the Asháninka; they found him to be cheerful and smiling but at the same time serious and dignified, never inopportune or overly curious. He recognized that civilization could be too heavy a burden for this society if it were associated with settlers and rubber dealers with no kind of control.[87]

A very different opinion would be expressed some years later by German ethnologist Günter Tessmann, self-identified as a follower of Leo Frobenius and Wilhelm Schmidt but without the poetry of the former or the scholarship of the latter. After an inspiring introduction proclaiming that his book begins the third chapter of Amazonian studies—the scientific chapter—what follows is a huge volume at the end of which the reader will be sure that he has read the work of a zoologist who missed his calling.[88] Tessmann reveals something zoological, especially in his examples, where he calmly states, "At times it seemed like I was looking at a highly evolved anthropoid ape; the Indian's brain was so deficient when it came to retaining facts, even when presented clearly and simply." Who was this indigenous informant? "He belonged to the Campa who had been relocated along the lower Ucayali by Mr. Iriarte, on whose hacienda I stayed for some time. All of the informants spoke fair Spanish and were to a point sufficiently sane."[89] Tessmann did not consider the fact that this particular informant was disturbed because of having been separated from his society for years, because of his situation as a slave talking to an individual who was a friend of his boss, or above all, because of the German's attitude:

> I never renounced my own personality when I was face-to-face with him. . . . I never tried to play the ridiculous game of pretending to be an Indian among the Indians. . . . I have never tolerated disrespectful actions or excessively drunken

> visitors, and without any hesitation I threw them out of my hut or tent. . . . [I]n short, I treated the Indians as they deserved to be treated.[90]

Around this same time, dozens of anthropologists were striving to play the "ridiculous game" of participant observation. An anthropologist like Tessmann cannot set aside his racism: "[T]his tribe [the Campa] will be civilized very slowly and only through the expansion of the light-skinned population."[91] A very short time later, this language would be spread throughout Europe in circumstances that were more dramatic than the visit of an ethnologist.

To support his negative opinion of the Peruvian jungle Indians, the German ethnologist quoted some late-nineteenth-century travelers and missionaries, which evidently allowed him to affirm that "the Campa are completely lacking in civilization . . . , [and] most are completely savage."[92] What is even worse, to Tessmann's inflexible mentality, is the mocking and disrespectful attitude of these Indians who take everything, even the most solemn things, simply and unceremoniously, showing a "surprising insolence" toward the authorities and settlers. Tessmann recommended a serious "moralization" campaign by the government; however, he said, things would not change.[93] Fortunately this German traveler's opinions had no repercussions in Peru, neither among scientists nor among lay people. Tessmann returned to Germany with his moralizing and civilizing ideas to join the ranks of those thinkers who proclaimed that "now in the Germans the meaning of life is genuine; now we can fulfill the role that was written especially for us" (Leo Frobenius, 1933). How this role was played is well known. Tessmann has left us a few thick volumes of less than reliable ethnological data and the most complete slander ever poured out against the Asháninka.

> Their most salient characteristics are a lack of vision of necessity, cunning or rather wickedness . . . , trickery, dishonesty, cruelty, evil, lack of joviality, distrust, lack of respect, insolence, and stubbornness. They never laugh at a simple joke; they only shout maliciously when they hear that something unpleasant

> happened to someone . . . ; they only have material goals that are the only thing that guides their actions.[94]

The material goals to which Tessmann refers were the little glass boxes or old shoes that he promised his informants if they gave him permission to photograph them naked.

. . . AND MANY MISSIONARIES

No other professional ethnologist would take an interest in the Asháninka, neither to denigrate them nor to assist the authorities in their administrative policies toward ethnic minorities. In fact, in Peru, as in most other Latin American nations, there was never any manifestation of the phenomenon of European (especially English) colonialist administration known as "Indirect Rule" or of the use of professional anthropologists as government advisers. The "Indirect Rule" policy assumed a knowledge of the traditional institutions of governed peoples and an interest in governing them through their own laws and cultural norms, but none of this happened in Peru.

Diverse historical circumstances had given the Andean and jungle Indians the status of apparent legal equality with the criollo class, a status that ended up becoming more of a burden than an advantage. In fact, with Independence the status that declared the inferiority of the Indians during the colonial period was eliminated; at the same time, however, the new republic also eliminated a detailed body of laws, which, although discriminatory, provided the Indians with at least partial protection from excessive exploitation by the criollos.[95] Independence, essentially a rebellion of the criollo colonists against the mother country, to which the indigenous masses were completely indifferent, was not followed by a period of "decolonization" or by a change in the conditions of the Indians; the most archaic structures remained as before, despite transformations in the political sphere. "Far from achieving decolonization . . . , the emancipation of the criollos—which was not the emancipation of the Indians—had as a result the culmination of colonization."[96]

From the time of Independence to the present, we find the jungle Indians in these conditions: theoretically equal to other citizens under the law, but for all practical purposes, the subjects of the colonial systems of apportionment and *encomiendas*. Naturally there never was, nor is there now, any interest by the politicians in Lima in improving the situation of the jungle Indians; the preference has always been to leave that portion of the population to the "care" of missionaries or to the exploitation of settlers in a frontier too far from the capital to be effectively controlled. It was therefore useless to ask republican Peru for governmental attention to ethnic minorities based on the principles of "Indirect Rule" or on the administrative suggestions made by anthropologists' research. It was also pointless to look, in what remained of the twentieth century, for serious state attempts to protect, help, or even "govern" the jungle populations.

The jungle had been and continues to be "the frontier of opportunities," being constantly and prematurely ravaged by criollo entrepreneurs, first in search of rubber and now in search of timber or coffee: a moving frontier whose Indian inhabitants also move at a pace that is too fast with respect to the use of the already incorporated lands. This lack of correspondence between the exhaustive exploitation of land already incorporated into the national economy and the conquest of virgin territory (taken from the tribal societies) has been accurately pointed out by Jacques Lambert[97] as one of the main causes of the deterioration of the traditional communities. In fact, those who can afford the luxury of buying tracts of forest that are far from population centers, and therefore costly to use and maintain, are the wealthy coastal criollos who generally reside in the capital and turn over their new lands to administrators. This discourages limited colonization by families of settlers who do not occupy more land than they can cultivate, and encourages the monopolization of large areas with sparse peasant population but abundant indigenous human resources. In this way, tribal communities are not only robbed of their lands but are also faced with the alternative of abandoning the area inherited from their ancestors and bestowed by their gods or becoming members of a class of dispossessed laborers.

The Indian moves from an organic and functional society, as his had been, into a situation of semiservitude and paternalistic relationships, which might attract him at first but in the long run binds him to the new type of latifundium, or large landed estate, through the precariousness of his new economic situation. In fact, in order to work for his boss and pay his debts, which are not freely contracted (because it is difficult for him to fight the temptation to possess "white" goods that entail prestige), he must neglect his own farming, hunting, fishing, and trading and in the end will become more and more tied to the hacienda and less and less free to return to his traditional life.

The relationships between the colonial *encomiendas* and the present-day large landed estates (latifundia) have been noted so often that it is unnecessary to reiterate them here;[98] however, it is important to examine a structural aspect that has remained invariable from the times of apportionment to the present: the personal relationships of dependency between the laborer and the owner or administrator, which even now may be accompanied by forced labor. We pause to examine this aspect because it also relates to the missions, which often imitate, in their organization, the models that society provides. Naturally the missions were not latifundia in the strict sense of the word,[99] but they copied the personal relationships of dependency, which created situations that were identical to those on the haciendas. The Indian taken as a youth and transformed into a "convert" was just one more peon, morally bound to the mission, with little hope of becoming emancipated and independent other than by escaping and returning to his tribal society; such escape was invariably classified as a return to savagery. Even sadder was the situation of women taken from their society: alone, with little hope of marrying and acquiring a clear and defined social position. Far from their society and their world, rejected or relegated to the role of servants by the white community, the Indians could do nothing but yearn for a return to the jungle or a trip to the city, where their past would remain as dark as their future.

Missionaries and hacienda owners were those who anachronistically held the monopoly on colonization of the jungle. Governments' roles were limited to supporting, according to their sympathies, one area of colonization or another, and they did not take part in planning this new conquest, whose details were at times left to the Franciscans.[100] The missionary continued to be the entrepreneur, as he had been during the centuries of colonial rule. He was interested in discovering areas appropriate for the establishment of towns; he built roads, introduced new plants and cattle, and experimented with new production. It was he who planned the emigration of Andean families to recently discovered lands and who usually and openly competed with the hacienda owner—his rival—who, though possibly lacking the official support of the government, certainly had its moral backing. The rivalry exploded the moment the two colonization entrepreneurs made contact. The hacienda owner devoted himself to trading slaves, making and selling liquor, and exploiting the Campa. The missionary had the support of the authorities to oppose these activities but did not have the material means to do so.[101] His role was limited to making general recommendations, as in a 1919 letter from the Prefect of Missions to the Commissioner of Pangoa: "The heathens should be respected by the civilized people. . . . Make every effort that the people who go to settle in that region have good records so that they will not be the object of hostilities or vexations for the indigenous people who inhabit it."[102]

The moment that the missionary ventured into Asháninka territory, the floodgates opened; in flowed coastal emigrants and Andeans, who could not always be selected as the 1919 letter advised. In 1932 from Satipo, the Prefect of Missions wrote to the treasury inspector:

> [M]ore of the extreme difficulties the Colony encountered included the arrival of an immense number of vagrants, citizens as well as foreigners, among whom were well-known thieves from the capital; well it seems that . . . a decision was made to send them to Satipo . . . , along with the bad elements thrown out of Madre de Dios and Pichis.[103]

A short time later these common delinquents would be joined by political prisoners. The colonization and "civilization" of the "Campa savages" was not being achieved as the missionaries had foreseen. Even the Austrian colony, which entered the area during the Leguía government, caused problems and endangered the success of the evangelization of the valley.[104]

To understand what happened in Satipo, what would happen later in other central jungle missions, and what is currently happening at the missionary outposts, one must consider the missionary institutions of the Peruvian jungle. How have the missionaries' actions been conducted from the beginning of the twentieth century to the present? What have the goals of the missions been, and how should the missionaries act among the "heathen" Indians? In reality there is no one specific doctrine that has served and still serves as a guide for the Franciscans in the jungle. Every few years old and new methods of evangelizing appear and disappear, all of which ultimately depend on the personality of one or another prefect or inspector. Different and often contradictory opinions succeed one another and are barely tried before being replaced by new attempts. But in all of these irregularities and with all of this lack of continuity in doctrine and action, some postulates remain clear:

> [T]hat the indigenous tribes that still remain in barbarism and idolatry be liberated from their savage life and introduced to civilization and the Christian religion. That those regions abundant in natural riches . . . may increase in settlers, population, and public establishments and their number of inhabitants grow.[105]

This is, then, a conquest of people, but above all of lands. People and lands are conquered for "civilization."

> The immense Peruvian territory is unpopulated; the Nation needs citizens; and because nothing can be expected from the adult savages in terms of their regeneration, we have no other recourse, as missionaries, than to dedicate ourselves to the education of the aboriginal children, far from their parents,

> inculcating in them in our homes the love of God, Country, and work.[106]

Lands are conquered with settlers and roads, advised a general inspector in 1931, but as has been seen, the settlers did not always represent the best of civilization, and the roads were dangerous entryways.[107] For the missionary, his task presents a logistical problem: How to dominate the Asháninka, first on a material level and then on a spiritual one, without taking risks or provoking rebellions?

In the missionary action of the last fifty years, it is easy to perceive the two contradictory tendencies enunciated by the Franciscans in their evangelizing postulates. On the one hand, they wanted to Christianize the Asháninka; on the other hand, they planned to make their tribal territory an area of settlement, where hundreds of immigrant families would settle and found cities. The missions were envisioned as exclusively indigenous towns, like the settlements of converted Indians the Jesuits had created in Paraguay in the eighteenth century. The missionaries wanted to keep the Asháninka away from all contact with whites, in a sheltered space where no lay person could penetrate. Not infrequently the missionaries achieved these goals, at least during the first years after the founding of the missionary outpost.

The missionary settled near some Asháninka families, offered work in exchange for manufactured goods, and then, unintentionally, began to stimulate trade in children: boys and girls purchased by the missionaries in exchange for machetes, shotguns, or other objects. The priests blamed the Indians for this trade, not realizing that they were the main instigators and the most responsible—unwittingly, of course—because they had placed at the disposition of the Indians economic goods that were too important to pass up. This trading of children was always and inevitably associated with the appearance of whites and missionaries. No source prior to the rubber era (late nineteenth century) mentions the sale of children by the Campa Asháninka. The rubber dealer, as has been seen, stimulated the raids, and then the missionary innocently became installed in a system he could rarely leave.

The farther the Asháninka groups were from the centers of white influence, the less selling of children occurred. By stating this we do not mean to deny the existence of practices of stealing young people among the Indians before the arrival of whites and especially before the rubber era, but we must give a new dimension to the phenomenon. Before the appearance of the whites' material goods (rifles, cloth, and machetes), the stimulus to carry out raids in search of slaves did not exist. Unlike other indigenous groups in South America, who organized their societies in a stratified manner and based their economy on the labor of a slave class, the Asháninka did not take this cultural route. With the appearance of the whites, however, some tribes (especially of the Pano group) and some Asháninka realized that one of the most sought-after commodities was the human being. Well paid and unquestioned, this new trade became extremely important during the rubber era. Trapped in this system by the desire and need (they were already necessities) for white commodities and by the fear of being left without the weapons that the whites were selling to other enemy groups, many Indians gave in easily in this unexpected situation. At present some continue to yield to the temptation of obtaining a shotgun in exchange for a child stolen from an enemy or from some person with whom they have accounts to settle. It is not true that the Asháninka sell their own sons and daughters, as has often been said. The prestige and social guarantee provided by children in this indigenous society completely preclude this possibility.[108]

As we have indicated, another goal of the mission was to transform virgin territory into colonization zones. Following their failure with Asháninka adults, who mysteriously, according to the missionary, could not resign themselves to living as civilized people, and the delayed successes with the youth they had taken in, the mission began to encourage the influx of Andean immigrants. In 1934, shortly after another rediscovery of the Pajonal, the Franciscans attempted to introduce thirty Andean families, who the apostolic vicar believed, "in union with the indigenous people of the place, will not only have their own life but will also benefit the neighboring jungles with their products."[109] The failures of the Satipo colony, where many Andeans deserted the mission in 1927 because of difficulties in adapting to the new environment, did not serve as a lesson. In 1935 the Oventeni mission on the Gran Pajonal had to be hurriedly abandoned because of the murder of a Campa by a settler.[110] In 1941, only after repeated problems due to interethnic relations and lack of foresight, the missionary authorities decided to halt and block Andean emigration to Asháninka territory. They recommended instead a return to the colonial systems of "closed" missions, in which all evangelizing efforts were limited to children.[111]

This measure would also be short lived. The towns founded by the religious orders were soon abandoned by the Indians, after which only a few children inhabited them. The very usefulness of the missionary's presence was arguable. Such mediocre results did not justify the excessive costs of maintaining the missions. Undoubtedly the formation of a settlement of colonists from the cordillera, who were more docile, more needy, and bound to the mission by a moral commitment, was the most appropriate solution and the one that was finally applied in the central jungle.

Missionary action in Asháninka territory in more recent times has been based upon this mosaic of varied opinions. It is beyond the limits of our ability and intention to express any judgment of a historical nature; nevertheless, we can identify some of the aspects frequently associated with the failure of the missionaries' work. We will try to outline some of these.

Why did the closed missions that were similar to the Jesuit settlements in Paraguay fail with the Asháninka? Times had changed and Asháninka society was not identical to that of the Guaraní. The missionary was attempting to place the Indian into an economic (sometimes monetary) system, in which the accumulation of goods is set forth as one of the principle goals. The same idea of private property exists among the Asháninka but is associated with only some goods and is never related to accumulation and capitalization; the jungle, the water, the plants, the animals, the salt—all the resources of the world—are goods that are utilized at some time in one's life.

They are then abandoned so that nature can complete its cycle. More than forty years ago, Betty Meggers demonstrated how, from an ecological point of view, the itinerant horticulture practiced in the jungle is the best solution.[112] Whatever the cause of the abandonment of lands and homes, for an Asháninka it is inconceivable and impracticable from any point of view to accumulate lands for cultivation and to take up residence there permanently. Yet this is precisely what the missionary is asking him to do: to establish sedentary residence near the mission and to take an active role in the mercantilist mechanism. Although at first the Indian may be attracted by the idea of obtaining goods in exchange for work done on mission lands, eventually his traditional economic system (which, we must not forget, is related to all the rest of his culture) will absorb him again.

Without a minimal, stable, reliable, native, manual labor force to ensure its survival, without a sufficient number of individuals to carry out evangelizing work of a certain value, the missionary found it necessary to organize colonization by peasants from the cordillera border areas. The peasants, generally from communities suffering from an ancestral lack of lands, took up residence around the mission and from that center moved out to occupy the lands in the surrounding radius. These lands were often usurped from the Indians and prepared for extensive crops, especially coffee. The settlers' farms required a great deal of manual labor for maintenance, weeding, and harvesting; because there were not enough Asháninka or because they were not interested in this type of work, the colonists resolved the problem by inviting friends and relatives from their hometowns to the area. These people came to work as laborers but after some time became independent and claimed their own plots of land. This cycle was repeated slowly, often being interrupted by the difficulties that the Andean encountered with unfamiliar crops and with a way of life and a climate that finally defeated him. In some cases the settler returned to his highland community; in other cases, after twenty or more years of living near the mission, it was not odd to find him completely assimilated into the local culture. Married to an Asháninka woman, he had become part of the native social network and adopted more than a few of the customs he had originally been called to fight against.

At this time, the mission was completely separate from the Asháninka society that had been the stimulus for its founding and the reason for its existence, and was surrounded by several Andean families who, little by little, were moving farther out and becoming more and more like the "savages." It was also on this occasion that the missionary or civilian authorities began to distribute land ownership deeds to the Campa who wanted to take up residence near the town. This initiative entailed a sad irony, which did not go unnoticed by the Asháninka. The same lands that they had been forced to abandon were now being distributed to the settlers and to the Asháninka, as long as they agreed to live in the town[113] and surrender their traditional way of life.

Up to this point we have limited our discussion to the consideration of exclusively economic mechanisms that can help us understand the reasons for the failures of the missions among the Asháninka. Obviously an exhaustive analysis should be focused on the functional aspects of the native society and of the developing society of the settlers and the mission. The study of the interrelationships of these two societies or "social processes" would have to be conducted at all levels because it is obvious that contact occurs not only against an economic and social backdrop, but also against a spiritual one. The missionary laid the groundwork for an inevitable break with the Asháninka the moment he assumed that he was dealing with godless people. The Asháninka's silence is confused with emptiness, his reserve with ignorance, and his struggles with anarchical rebellion.

Although the missionary had not obtained significant evangelical results during almost four centuries of presence near this society, in many cases it was precisely owing to this presence that contact with whites did not have a tragic outcome. In this sense, one must look at the positive side of Franciscan action in this chapter of shameful western aggression against native cultures.[114] The mission functioned, at times, as a buffer between the settlers and the Indians, although some missionaries tired of this exclusively mitigating function and of the scarcity of catechistic achievements and advised giving up the enterprise: "[L]eave them [the Asháninka] alone. They tend to disappear, to flee from the light of civilization; the white man's breath poisons them and kills them."[115] In fact, the white man's breath does kill them, especially when it is accompanied by the prejudice and ignorance of those of us who today may feel far removed. "Experience teaches us that the savage does not climb but instead descends, and that he descends to the last rungs of animality, where he dies. For him to rise, he needs the help of a superior race," a Franciscan calmly wrote in 1942.[116] Further distancing himself from the truth, which a moderately informed individual could have glimpsed even in 1942, he added that

> in the education [of the Campa], it would be useless and even counterproductive to communicate elevated ideas and superior tendencies to them because they would turn out like the crafty Indians of the Sierra, pretentious, petulant, despotic with their own people, insolent toward whites, disobedient with authorities, liars and hypocrites as well as sneaky and cowardly.[117]

Years have passed since 1942, but the changes have been few. Old judgments are still in effect, and there are no apparent efforts to reconsider them. Even today the first contact with isolated Asháninka and the establishment of the mission are left to a Franciscan monk, who will repeat the same errors that have caused death and suffering for four centuries.

In 1939 Maxime Kuczynski-Godard, a leading expert on the Peruvian jungle, criticized from a medical perspective the missionary practice of concentrating several families into one settlement:

> It is very interesting to compare the physical condition of the Campa Indians, especially the adolescent children, in the higher population-density areas such as Susiqui with that of the Campa who live an independent life. . . . In most cases

> the independent Campa seem clearly to be in superior physical condition . . . ; not only does malaria seem to be less frequent, but one finds at least some number of adults free of ankylostomiasis.[118]

The death rate among children up to twelve years of age at the Quimiriaqui and Susiqui missions was between 53 and 56 percent. In Metraro mortality was 47 percent for those persons living at the mission, and 25 percent for those who lived in isolation.[119] Ankylostomiasis and ascariasis with pulmonary complications were frequent causes of death; nevertheless, among the Asháninka in the isolated areas, they were less common than among those who had been gathered into settlements. According to Kuczynski-Godard, at the Adventist center at Susiqui, 88 percent of the Indians suffered from ankylostomic infection because the equilibrium between host and parasite possessed by all jungle inhabitants had been destroyed by the concentration of too many people in too small a space.[120] The same researcher also recommended the adoption of the Asháninka-style dwelling, which was "open and accessible to air and sunlight, which are undoubtedly of extreme hygienic importance with regard to all of daily life and especially to the danger of malaria."[121]

Missionaries (both Catholic and non-Catholic), settlers, and certain institutes have always ignored researchers' opinions, and naturally they ignored those of Kuczynski-Godard. Today, as always, the Indians are gathered into villages; a mission is constructed there and sometimes an airstrip, customs are prohibited, and there are punishments, threats, and the delivery of the germs of physical and spiritual destruction. The traditional way of life, which had allowed the Asháninka to survive for thousands of years, is replaced within a few years by hybrid ways that are imposed upon them by force. Tradition is a path traveled by one's ancestors that must continue to be traveled; this path has patterns, rules, and norms that are conditions necessary to individual and collective existence. When this way is blocked, when the validity of the ancestral legacy is denied, when all possible means are used to force people to follow another path, a crime of aggression is committed. The reasons and name given to it are of little importance. One must counter this attitude of force with one of understanding and respect toward ways of thought and behavior that belong to another tradition and other historical and cultural circumstances. "Understanding," however, assumes questioning our own historical situation; it assumes a clear and disinterested awareness of the limits implicit in our own culture; it assumes pondering the "superstitions" about "progress," "civilization," "science," and the many other idols that accompany our own thoughts. Understanding is opening ourselves to new experiences and diverse spiritual subjects; it is being willing to value cultural phenomena that are apparently incompatible with our own tradition only to discover, without even trying, a unity that transcends all the limits of one specific historical and cultural moment. We must move toward these ways if we truly seek a synthesis and not a toll of traumatized and deprived peoples trapped by circumstance within national borders.[122]

To the colonizer and the missionary (Catholic or not, as all are individuals of "modern" mentality), it is incomprehensible that the Asháninka refuse the material and moral "progress" that is offered to them. They adopt a few material tools that do not upset their concept of the Universe, but they do not allow themselves to be dazzled by the constant change, instability, agitation, and movement that constitute the essence of what the modern West considers "progress." This permanent lack of balance exalted as an ideal, this constant search for novelty for novelty's sake, is considered an export that all peoples (especially "primitive" ones) should welcome. When indigenous people resist these changes, it is alleged that the "savages" have an innate incapacity for all that "civilization" represents, whereas in reality their reaction is first and foremost a fundamental spiritual rejection. It is the rejection of the materialistic conception of life and the universe, a materialistic conception that inevitably accompanies the secular actions of the missionaries and is immediately obvious to the Asháninka, because the last thing the missionaries plan to do is initiate a theological or cosmological dialogue with the "savage" that might offer a less distorted image of the whites. The white man acts; he is completely possessed by the desire for exterior activity. He destroys the jungle, thus driving away the animals; he reroutes the rivers, dries up the small lakes, and disrespects a cosmic order that the divinity wished in the beginning and that humans have tried to maintain year after year, century after century. At times the Asháninka oppose the desecrators violently; at other times they opt for passive resistance or withdraw to the deepest jungle; but they always seek in the legacy of their tradition the eternal values that may provide an explanation and a reason for the new events and the new situation. In their traditional knowledge, in their myths, the Asháninka pursue an explanation and a solution, which are valid provided they are revealed *ab origine*, because the myth reveals a mystery, announces the appearance of a new cosmic "situation," and offers an account of how something has come to be, which implies the *why*. Myth offers exemplary models for all of the most significant existential situations; therefore the white man's presence and his aggression also become understandable and "bearable" if they are related to "sacred history," to mythology.[123]

THE MYTH OF THE WHITE MEN'S ORIGIN

The *virakocha* [whites] were in a lake. Near there lived the Asháninka [Campa]. One day a Campa heard the barking of a dog coming from the lake. "Good," he said, "I'm going to catch it," and in order to do so he took along some plantains. But the plantain is food for people, and the dog refused to eat them. Instead, all the *virakocha* came out of the lake and began to chase the Campa and kill them. They killed all of them. The lake had dried up. The only survivor was a *shiripiári* who chewed tobacco [a shaman].

This *shiripiári* called Tzího [the vulture, *Cathartes aura*]: "Look, the *virakocha* have killed all my brothers." "Where?" asked Tzího. "There on the pajonal." Then Tzího gave the *shiripiári* the *ivénki* [*Cyperus piripiri*, the magical herb], and the *shiripiári* killed all the *virakocha*. Only one survived and fled

> downriver [to the Ucayali], and now there are many *virakocha* there. [Meanwhile] on the pajonal, Tzího was eating the dead *virakocha*; he cooked them and ate them.[124]

Paraphrasing a concept expounded by Mircea Eliade, we can state that Asháninka myths are *myths* more than they are *Asháninka* because "they belong to a particular category of spiritual creations of ancient man; consequently, they can be compared to any other group of traditional myths."[125] In this regard all contact with myth is, above all, contact with a particular type of language whose content surpasses the limits of a concrete temporal and spatial situation. The structure of a myth must be examined more than the details; variations in the latter, which depend on the source, are irrelevant unless those variations affect the essential message of the myth. In 1928 Vladimir Propp wrote this about magical stories:

> The term *morphology* means a study of forms. In botany, *morphology* means the study of the component parts of the plant, its reciprocal relationships, and its relationships to the whole; in other words, the study of the structure of the plant . . . ; it is possible to examine the forms of the fable [or myth] with the same precision with which one studies the morphology of organic forms.[126]

The structures, the functions of the parts, and the symbols, as "signs of a transcendent reality that defy their concrete limits and cease to be isolated fragments, being integrated into a system,"[127] constitute the focus of the examination of myth. For these reasons "the validity of the mythical account is situated outside time and space; it is valid everywhere and always";[128] therefore there are no "false" myths.

> Myth is a true story because it is a sacred story, not only because of its content, but also because of the concrete sacred forces that it mobilizes. . . . Myths cannot be false stories. Their truth is not of a logical order nor of a historical order; it is, above all, of a religious order. . . . It is a true story because of its content, the account of events that really happened,

> beginning with the grandiose origins—the origin of the world and humanity, the origin of life and death, the origin of plants and animals, the origin of hunting and agriculture, the origin of fire, the origin of worship, the origin of initiation rites, the origin of shamanic societies and their therapeutic powers—events distant in time, which gave beginning and foundation to the present life and from which the present structure of society originates. . . . The divine or superhuman characters who operate in myth, their extraordinary undertakings, their amazing adventures, this entire marvelous world is a transcendent reality that cannot be questioned because it is the antecedent and sine qua non of present reality.[129]

For members of "primitive" or traditional societies, myth is the only valid revelation of reality; "it proclaims the appearance of a new cosmic situation."[130] Therefore all new events and situations (the arrival of the white man, the *virakocha*, in our case) can be explained—or perhaps it should be said that they can be "endured"—through a prolongation and complementation of the cosmogonic myth, through the origin myth that "tells how the world has been modified, enriched, or impoverished."[131] This is a representation, a "creation." It tells how "something" began to "be." Therefore, "myth is identified with ontology; it speaks only of *real things*, of that which has *really* happened, of that which has been completely revealed."[132]

All that is contained in myths, all that has been done by the gods, demigods, man-gods, and ancestors, belongs to the sphere of the sacred and forms part of *Being*. In contrast, what men do of their own initiative, without mythical models, belongs to the profane sphere:

> [I]t is a vain and fallacious activity, definitely unreal. The more religious the man, the greater number of exemplary models he will have at his disposal to standardize his behavior and actions. Or also, the more religious he is, the more he becomes grafted to the real, avoiding, whenever possible, the risk of being lost through actions that are not very exemplary, that are *subjective*, in a word aberrant.[133]

Every myth is etiological, not in the old sense of the word—that it "explains" a fact—but in the sense that it provides this fact with support, with a guarantee:[134] "[I]t was done this way in the beginning; we do it the same way now." Thus it was in principio; thus it should be now. Therefore "the principal function of myth is to establish exemplary models for all rites and all significant human activities. . . . Behaving as a fully responsible human being, man imitates the exemplary actions of the gods; he repeats their actions, whether a simple physiological function . . . or a social, economic, or military activity."[135]

We should briefly examine the idea of time as it is presented in a mythical context. The acts of members of a "primitive" society, to the extent that they repeat original paradigms that occurred *in illo tempore*, are related to primordial time,

> not as a very remote time in the past, but rather as a prototypical time in which everything already happened and that today does not begin again but is just repeated. Primordial time is creative; it creates what happens today. And all this is achieved through the repetition of their myths . . . ; everything is already present in the beginning. . . . Everything is contained in the primordial era.[136]

Nothing that appears in reality or in life is totally new; even the aggressive *virakocha*, recently arrived in the guise of a settler or soldier, was already in existence, was already present before coming to light. "There are no new times, there is no moment that has not already been lived. There is only primordial time, today as in the past and in the most distant future."[137]

The new situation can be endured because it is contained in the "sacred story"; the suffering ("the *virakocha* have killed all my brothers") acquires meaning; it goes back to a prototype, to an order whose value is unquestionable. Suffering as an event, a historical fact, caused by an invasion or a cosmic catastrophe, can be endured precisely because it does not seem gratuitous or arbitrary, because it is not owed to chance but to explicable reasons, which are contained within a system that can be known.[138] When suffering becomes coherent, it becomes bearable. "The primitive struggles against that *suffering* with all the magical-religious means at his disposal,[139] but he endures it morally because *it is not absurd*."[140] If it is not the myth that justifies it and makes it comprehensible, it is the recognition that suffering is the consequence of a deviation from the norm.[141]

In Asháninka myth, breaking the rules is apparently trivial and unimportant; at least it is not proportionate to the fatal consequences that it carries for all of Asháninka humanity. The Indian guilty of the catastrophe simply used the wrong bait. He used plantains, but that "is food for people, and the dog refused to eat them." Humanity was lost because of a few plantains, or as G. K. Chesterton said, "An apple is eaten and the hope of God is gone."[142] From that primordial moment, from that break with the cultural norm (expressed in symbols and therefore of transcendentally significant value and valid at all levels of the real),[143] the life of the Christian, like that of the Asháninka, is destined and marked. Each Christian has eaten from the tree; each Asháninka suffers the consequences of that primordial "error."

Questions may arise as to whether this is legend or history, mythical or real. Does the lake symbolize the sea? Is there any relation to the fact that the Spaniards arrived from the sea? How could the Asháninka have known these things? But all these questions are false or incorrectly posed, "since myth and so-called reality are indissolubly intertwined. . . . Myth is life and life is myth."[144] As has been stated, the language of myth is symbolic, which does not exclude interpretations on other levels. René Guénon has written that

> too frequently there is a tendency to think that admission of a symbolic meaning must entail rejection of the literal or historical meaning; such an opinion results from ignorance of the law of correspondence, which is the foundation of all symbolism and by virtue of which each thing, proceeding essentially from a metaphysical beginning from which all its reality is derived, translates and expresses that beginning in its own way and according to its order of existence, in such a way that,

> from one order to another, all things are linked and correspond in order to take part in the total and universal harmony, which is, in the multiplicity of the manifestation, like a reflection of the very unity of the beginning. It is because of this that the laws of an inferior sphere can always be taken as the symbol of a superior order, because it is in this that they have their profound reason, which is at the same time their beginning and their end.[145]

Saint Paul has synthesized these concepts in the formula *Per visibilia ad invisibilia*:[146] from the observation of the perceptible, from the order of visible phenomena, to the universal, the fundamental. Through symbolism, universal content is expressed, transcending and explaining concrete historical and cultural circumstances, and the operation is performed analogically. Goethe said, "In the symbol, the particular represents the general, not as a dream or shadow, but as a living and immediate revelation of the unfathomable." It is not our intention to further expand on matters of symbolism, but it is important to point out the difficulties inherent in any hermeneutics of a myth, no matter how simple the myth may seem—difficulties that derive from our historical condition as "modern men" distanced (only at a "conscious" level, as Carl Jung has demonstrated in several of his works) from the symbolic world. If a myth, a ritual, a cosmology, or any other religious structure of a people seems to us to be simple and devoid of content at an ethnological level, and a "functional," purely anthropological analysis seems sufficient to us to explain and understand it, this is because we settle for the primary interpretive levels, which are necessary but are not the only ones.

The whites were in a lake, in the water, which is *fons et origo*, the origin of all existential virtualities and possibilities. The waters symbolize the primordial substance from which all life forms are born and to which they all finally return through regression or cataclysm at the end of a historical or cosmic cycle.[147] The waters of the pond, of the small lake (on the Gran Pajonal there are no large lakes, and what the Asháninka call *lakes* are really just small ponds), symbolize the origin of material and at the same time the entryway to the subterranean world, which is the home of the Nónki, the great monstrous serpent symbolized in the rainbow. The lake is the entrance to the subterranean abyss of the Nónki, source of death and disease, who is defeated only, in primordial time, by a heroic shaman. From the waters, protomaterial par excellence, and from the lake come the whites. In its function as the *virakocha*'s origin, the lake becomes exhausted and dries up: [I]t has produced and fulfilled all of its procreative power; at the same time, Asháninka cosmology does not appear to be concerned about the distressing idea that other lakes might be the origin of more whites. They were born once and for all *in illo tempore*, and the lake that produced them no longer exists.

It is useful to add that "any analysis risks fragmenting and disintegrating into separate elements what, to the consciousness that has represented them, form a single unit, a Cosmos."[148] The symbols implicit in the Asháninka conception indicate and evoke an integral series of realities that are separable only in our study, which is therefore inadequate and incomplete. In the mind of an Asháninka listener, the water-lake combination obviously has a resonance that the anthropologist can not grasp in all its nuances; the same is true for any other spiritual or simply cultural (in the broad sense of the term) symbolic element that one wishes to examine. The member of a traditional society feels the fundamental unity of all "works," whether of a "physical-natural" order or of a "spiritual or historical" order;[149] this inextricable unity that he perceives intuitively and analogically, when analyzed logically, may lose meaning to the point of appearing to us as a "superstition" (that is, as *vana observatio*), the vestige of an ancient system of thought that now, alone and without a function, has completely lost meaning. Such is not the case, however. For the Asháninka, myth is completely functional and valid; moreover, it is the only tenable explanation of reality. The Nónki—monstrous dragon; primordial serpent; symbol of the cosmic Waters, of Darkness, of the Abyss, of Death, that is to say of the amorphous and the virtual—is associated with these new beings, the *virakocha*, who were not created by the God Oriátziri[150] with the rest of the universe, nor were they lost and transformed into animals, as was a large portion of primordial Asháninka humanity; instead they appeared by mistake and contrary to the will of Asháninka humanity. The white man is homologated to the Nónki and is identified symbolically with the enemy of humanity that causes death and that, it has been said, was vanquished in primordial time by a heroic shaman.[151] For this reason it is a shaman (assisted by Tzího) who triumphs over the whites.

If we continue the hermeneutic analysis of the myth, we meet a character, the dog, which in other Asháninka myths is presented as negative and evil. Once dead, the dog will do everything possible to convince Oriátziri that, here on earth, humans treated him badly, denying him food and meat, which should have been his just reward for assisting in the hunt. The dog is evil: "[W]hen we Asháninka die and go there [into the world beyond], the dog [who awaits us] has piled up for us the bones of all the animals we had hunted with him in life, and he says to us, 'Let's see if you like to eat bones, as you used to give me there on the Pajonal.'" The dog, not born like the other animals of the Asháninka world, an "exception" to the cosmogony, is related to death. He is the one who welcomes the dead man, like an initial test that the new being must pass, an initiation. This same dog is associated in the myth of the origin of the *virakocha* with the white[152] invader and aggressor.

Later the character of the Asháninka myth commits the error, the "sin," which is the cause of the ills that afflict present-day humanity. The error is essentially a failure to follow the rules, committed out of ignorance, by being unaware of the exact nature of the dog. Here too the symbolism is broad. Ignorance is the cause of perdition, although in this case, the ignorance would not be culpable because whites and the dog did not belong to the universe created by the divinity. In this sense the myth is truly standard: being familiar with things so one may act in accordance with their nature and thus avoid breaking the traditional rules that are supported by the archetypal actions of the divinities. To act correctly means to imitate the exemplary models of mythical events. Myth, Bronislaw Malinowski has said, "expresses, exalts, and codifies beliefs; it guards and legitimizes morality; it guarantees the efficiency of ritual and contains practical rules for teaching man."[153]

Because of the error, a negative force is unleashed and humanity is exterminated. It is not necessary to know the *why* of the whites' attitude, although it is constantly confirmed; it is sufficient to narrate the *how*. The one who survives (as in all other Asháninka eschatologies) the extermination—the conclusion of one humanity and one cosmic cycle—is the heroic shaman, the initiate par excellence, the one who chews tobacco[154] and therefore the one who "knows" and has the "vision." Knowledge saves him. As an initiate he can avoid defeat and prepare the final victory that will also be the beginning of a new Asháninka humanity. This sort of native "gnosticism" is confirmed by the next action of the shaman, who calls Tzího, the vulture, to help him fight the white men. The initiate, the shaman, knows the "world" perfectly and knows whom to call for help. We must not forget that we are dealing with a unified cosmos in which men, animals, plants, lands, sky, water, and fire form a whole, the sacred medium: "[W]hat the primitive sees in the environment with which he associates and intertwines ever more closely is the revelation of a power."[155] The animal is a numinous manifestation because of its mysterious and unknown character. Tzího helped in two ways: by bringing the magical herb and by eating the whites' corpses.

Universal mythology frequently presents us with characters with a protective function, the good spirit that provides the hero with the amulets or magical formulas that help him overcome the initiation crises or defeat the dragon that he must destroy.[156] In the shamanic context, animals generally fulfill this protective, helpful, and in a way, initiating function. In Asháninka culture there is an entire category of birds that are related to the supernatural powers of the shaman. Tzího is one of these birds. The ordinary Asháninka hunter cannot kill him; if he needs to do so to obtain the feathers, which are especially propitious for his hunting arrows, he must then observe mourning as he would at the death of a relative. The fact that birds and animals possess language and magical powers should not surprise us; all this is possible for a shaman or for any character in the myth: "[W]here there is shamanism, time and the mythological realm are here and now."[157] The heroic *shiripiári* receives from Tzího the magical plant, the *ivénki* that cures, that protects against demoniacal forces, and that aids in the hunt and in war. The Ashéninka identify more than fifty types of *ivénki*, each with its specific properties, each with a certain purpose. In other myths the hero receives the magical gift from other sacred animals. Kontáwo tricks the Nónki with the help of the jaguar, Manítzi, who gives him the magical *ivénki*. These are symbolic structures that represent the path of the shaman toward esoteric knowledge, which he achieves with the help of protective beings. Again, as wisdom saved him from white aggression, it is the mystically acquired knowledge that permits the hero to defeat the enemy. All of the *virakocha* are killed, except one who escapes and flees to the Ucayali River (Kirinka means "downriver"), the place where the moon goes fishing during the three days when it disappears (Kásri means "moon," is masculine, and represents all that is related to death; it receives dead Asháninka and delivers them, rejuvenated, to their wives). There at the Ucayali is where the white descendants of the only survivor live; there are many of them, and they live near the great river. The white men are thus associated with death and with one of the places through which the dead have to pass on their long journey after death. This portion of the myth, however, is also etiological because it explains the presence of the whites along the Ucayali River, where the haciendas and a few towns with settlers are located.

The myth concludes with the image of the carrion-eating vulture eliminating the corpses of the white men killed by the shaman in combat. Tzího cooks the dead, submits them to the purifying and transforming action of fire, and finally incorporates them and absorbs them, thus preventing their return to the river (the common form of "burial" for the Asháninka), the renewer of life.[158]

All of this has a function and a purpose. The myth offers a way to endure and explain the new situation, the presence of the whites. The myth provides hope. Salvation lies in the just use of traditional norms—in adherence to culture itself—which is nothing more than the sum of the paradigmatic actions performed by the gods and heroes. The Asháninka, who firmly believes in the efficacy of the *ivénki*, who believes in Tzího and the shaman, has the assurance of final victory over the aggressors. On several occasions the *virakocha* may win the battle, but these will always be temporary victories. As in the myth, the final triumph belongs to the shaman because thus it was in the beginning, and thus it will be evermore.

HEROIC SHAMANISM

Based on the foregoing, it is easy to conclude that Asháninka culture is embodied in the shaman; he is the earthly representative of divine wisdom, the guardian and interpreter of tradition. "The realm of myth from which . . . the entire universe proceeds and the realm of the shamanic trance are one and the same," Joseph Campbell has said.[159] The shaman's power over "nature" is unquestionable; he can use it to benefit or harm the community; because of this the community fears and respects him, admires and believes in him. Why should they not have faith in his powers when he proves them at every turn? The shaman heals, defeats death, or sends it to his enemies. The shaman is the hero who has overcome all the obstacles and trials on his initiation path; he has become the husband of the tobacco (*shiri* means "woman"), which facilitates his magical flights; he has achieved dominion over other hallucinogenic plants, can transform himself into a bird, can travel to the world of the dead, or can repeat without difficulty the actions that the divinities carried out in the beginning of time. A *shiripiári* from Oventeni, who died some years ago, tried to re-create the flood by blocking the three rivers that flow into the valley and then opening them suddenly so that the force of the water would carry away all the whites and Andeans of the mission. This is what Oriátziri had done *in principio* when he destroyed all of humanity; therefore the shaman, tired of the white men's abuses, could act in the same manner.

The shaman is a mythological hero who lives among the Asháninka today. From his perspective he feels, in a way, a bit removed from his society and its hazards. He has reached (through his search) the center of his society, his cultural world, and his historical circumstances; he has transcended them and reached the heart of that universe of which his group is but one more manifestation. Precisely for these reasons he has the ability to help his people. The shamanic vocation or calling and the corresponding crisis do not represent a break with society and the world (in the psychopathological sense that, in some cases, has been ascribed to the phenomenon), but rather "the disconcerting intuition of its depth, and the break takes place with regard to the relatively trivial attitude toward the human spirit and toward the world that seems to satisfy the great majority of men."[160]

The shaman is a living mythological hero because he has repeated and constantly repeats the feats of semidivine beings just as they are explained in the myths. "[M]yth is life and life is myth": The maxim works even better in the case of the *shiripiári* who has recurring daily mythical experiences. Fundamentally for this reason, the shaman represents the "authentic man" of Asháninka humanity; he has been able to make his life an *imitatio dei*; the closer it is to the world of the sacred, the more "real" it is. More than any other member of his society, he has access to the sphere of the exemplary and therefore to the primordial, to the perfection of the archetypal. By following the shaman's advice and repeating the actions that he recommends, one can reach the "perfection of the primordial . . . time sanctified by the divine presence,"[161] a perfect time and world that can be realized—contrary to the "irreversibility of history"—because the action that repeats a divine paradigm is all that is "real" for the traditional man.

"Mythical or sacred time[162] is qualitatively different from profane time, distinct from the continuous and irreversible time of every day, from desacralized existence."[163] It is not a rejection of one's own historical situation, but it does represent a rejection of "history" in the modern sense of the word;[164] it is instead a matter of understanding time in light of the permanent and stable, that which never changes because it is divine. "The *historical situation* does not necessarily imply *history* in the broad sense of the term; it only implies the human condition as such, that is, a condition governed by a certain series of attitudes."[165] Acting as in primordial time and performing the acts that the *shiripiári* recommends (chewing the magical *ivénki* and blowing it against the whites, for example), means installing oneself in absolute reality, on the ontological level; it means transcending one's own situation and "the obtuse and temporal self-sufficiency that is the fate of all men because all men are *ignorant,* that is, they identify the real with their own particular situation. Ignorance is principally this false identification of the real with what each one of us believes to be or believes to possess."[166]

The *virakocha* are not just any hacienda owner, missionary, or settler; they are not just the concrete persons who invade lands or commit crimes against society. Beyond this concrete historical situation is the ultimate reality: The *virakocha* are the darkness, the Nónki, and the aquatic monster that must be defeated in a heroic struggle. The whites are the precosmogonic chaos and the chaos at the end of each cosmic cycle. Just as traditional Asháninka eschatology identifies a sign of the end in the whites' arrival, so too the shaman represents salvation. Heroic shamanism fulfills a soteriological function; the myth and its social catalyst, the shaman, are redeemers. Transcending time, transcending historical circumstances, regaining the mythical *great time*, and acting in accordance with it not only assure the ultimate victory, but also put the Asháninka in contact with the ultimate reality. Therefore all that happens—*history*—is explainable and tolerable.

When all is said and done, all Asháninka know that the universe has been created, destroyed, and re-created several times. Death and birth are present in Asháninka daily life. At the end, the world in which we live (Kipatzi) begins to stink, to give off an unpleasant odor because it is rotting; the weary, beneficent divinity grants a dissolution, an *Omóyeka* in Asháninka terminology.[167] A powerful earthquake will invert the cosmic order. The world below—the consumed, foul-smelling, rotted, chaotic, and in a word, profaned earth—will go up (Henóki) and be renewed by its closeness to the divine. The celestial world—the world above, new and sacred, the perfect cosmos—will be put down and a new humanity will be reborn. Other myths speak of destructive floods. Beyond the symbol, the meaning is obvious. In other cases the white man is the sign of this eschatology.

Although these thoughts offer the Asháninka an explanation, in no way do they prevent him from taking action or fighting. The Asháninka's rejection of "history" in the modern sense of the term is fundamentally a refusal of the "new" and of meaningless change or norm-transgressing change.[168] The struggle, supported by a mythical antecedent, not only can be carried out but also becomes a "holy war." There are the usual battles against the invaders: opposition or simple resistance. Juan Santos, Amachegua, and all the unknown Asháninka who have opposed the white invasion indicate to us the operative function of this aboriginal concept. There are the *shiripiári* with their explanations and their conduct, who are simple masks of ultimate reality, but also living masks who do not abandon their role in the world and are willing to rebel to restore and prolong the primordial order, which is physical, social, ethical, and metaphysical all at the same time. This is an order that is known to be periodically lost because this is the way it has always been, but this order must be restored by acting as the gods have acted. The world is born, grows, and ends. Men, animals, plants, the moon, the sun—everything is born, dies, and is reborn. But always, even after the worst cosmic cataclysms, a mythical ancestor, a heroic shaman, finds the solution and gives origin to the new humanity. After the flood, in which all humanity died, the shaman and his wife float on a raft that has saved them. They are the only ones who listened to and followed the advice of the divinity. But all is darkness, and the waters do not recede. The hero then orders his wife to construct a moon of white cotton and place it on the raft. Shortly thereafter the trick[169] works: "[A]fter the moon comes the sun," and with the sun everything dries and the new world is reborn.

The Asháninka, therefore, fully accept the responsibility of collaborating in divine designs. This is responsibility on the cosmic level: to save and take care of plants, animals,[170] and the universe in general; to participate in the creation, re-creation, and maintenance of the world. This is the responsibility of preserving the cosmos in its present condition; in this cosmos the whites are unnecessary or are representatives of (or at least symbolically associated with) the negative forces against which it is right to struggle.[171]

Some themes of Asháninka culture, which concur principally in the type of response that this society has given for several centuries to the presence of the white man, are readily apparent. Among them are the cyclical concept of time and the eschatological concept of the universe inherent in Asháninka culture and thought, which permit us to glimpse an explanation for this society's resistance to the whites' presence and the changes this has caused. A cyclical concept of time is characteristic of most traditional societies. We do not necessarily have to link it to the millenarian Christian tradition to see within it the seeds of a diffuse and latent messianism that can acquire historical consistency when the right circumstances present themselves. To the religious mentality of a traditional person, the idea of time has a resonance that is completely different from that which it has for a "modern" or "historical" individual. For the Asháninka, time is not homogeneous. There is a sacred time (that of sacred acts, myth, or action that repeats a mythical act, for example), and there is a profane time (that of the normal course of all acts that do not have special religious significance). Sacred time, by nature, is reversible; that is, "it is a primordial mythical Time that has become present."[172] In the same sense, this sacred time can occur in the future as long as the members of the community desire it and are willing to achieve it through adherence to the traditional, which is the paradigmatic and divine. The more mystical the society, the more its members can freely flee from the present toward the past (which is primordial) or toward the future (which is also primordial because the eschatology contains two poles or moments: the end of the old world and the creation of the new order by direct intervention of the divinity or the *beginning*). This is obviously not a denial of the immediate situation or an escape from reality; we have seen this fact in the preceding pages and in the historical chapters. Juan Santos or the present-day shaman represents this projection toward the future; they are or can be the "messiah," who enters sacred time and brings the perfection of primordial (or eschatological, in the aforementioned sense) time. The concrete historical figure may disappear—Juan Santos died and so do the shamans—but this historical figure as such is not important. He has been only the personification of an archetype. What is present in the mind of the Asháninka is the principle, not its concrete incarnations.

Another recurring theme in the action of Asháninka society through the centuries is intimately related to the concept of time. The function of the shaman is not limited to the therapeutic aspect (even if we consider the term in a very broad ethnological sense), but, as has been demonstrated, it is eminently soteriological. The shaman is a mythical hero, a divine trickster, and in a certain sense a messiah. Because he is in almost permanent contact with sacred time, salvation is present in him, now or in the future that he foretells. For the typical Asháninka, the code of conduct with respect to western society has been and is an *imitatio dei* carried out through an *imitatio* of the shaman. Although it is true that "messianism does not manage to overcome the eschatological valuation of time"[173] because the solution is placed in the future, it is also true that in the case of Asháninka thought, this future is eternally present (potentially) in the figure of the shaman, who can put it into effect from one moment to the next, as circumstances may require.

PACHAKAMÁITE

In messianic and millenarian phenomena, there has often been a desire to see the expression of frustration or deprivation of a social and economic nature among the aboriginal populations after their contact with whites. This is true, but only as long as this viewpoint does not obscure or deny other approaches and perspectives.[174] In the case of Asháninka society, there is an obvious tension between its members and the whites and Andean settlers brought by the missionaries. It is also clear that the introduction of western goods by the settlers—goods that in large part remain beyond the reach of the native economy—contributed to creating a sense of deprivation and frustration; nevertheless, an exclusively economic viewpoint will give us only a partial explanation of the phenomenon. This phenomenon is complex and, as previously noted, has to do with the entire cosmovision of the society. It is reasonable to wonder, with Sylvia Thrupp, why some native societies that have been conquered and economically dominated by whites have not reacted with messianic responses.[175] It would seem necessary to look for the reasons for a messianic cultural attitude first in the mythological-doctrinarian contexts of the population in question, in their concept of time, in their ethical and soteriological concepts, and in the functions of their religious institutions, and then combine these cultural elements with the deprivations of an economic nature. It is not our intention here to linger over the study of the millenarian manifestations that can be perceived in the society of the Gran Pajonal Asháninka; nevertheless, we wish to note a myth that clearly translates the spiritual situation of the Asháninka who are facing white and Andean settlers. This is a myth of men as opposed to origin myths, which are a preferentially feminine patrimony. This is a myth of men because it refers to the masculine activity par excellence: the acquisition of goods, or trade. It is a myth of a traveling adventurer who goes in search of his divinity on a path that is difficult and full of real and symbolic obstacles, all for the sake of being able to trade with that divinity.[176]

> Pachakamáite is Páwa [Father and God] and lives downriver. He is not a *virakocha*; he is not a *chori*. He is the child of the Sun, and Mamántziki is his wife. Pachakamáite makes everything: machetes, cooking pots, gunpowder, cartridges, salt, shotguns, ammunition, axes. Because previously the Asháninka were poor and had nothing; they had no machetes, axes, nothing. Where did the Asháninka get everything? Back then they would go there, to Pachakamáite, and there they got everything. That is the way it was before, before; now we do not know. In the past the Asháninka used to know.

The Asháninka would go downriver from the Pajonal and would take *mate* gourds that they put on their heads so that Piri [the bat] would not bite them. Because on the way to Pachakamáite you must pass through caves full of huge bats. Then you meet Oshéro, the great crab, as large as an Asháninka. Oshéro is in the middle of the path and does not allow you to pass. You must take him some annatto; you give it to him and he allows you to pass.

Then the Asháninka reaches Pachakamáite but cannot sit down. He has to keep walking, always walking [without sitting down]. And Pachakamáite says to him, "What do you want?" And there in Pachakamáite's house there is everything: machetes, shotguns, ammunition, axes. And the Asháninka, without sitting down, says, "I want this and that. . . ." If he sits down, then when he has to leave he tries to get up and cannot; he is stuck to the floor. The Páwa Pachakamáite does not allow him to leave and then there is an earthquake.

Also on the way is Pokinántzi, measles,[177] who is looking for a husband and seeks out the Asháninka. You must take feathers of [the birds] Hankátzi, Ttamíri, and Herótzi and drop them behind you on the path. [The] measles [that is] behind wants to capture the Asháninka but sees the feathers and begins to pick them up; thus the Asháninka is able to escape.

Where is Pachakamáite? Far, far away, farther than Iquitos, but the path has been blocked by the palisades of the *virakochas'* and the *choris'* rafts. Before the Asháninka knew how to get there, but now they have all died.

All the things that the *choris* and the *virakochas* bring—the machetes, mirrors, axes . . . —are given to them by their "owner." He gives them to them for us, the Asháninka, so that we can hunt and farm, but the *choris* and *virakochas* sell us the things. They say they cost money, that they pay for them, but that is a lie. Their "owner" gives them to them for us, the Asháninka.[178]

This story contains several points that are worthy of hermeneutical examination, but as indicated above, all that concerns us here is the message that Asháninka society, confronted over a long period of time by our civilization, wished to express in it.

We must distinguish methodologically some terms that are not univocal, although at times they may be used indiscriminately. We refer to millenarianism, messianism, prophetism, and cargo cults—phenomena that, though presenting parallel morphologies, cannot be confused as a single religious form. In conjunction with our study it is obvious that, upon the basis of a cyclical-eschatological (and therefore in a broad sense millenarian) concept, Asháninka thought has occasionally developed forms of messianic escapism and salvation. The periodic cosmic cataclysms and consequent renewals of the world can be performed and accelerated through the direct intervention of a divine envoy, who simply carries out what was already said in the mythical traditions; he is the messiah of the heroic tradition, who enters "history" and makes it sacred, that is, giving "reality" to what would otherwise be only a profane temporal flow. Not all millenarian traditions are necessarily messianic, but in the case of Asháninka spirituality, the hope for the arrival of a divine savior, who directly intervenes in profane life to purify it and restore primordial order and justice, constitutes one of the most important core points. In the preceding pages we have seen how the shaman largely fulfills this at once prophetic and salvific function. In this sense, Asháninka society has paradise within its reach. Beyond the *shiripiári*, who is occupied in his daily tasks and service to the community, there appears from time to time the hero, who prophesies the eschatology and the (re)establishment of the new and old order. The wait then becomes impatient; added and sometimes opposed to the hopes and explanations offered by the myth is action, in some cases the extreme solution of war. But not always do there appear the Ignacio Torotes or Juan Santoses, who pull the Indians with them into a holy and liberating war in search of primordial time; then the myth, that "present and lived reality . . . , that celebration in word . . . , that typical and eternal event . . . , that timeless time,"[179] again takes its place, offered to the Asháninka as a testimony of truth and as support for their existential situation. Their own condition is explained in the mythical account and therefore becomes understandable and bearable.

What is this condition for the present-day Asháninka of the Gran Pajonal? Let us follow the myth of Pachakamáite, which stresses the aspects that the Asháninka themselves consider most important. Pachakamáite is the Father. He is God. He is the child of the Sun and the husband of Mamántziki.[180] He is neither creator nor demiurge; rather he is the manufacturer and possessor of all those goods that the missionaries and colonists have, even of salt, which can no longer be obtained, as in ancient times, by traditional means. Previously the Asháninka were poor; they did not possess many things, but they could obtain them by traveling to Pachakamáite, that is, by trading and exchanging with other tribes and Andeans.[181] In this era, however, these things are no longer known because "we, the Asháninka, have declined." The way was not easy; as always the conquest of goods—material as well as spiritual— presumes the overcoming of obstacles and trials. It was an initiation path because one cannot reach the Divinity without suffering, without fear (the sacred is *tremendum*; *tremor* means "fear"),[182] without passing through a death (the symbolism of the dark cave alludes to this aspect and is also found in the rites of passage of women, who have to die to one life and be born to a new one through a period of darkness) and fighting the monsters that guard the secrets. The annatto, the sacred paint, can help. The Asháninka therefore never fail to paint their faces and garments before starting out on a trip. The third test is conducted directly by Pachakamáite, prohibiting the traveler from sitting down, taking up residence there, and forgetting that his absence from his home and society is only transitory and that the return from his real or mystical journey is indispensable because others depend on him.[183] The punishment for breaking this rule is serious, so much so that the god may cause an earthquake.

A fourth test awaits the *ayúmpari*,[184] who has had the courage to abandon the security of his known world to search for the unknown, drawn by the adventure and the reward that has both individual and social value. The material goods of the whites constitute the prize in this case, not because they are the whites' objects, but because the Asháninka sees the decline of his sacramental life symbolized in the impossibility of obtaining them through the traditional means of intertribal and extratribal trade. It is true that the objects of European origin did not exist before the arrival of the *virakochas*, but obviously it is to the frustration of sacred trade that the symbolism of the myth alludes, and not to specific objects. Salt, included among Pachakamáite's goods, as has been seen in the historical portion of this study, was part of the native patrimony, now usurped and desecrated at its source. It has been transformed into an unattainable good possessed by a god whom the whites and Andean settlers have isolated, blocking the way that leads to him. The fourth test must be overcome with the magical flight[185]—not from the god Pachakamáite, who has benevolently provided the gifts—but from Pokinántzi, the demoniacal illness brought by the whites, which lies in wait on the return path to ambush a husband and drag him off to her kingdom of darkness.[186] Some bird feathers, however, distract the illness and permit the hero to escape and return home.[187]

In its original or traditional form, the myth probably ended here. The hero voluntarily left his home and social circle and advanced toward the dangerous threshold of adventure (whether real or symbolic, it matters little because each listener interprets the myth on his own level, "since the spirit perceives what belongs to the spirit"),[188] where he must pass one test (Piri) followed by another (Oshéro) and finally can reach the victory, that is, the encounter with the benevolent deity. Once the reward is obtained through another test (that of not sitting down), the final task remains: that of returning to society and leaving behind all of the transcendental (good or evil) forces that would upset the order of the community. The hero's return signifies a benefit for all because *everyone* shares in the gifts of the divinity through trade.

We can confront the myth with a historicist attitude; we can wonder whether there ever existed an Asháninka hero who had this adventure, "but that would not help us, because what concern us now are problems of symbolism and not of historicity . . . ; the underscoring of the historical element would only lead to confusion, would only serve to obfuscate the message of the image."[189] We must not forget that symbols are simply vehicles of communication and should not be confused with the content or message. Because they occur in a specific space and time, symbols are adapted to that specific human understanding; the task is "to preserve the transparency of the symbol in order that it not obscure the very light that it is supposed to reflect."[190] The light is inexpressible; it is *árreton* and can be expressed only with language that is irremediably concrete, linked to a historical and cultural situation. But beyond the language is the symbol, which, as its Greek root indicates, is meant "to reunite," "to approach," and "to relate"; "the symbol unifies the distinct orders of reality, referring them to its foundation."[191]

Through the vehicle we can examine the profound significance of the story and see in it the expression of the drama of a society to which our civilization is denying part of its cultural life—its sacred trade—and therefore, its sacramental life. To the Asháninka, culture is, in a way, the fixing and confirmation of the given: exactly the opposite of development, which is understood as constant change and ever greater separation from the archetypal and established.[192] The ancient and divine order has been profaned and broken by the actions of the *virakochas* and *choris*, who impede, with their presence and the obstacles they have placed in the path, the pilgrimages to the god and sacred trade. Here we come to what, at this moment, we consider the focal point of the message.

> Where is Pachakamáite? Far, far away . . . , but the path has been blocked by the palisades of the *virakochas'* and the *choris'* rafts. Before the Asháninka knew how to get there, but now they have all died. . . . That is the way it was before, before; now we do not know.

We find the clear idea of a decline with respect to the knowledge of the men of the past, a decline caused, or at least maintained, by the whites and Andeans. The god has always been far away but now there is, between him and the Asháninka, an insurmountable obstacle that explains the poverty of the native society in the material as well as the spiritual realm. The characteristic of native "gnosticism" reappears here: It is knowledge that saves; "now we do not know; before the Asháninka knew." The contact with the divinity and the sacred, the free practice of exchanging goods, and the hazardous journeys through mysterious lands in search of material goods and interior routes are part of a lost existence that can only be found again through an ever greater adherence to tradition. To restore the primordial and reestablish it *sicut erat in principio*—not because of an illusory idealization of the past, but because the primordial was divine and pure—should be the action of Asháninka society. To seek the primordial does not mean to deny the future; it means to live it according to the beginning, the archetype, and to cast from the path all that is not contained in the beginning. In this sense there is not a past, present, and future that the Asháninka see as qualitatively different (as in the case of the man of "historical" mentality), but an eternal "timeless time" profaned by the appearance of the white man. The traditional culture demands this pursuit of the primordial cosmos, of order, and of the distant Pachakamáite: as it was in the beginning, *et nunc et in saecula saeculorum*, rejecting the profane by all possible means. The old shaman of the Chenkári hills trusts all the jaguars (deceased shamans) of the subterranean world to fight against the settlers; against their strength the white men's weapons will be powerless, and they will have to surrender. They brought the three diseases that are killing the Asháninka; they do not believe in the *shiripiári* or his powers; they deny him because they do not know him. Omága, the young Asháninka, is convinced that the only one who can save the traditional order is the *shiripiári*, and all the other Asháninka are of the same opinion.

Perhaps the most serious fault of the *choris* and *virakochas* is denying the Asháninka the divine gifts: the objects of western origin that are considered an offering from their "owner," the god Pachakamáite, to the Indians. Not only have the whites and Andeans isolated him with their palisades, but they also refuse to turn over the merchandise that the god sends for the Gran Pajonal Asháninka. The theme of the cargo cult, which is particularly common in Melanesia, is presented to us in this case with the modifications of a different cultural situation but with the same structural base. In our case, it is not the boat of the dead loaded with axes and knives that is awaited, but the plane that lands from time to time in Oventeni, from which numerous objects mysteriously appear but never reach the hands of the natives. In Melanesia, the generous donors are dead ancestors, who have been denied status by a foreign social and spiritual system. In our case, the donor is Pachakamáite, a complex symbol that encompasses the meaning of traditional intertribal and extratribal trade and the cultural interdependence with the pre-Hispanic Andean area.[193]

The axes, machetes, shotguns, and other metal instruments are sent through the *choris* and *virakochas* by the god so that the Asháninka can cut down trees, prepare fields for the planting of cassava, and hunt more easily; but the settlers maintain that they have to pay to obtain the instruments, and this is not true. There is a rejection of the money and mercantilism that characterize the actions of the missionaries as well as settlers in general. This rejection of one of the most typical elements of modern western culture represents the refusal of this aboriginal society to enter a system that is completely secular and alien to their cultural perspective. This phenomenon is not uncommon in nativist renaissances. In 1940 in the New Hebrides, the prophet Manequevi announced the imminent transformation of the island and the way of life of its inhabitants. "Eternal youth and abundance would reign among them, but this would be realized only after the expulsion of the Europeans, and after all the money imported by them, down to the last penny, had been destroyed or returned to its introducers."[194] Implicit in the rejection of money is the rejection of forced labor in the white establishments as a means of obtaining the instruments that belong to the Indians by divine mandate. The reaction reaffirms, consolidates, and defends the traditional culture through an entrenchment in retrospective postures and the formation of "an absolutely new cultural consciousness . . . ,

[a] form of intelligent syncretism . . . , [a] policy of intelligent parasitism . . . , in the face of the work requested by the whites. . . . This is, in the practical as well as in the cultural sphere, a behavior of preservation, almost of biological defense."[195]

These new cultural forms, these "cargo cults," these types of messianism (it is hoped and expected with growing certainty that the situation will be resolved any day, whether by the disappearance of the white intruders or by reestablishing contact with Pachakamáite), manifest the vigor and vitality of Asháninka society, which does not give up even after four hundred years of domination and which seeks in its traditional cosmovision the explanations and strength to endure and overcome the desecration by the whites.

To the modern western man, the world is nothing but an object to be used, according to Martin Heidegger;[196] the white man has demonstrated that to the Asháninka—and continues to do so—by his attitude. The jungle, the rivers, the animals, and the plants are objects devoid of transcendental meaning; they are there to be used and exploited until they run out. At times they represent nothing more than obstacles to an assumed "freedom" of action. Material instruments are also means of creation and more frequently of destruction, but they have no other meaning. Just as our civilization has secularized nature, so too has it secularized labor and its fruits; beyond the physical use of a machete, for example, no transcendent expression is perceived. For the Asháninka, however, every object, no matter how small, has a place in the universe; acting with it, on it, or through it means causing a more general movement that has repercussions on the natural and social order, in a word, on the cosmic order. Here is an example: Using a machete to cut down a tree (all plants have a "history" and a name, even those that are "no good") always means acting upon the entire world. The tree has a spiritual "owner." Certain insects feed on its leaves; these insects in turn are the food of a bird, in whose rotted interior edible worms develop; and so on. This chain of relationships, of living fractions of a whole, is known and thoroughly understood by the Asháninka. The metal instrument that is used is the fruit of an exchange with another *ayúmpari*; it is possessed provisionally because it can be demanded by a creditor or exchanged for some days of hospitality. This sharing of the world (it is difficult to speak of "nature"; instruments of industrial origin are considered to be part of the "natural" world because they are sent by Pachakamáite) by all members of the community, this state of being not outside the "subject" but part of the subject, is the substantial difference between the vision of the natives and that of the settlers. One can act upon the world and the gods, as they do upon men. The world is not given to the Asháninka, but rather the Asháninka encounters it and "makes it a sharer in himself after having modified it sufficiently. The *world* is therefore essentially a *celebrated*, not an *accepted* world."[197] In this *celebrated* world the Asháninka finds that several parts—the white man's instruments, which are divine gifts and therefore sacramental objects—are denied to him. The white man has profaned the world; he prevents the Asháninka from possessing it and "celebrating" it. The white man constrains the world, reduces it, and mutilates it by interceding between god and men and by raising up a new god and usurping his functions. The myth of Pachakamáite that we have chosen to conclude this study clearly expresses the decline and loss that the Gran Pajonal Asháninka perceive in their new situation with respect to the ancient traditional order.

At this moment the new pages of an old story are being written in the central jungle of Peru. Our work has ended, but, as we all know, everything that ends is merely a beginning.

Notes

ABBREVIATIONS

AGOF Archivo General de la Orden Franciscana, Rome.

BNSM Biblioteca Nacional del Perú, Sección Manuscritos, Lima.

BSG *Boletín de la Sociedad Geográfica de Lima.*

GSI García, Domingo, and Manuel del Santo. "Carta escrita por los padres fray . . . misioneros apostólicos del colegio de Santa Rosa de Ocopa, y misioneros de infieles del Cerro de la Sal. . . ." In *Historia de las misiones franciscanas y narración de los progresos de la geografía en el oriente del Perú*, compiled by Bernardino Izaguirre, vol. 2. Lima: Talleres Tipogr. de la Penitenciaría, 1922.

HSAI Steward, Julian, ed. *Handbook of South American Indians.* 7 vols. Washington, D.C.: Smithsonian Institution, 1946–59.

IHM Izaguirre, Bernardino, comp. *Historia de las misiones franciscanas y narración de los progresos de la geografía en el oriente del Perú.* 14 vols., Lima: Talleres Tipogr. de la Penitenciaría, 1922–29.

JERG Jiménez de la Espada, Marcos, comp. *Relaciones geográficas de Indias.* 4 vols. Madrid: Tipogr. M. Hernandez, 1881–97.

LCCL Larrabure y Correa, Carlos, comp. *Colección de leyes, decretos, resoluciones y otros documentos oficiales referentes al Departamento de Loreto.* 18 vols. Lima: Impr. La Opinión Nacional, 1905–9.

LJS Loayza, Francisco A. *Juan Santos, el invencible.* Manuscripts from 1742 to 1755. Lima: Editorial D. Miranda, 1942.

LMDP La Marca, Juan Bautista de. "Diario y padrón de la gente del Paxonal, que el P. fray . . . , actual misionero, congregó al gremio de Nuestra Santa Madre la iglesia católica apostólica romana. Año de 1733." Lima: Biblioteca Nacional del Perú, Sección Manuscritos, 1733.

MJL Maúrtua, Víctor M., comp. *Juicio de límites entre el Perú y Bolivia.* 15 vols. Barcelona: Impr. de Henrich y Comp., 1906.

INTRODUCTION TO THE ENGLISH EDITION

1. The Campa Asháninka of the Gran Pajonal area speak a dialect variation of the Asháninka language that belongs to the pre-Andean Arawak linguistic family. For millennia this has been an oral language that only recently has been written using the Latin alphabet. For the Campa Asháninka words that appear in this book, I have kept my own system of transcription, which I devised during my fieldwork. It is a nonrigorous and simplified version of the various systems used by Catholic missionaries, missionaries of the Summer Institute of Linguistics, and the Wycliff Bible Translators. My system of transcription is based on Spanish phonology. Accents simply indicate the prominence of a vowel or syllable in the pronunciation. What follows are the vowels and consonants whose Spanish pronunciation differs from that of English:

a is pronounced *a* as in *America*
e is pronounced *e* as in *bet* or *Peggy*
i is pronounced *ee* as in *beet*
o is pronounced *o* as in *bought*
u is pronounced *oo* as in *boot*
ch is pronounced *ch* as in *chase*
h is pronounced as an aspirated *h* (as in the Spanish *jota*)
sh is pronounced *sh* as in *short*
tz is pronounced *zz* as in *pizza*

2. Bodley, Denevan, Elick, Lehnertz, and Weiss conducted their research in the late 1960s and early 1970s. John Bodley finished his Ph.D. dissertation in 1970: "Campa Socio-economic Adaptation" (University of Oregon; University Microfilms, Ann Arbor). In 1969 he published a short article: "The Last Remaining Independent Campa," *Peruvian Time*, vol. 29, no. 1498 (5 September). Other works include the following: John Bodley, "A Transformative Movement among the Campa of Eastern Peru," *Anthropos*, vol. 67 (1972), pp. 220–28. John Bodley, *Tribal Survival in the Amazon: The Campa Case,* IWGIA Documents, no. 5 (Copenhagen: International Work Group for Indigenous Affairs, 1972). William M. Denevan, "Campa Subsistence in the Gran Pajonal, Eastern Peru," *Geographical Review* (New York), vol. 61, no. 4 (1971). John Elick, "An Ethnography of the Pichis Valley Campa of Eastern Peru" (Ph.D. dissertation, University of California, Los Angeles, 1969; University Microfilms, Ann Arbor). Jay F. Lehnertz, "Cultural Struggle on the Peruvian Frontier: Campa-Franciscan Confrontations, 1595–1752" (Master's thesis, University of Wisconsin, 1969). Jay F. Lehnertz, "Juan Santos, Primitive Rebel on the Campa Frontier (1742–1752)," in *Actas y Memoria*, no. 4 (Lima: 39th International Congress of Americanists, 1972), pp. 111–26. Jay F. Lehnertz, "Lands of the Infidels: The Franciscans in the Central

Montaña of Peru, 1709–1824" (Ph.D. dissertation, University of Wisconsin, 1974; University Micrifilms, Ann Arbor). Gerald Weiss, "The Cosmology of the Campa Indians of Eastern Peru" (Ph.D. dissertation, Columbia University, 1969; University Microfilms, Ann Arbor). Gerald Weiss, "Campa Cosmology," *Ethnology* (Pittsburgh), vol. 11, no. 2 (1972).

3. Stefano Varese, "Celebración del desencuentro," in *A los quinientos años del choque de dos mundos: Balance y perspectiva*, compiled by Adolfo Colombres (Buenos Aires: Ediciones del Sol, 1989).

4. Stefano Varese, *La Sal de los Cerros* (Lima: Universidad Peruana de Ciencias y Tecnologías, 1968).

5. Currently this corporation is part of Exxon.

6. The price that some of us had to pay for this decision turned out to be excessive. I was never able to return to my academic career at the National University of San Marcos and eventually, in 1975, I left Peru to accept an opportune invitation by Mexican anthropologist Guillermo Bonfil Batalla, at that time director of the National Institute of Anthropology and History. This fortunate invitation extricated me from the uncomfortable position of being considered a collaborator of a fallen revolutionary regime.

7. Stefano Varese, *Estudio sondeo de seis comunidades Aguaruna del Alto Marañón* (Lima: Dirección de Comunidades Campesinas, Ministerio de Agricultura, 1970).

8. Stefano Varese and Sergio Chang, *Las sociedades nativas de la selva: Diagnóstico socio-económico preliminar del área rural peruana*, reporte oficial (Lima: Sistema Nacional de Apoyo a la Movilización Social, Dirección General de Organizaciones Rurales, 1972).

9. Stefano Varese, *The Forest Indians in the Present Political Situation of Peru*, IWGIA Documents, no. 8 (Copenhagen: International Work Group for Indigenous Affairs, 1972). Stefano Varese, "Inter-ethnic Relations in the Selva of Peru," in *The Situation of the Indians in South America: Contribution to the Study of Inter-ethnic Conflict in the Non-Andean Regions of South America*, edited by W. Dostal (Geneva: World Council of Churches, 1972). Stefano Varese, "Au sujet du colonialisme ecologique," *Les Temps Modernes* (Paris), no. 316 (April 1973). Stefano Varese, "La selva: Viejas fronteras, nuevas alternativas," *Participación* (Lima), no. 5, year 3 (1974). Stefano Varese, *Las minorías etnicas y la comunidad nacional* (Lima: Ediciones del Centro de Estudios de Participación Popular, 1974).

10. Alberto Chirif and Carlos Mora, *Atlas de comunidades nativas* (Lima: Sistema Nacional de Apoyo a la Movilización Social, 1976).

11. Michael Brown and Eduardo Fernández, *War of Shadow: The Struggle for Utopia in the Peruvian Amazon* (Berkeley: University of California Press, 1991), p. 206.

12. Abraham Lama, "Asháninka Displaced from Their Lands," press release, InterPress Third World News Agency (IPS), 22 April 1998. The Communist Party of Peru (CPP), known as "Shining Path," has a radically different version of the story. In a short mimeographed document titled "History of the

Asháninka Nationality," issued probably in 1993, the CPP argues that as soon as 1986 the first Open People's Committee was established in the Asháninka village of Selva de Oro along the Mantaro River. "By 1990, the Peoples' War had reached out to all Asháninka communities and to hundreds of people's committees. Democratic elections were held to elect civilian and military authorities for the New State" (pp. 2–3).

13. Brown and Fernández, *War of Shadow*, p. 209.

14. To illustrate the degree of conscription exercised in the region by a combination of drug cartels and the Shining Path, an official report of the Peruvian army mentions that between 1994 and 1995 thirty-four Asháninka villages were freed from the oppressive control of drug traffickers (Lama, "Asháninka Displaced").

15. Brown and Fernández, *War of Shadow*, p. 209.

16. Ibid., pp. 209–10.

17. "Peruvian State Targets Abandoned Lands of Asháninka. Interview with Mino Eusebio Castro," *Abya Yala News* (Oakland, Calif.), vol. 9, no. 1 (Spring 1995).

18. Ibid.

19. Eric J. Hobsbawn, *Primitive Rebels: Studies in Archaic Forms of Social Movements in the Nineteenth and Twentieth Centuries* (Manchester, England: Manchester University Press, 1978).

20. Dipesh Chakrabarty, "Subaltern Studies and Postcolonial Historiography," *Nepantla: Views from the South*, vol. 1, no. 1 (1999), pp. 9–32.

CHAPTER 1: ETHNOLOGY

1. Daniel G. Brinton, *La raza americana* (Buenos Aires: Edit. Nova, 1946), p. 224.

2. Paul Rivet and Charles Tastevin, "Les langues du Purus, du Juruá et des régions limitrophes. I, le groupe arawak pré-andin," *Anthropological Papers*, vol. 73, no. 8 (undated), pp. 857–59.

3. Chestmir Loukotka, *Clasificación de las lenguas sudamericanas*, Edición Lingüística Sudamericana, no. 1 (Prague: 1935), p. 21.

4. Alden J. Mason, "The Languages of South American Indians," in HSAI, vol. 6, p. 213.

5. Julian Steward and Louis C. Faron, *Native Peoples of South America* (New York: McGraw Hill, 1959), p. 22.

6. Olive A. Shell, *Grupos idiomáticos de la selva peruana*, Publicaciones del Instituto de Filología de la Facultad de Letras, Estudios, no. 7 (Lima: Universidad Nacional Mayor de San Marcos, 1958), pp. 4–7. The Arawak filiation of the Mashco also accepted by Loukotka (cf. *Clasificación*) has been questioned by Robert L. Carneiro in "Little-Known Tribes of the Peruvian Montaña," in *Bulletin of the International Committee on Urgent Anthropological and Ethnological Research*, no. 5 (Vienna: Heine-Geldern Edit., 1962), p. 83.

7. P. Rivet and C. Loukotka, "Langues de l'Amerique du Sud et des Antilles," in *Les langues du Monde*, edited by A. Meillet and M. Cohen (Paris: H. Champion, 1952), p. 1106.

8. Shell, *Grupos idiomáticos*, p. 3.

9. The Campa of the Lower Perené repeatedly assured us that they and the Machiguenga of the Urubamba did not understand each other.

10. Mason, "Languages," p. 213. Antonio Tovar, *Catálogo de las lenguas de América del Sur* (Buenos Aires: Editorial Sudamericana, 1961), pp. 128–29.

11. The young Indian converts at the Franciscan missions use the term *Campa* derogatorily toward their former relatives and friends, thereby further deepening the divide created in their people's tradition.

12. Stiglich, Von Hassel, Farabee, and Grubb are examples.

13. Steward and Faron (*Native Peoples*, pp. 17–21) provide an interesting clarification regarding the word *tribe*, especially as it relates to South American ethnology, and come to the conclusion that its use is not advisable.

14. Claudio Osambela, "El oriente del Perú," in BSG, vols. 1, 6, nos. 4–6 (1896), p. 220.

15. César Cipriani, *Informe del ingeniero sobre la ruta Perené-Ucayali*, Ministerio de Fomento, Junta Consultiva del Ferrocarril al Oriente (Lima: Imprenta del Estado, 1906), p. 57.

16. Jorge M. Von Hassel, "Las tribus salvajes de la región amazónica del Perú," in BSG, year 15, trim. 1, vol. 17 (1905), pp. 31–32. Charles C. Eberhardt, *Indians of Peru*, Miscellaneous Collections, vol. 52 (Washington, D.C.: Smithsonian Institution, 1907), p. 184. Otto Nordenskjold, "Explorations chez les indiens Campas dans le Pérou," *Meddelande fran Geografiska Foreningen i Göteborg* (Gothenburg, Sweden), vol. 3 (1924), p. 6.

17. Kenneth G. Grubb, *The Lowland Indians of Amazonia* (London: Word Dominion Press, 1927), p. 86. Pedro W. Fast, *Distribución geográfica de 30 naciones aborígenes en la Amazonía peruana* (Lima: Ministerio de Educación Pública, 1961), p. 4.

18. John H. Rowe, "The Distribution of Indians and Indian Languages in Peru," *Geographical Review* (New York), vol. 37, no. 2 (1947), p. 213.

19. Further demographic data on the Campa can be found in an article by Edmundo Rey Riveros, "El censo y los aborígenes selvícolas de nuestra Amazonía," *Revista Militar del Perú* (Lima), nos. 613, 633, 634 (July, August, and September–October 1956; reprinted 1957), pp. 7–16 passim. See also appendix 1 in this same text.

20. Denevan, "Campa Subsistence."

21. Betty J. Meggers, "Ambiente y cultura en la cuenca del Amazonas: Revisión de la teoría del determinismo ambiental," in *Estudios sobre ecología humana*, Estudios Monográficos, no. 3 (Washington, D.C.: Unión Panamericana, 1960). The original English version of this article was published in 1956.

22. Robert L. Carneiro, "Slash-and-Burn Agriculture: A Closer Look at Its Implications for Settlement Patterns," in *Men and Cultures*, Selected Papers of

the 5th International Congress of Anthropological and Ethnological Sciences, September 1956 (Philadelphia: University of Pennsylvania Press, 1960).

23. Ibid., pp. 231–34.

24. In fact the only form of polygyny we found on the Gran Pajonal was preventive sororal or sororate, the only form compatible with the type of residence.

25. The phenomenon of *trade*, or exchange of goods, would merit a separate description because it represents one of the most important aspects of Campa society and culture.

26. Marshall Sahlins, *Tribesmen* (Upper Saddle River, N.J.: Prentice Hall Inc., 1968).

27. Otis Dudley Duncan, "The Ecosystem Concept and the Problem of Air Pollution," in *Environment and Cultural Behavior: Ecological Studies in Cultural Anthropology*, edited by Andrew Vayda (New York: Natural History Press, 1969). Most of the following analysis was inspired by the work of Clifford Geertz, "Two Types of Ecosystems," in Vayda, *Environment*.

28. Harold Conklin, *El estudio del cultivo de roza*, Estudios Monográficos, no. 11 (Washington, D.C.: Unión Panamericana, 1963).

29. Utomo Kampto, cited in Geertz, "Two Types of Ecosystems," p. 14.

30. Donald Lathrap, *The Upper Amazon* (London: Thames and Hudson, 1970).

31. For a more detailed discussion of this point, see also Varese, "Inter-Ethnic Relations"; and Varese, *Forest Indians*.

32. Weiss, "Campa Cosmology," p. 157.

33. John H. Bodley, "Campa Social Organization," unpublished manuscript, personal communication, 1969; Bodley, "Campa Socio-economic Adaptation."

34. Bodley, "Campa Social Organization."

35. Ibid., p. 17.

36. Ibid., p. 14.

37. In this case there is a difference between the ideal culture, which seems to have forgotten or seems to deny the importance of this type of knowledge, and the real culture, in which there are constant manifestations of a notable knowledge of family ties. The data that we offer in the social aspect is provisional and subject to possible revision after further field research.

38. These encounters take place in the pajonal fields. The two groups station themselves forty or fifty steps away from each other and begin to shoot blunt arrows at each other. The skill consists of dodging them by jumping, crouching, and utilizing one's garments as protection. In the excitement someone begins to use arrows with real points, and soon the collective duel can become a battle, with wounded or a death that must be avenged immediately or in a subsequent battle. The women, along with their children, cheer their men on from a few yards behind them and pick up the lost arrows; upon seeing blood spilled, they intervene to calm tempers and take their men home.

39. We have transcribed the classification and tribal names according to the reports and from the point of view of the Gran Pajonal Campa.

40. Stefano Varese, "Dos versiones cosmogónicas Campa: Esbozo analítico," *Revista del Museo Nacional* (Lima), vol. 36 (1970).

41. Cf. Mircea Eliade, *Trattato di storia delle religioni* (Turin: Edizioni Einaudi, 1954), p. 446. See also these other works by Eliade: *El mito del eterno retorno: Arquetipos y repetición* (Buenos Aires: Emecé Editores, 1952); *The Two and the One* (London: Harvill Press, 1965), chap. 5; and *Il sacro e il profano* (Turin: Edit. Boringhieri, 1967), chap. 2.

42. Gustave Van Der Leeuw, *La religión dans son essence et ses manifestations* (Paris: Payot, 1955), pp. 342–47.

43. Ibid., p. 343.

44. Cited in Van Der Leeuw, *La religíon*.

45. Ibid., p. 344.

46. Ibid., p. 345.

47. *Bixa orellana.*

48. Van Der Leeuw, *La religíon*, p. 397.

49. Ibid., pp. 399–403.

50. Eliade, *Il sacro*, pp. 94–127 passim.

51. Steward and Faron, *Native Peoples*, pp. 343–46.

CHAPTER 2: MYTHICAL AND MYSTICAL

1. Víctor M. Maúrtua, comp., *Exposición de la república del Perú presentada al Excmo. Gobierno Argentino en el juicio de límites con la república de Bolivia, conforme al tratado de arbitraje del 30 de diciembre de 1902*, vol. 1 (Barcelona: Imprenta de Henrich y Comp., 1906), p. 214.

2. Raúl Porras Barrenechea, "El descubrimiento del Amazonas," in *El Perú y la Amazonía* (Lima: Instituto Raúl Porras Barrenechea, Universidad Nacional Mayor de San Marcos, 1961), p. 4.

3. Ricardo García Rosell, *Conquista de la montaña. Sinópsis de los descubrimientos, expediciones, estudios y trabajos llevados a cabo en el Perú para el aprovechamiento y cultura de sus montañas* (Lima: Tipografía La Prensa, 1905), pp. 10–11.

4. Porras Barrenechea, "Descubrimiento," pp. 4–5.

5. Ibid., p. 2.

6. In August 1643 Franciscans Gaspar de Vera and Juan Cabezas reached the Tepqui and Comanahua tribes located along the Magdalena and Santa Marta Rivers, both western tributaries of the Huallaga. There they received word of a neighboring nation of Ingas, where the priests were courteously welcomed and given lodging. In the language of these Indians, a machete was called *espada* (sword) and the mock-pearl glass beads *castilla*. Cf. Bernardino Izaguirre, comp., *Historia de las misiones franciscanas y narración de los progresos de la geografía en el oriente del Perú*, vol. 1 (Lima: Talleres Tipográficos de la Penitenciaría, 1922), pp. 125–26.

7. Antonio Vasquez de Espinoza, *Compendio y descripción de las Indias Occidentales* (Washington, D.C.: Smithsonian Institution, 1948), pp. 535–36.

8. Cf. Maúrtua, *Exposición*, vol. 1, pp. 203ff. and 247ff. See also Vasquez de Espinoza, *Compendio*, p. 569; this author generally uses the word *Chuncho* to refer to the Indians east of the highlands and Cuzco.

9. Marcos Jiménez de la Espada, comp., *Relaciones geográficas de Indias*, vol. 2 (Madrid: Tipografía M. Hernández, 1885), app. 3, p. 104. By the word *Chuquiambo*, Cabello de Balboa surely intended to indicate *Chuquiabo*, the valley where the city of Nuestra Señora de la Paz is located. Cf. Cosme Bueno, *Geografía del Perú virreynal (siglo XVIII)* (Lima: D. Valcárcel, 1951), pp. 116–17.

10. See Miguel Cabello de Balboa, "Carta del P. Miguel Cabello de Balboa al virrey, marqués de Cañete, sobre la conversión de los indios Chunchos, 11 de setiembre de 1594," in MJL, vol. 8, pp. 140–46.

11. Gregorio de Bolivar, "Relación de la entrada del padre fray Gregorio de Bolivar, en compañía de Diego Ramírez de Carlos, á las provincias de indios Chunchos, en 1621," in MJL, vol. 8, pp. 205–37. This expedition is also referred to by Pablo Joseph de Arriaga, "La extirpación de la idolatría en el Perú, Lima, 1621," in *Colección de libros y documentos referentes a la historia del Perú*, vol. 1 (Lima: Imprenta y Librería Sanmarti y Cía, 1920), p. 192.

12. Juan Alvarez Maldonado, "Relación verdadera del discurso y subceso de la jornada y descubrimiento que hizo desde el año de 1567 hasta el de 1569," in MJL, vol. 6, p. 60.

13. Felipe Guacra Paucar, "La descripción que se hizo en la provincia de Xauxa por la instrucción de S. M. que a la dicha provincia se envió de molde, mayo de 1582," in JERG, vol. 1, pp. 79ff.

14. Ibid., p. 86.

15. Diego Dávila Brizeño, "Relación de don Diego Dávila Brizeño, corregidor de Guarocheri, al virrey del Perú don Hernando de Torres y Portugal, conde de Villar, en que se describe la provincia de Yauyos, enero de 1586" (our title), in JERG, vol. 1, pp. 62ff.

16. Ibid., p. 72.

17. "Relación de la ciudad de Guamanga y sus términos. Año 1586" (no author listed), in JERG, vol. 1, p. 110. The river alluded to is the Mantaro, not the Marañón.

18. Diego de Porres, "Memorial del padre fray Diego de Porres a S. M. pidiendo mercedes por sus servicios, año de 1582," in MJL, vol. 1, pp. 82–86.

19. Jiménez de la Espada, *Relaciones geográficas*, vol. 4, last appendix, p. 186. Nevertheless, Father Font, in a letter written from the jungle of Jauja in November 1595, that is, eight years before his final statement, uses the name *Andes* to refer exclusively to the jungle and not to the Indians. The expression is still polysemous. See Jiménez de la Espada, *Relaciones geográficas*, vol. 2, app. 3, p. 93.

20. Diego de Córdova Salinas, *Crónica de la religiosissima prouincia de los Doze Apóstoles del Perú, de la orden de nuestro Seráfico P. S. Francisco de la Regular Obseruancía; con relación de las prouincias que della an salido, y son sus hijas. Compuesta por*

su historiador el P. Fray Diego de Cordua Salinas, predicador y padre dela mesma prouincia natural de la ciudad de Lima, metrópoli del Perú . . . , book 2 (Lima: Jorge López de Herrera, 1651), p. 127.

21. Referring to the distance between Huamanga and the new lands he discovered, Contreras says, "[I]t is exactly forty leagues: twenty of mountainous country and Baquerías of Guamanga and of Guanta, twelve of Andes or upper jungle that encloses and divides these two worlds, and eight of Aucaya jungle lands" (Fernando Contreras, "Representación de Fernando Contreras a S. M. sobre la reducción de los Aucaya, Austria-América, nueva provincia de los Minarvas, 10 de mayo de 1651," in MJL, vol. 5, p. 61).

22. With regard to the name *Andes, Antis,* or *Anti,* Stiglich's opinion is of interest. He states that the term *Antis* corresponds to the Campa who live along the Antis or Auchiqui stream, which empties into the Perené. The Inca generals called the Mountain of Salt range *Antis,* and hence used the same name for the Campa Indians who lived there. Later it was discovered that the Indians of the Urubamba and the Pilcopata spoke a similar dialect, and they were called *Cuchoa Antis,* after the mountain range near Cuzco. Cf. Germán Stiglich, *Informe del jefe de la comisión exploradora de las regiones del Ucayali, Fiscarrald y Madre de Dios* (Lima: SPI, 1904), p. 67. See also Luis E. Valcarcel, *Etnohistoria del Perú antiguo* (Lima: Universidad Nacional Mayor de San Marcos, 1959), pp. 112–13.

23. Fernando de Armas Medina, *Cristianización del Perú* (Seville: Escuela de Estudios Hispano-Americanos de Sevilla, 1953), pp. 33, 43.

24. In a report by Father José Teruel, provincial intern and rector of the College of Lima, to Viceroy Velasco, written in 1602, the name of one of the Jesuits who accompanied Hurtado de Arbieto appears: Father Montoya. There is no information available on the other two. Cf. Jiménez de la Espada, *Relaciones geográficas,* vol. 4, last appendix, p. 166.

25. Francisco de Toledo, "Provisión del virrey don Francisco de Toledo concediendo á Martín Hurtado de Arbieto, á su petición los privilegios de conquistador. Arequipa, 4 de noviembre de 1575," in MJL, vol. 7, p. 211.

26. Ibid.

27. Cf. Víctor M. Maúrtua, comp., *Juicio de límites entre el Perú y Bolivia,* vol. 5 (Barcelona: Impr. de Henrich y Comp., 1906), p. 242.

28. Anonymous, "Información de servicios de Francisco Valenzuela, 1578–1592. Declaración del testigo don Gerónimo de Marañón," in MJL, vol. 7, p. 109.

29. Francisco de Toledo, "Relación de los yndios de guerra que están en las fronteras de los yndios christianos de la governación del reyno del Pirú. In carta del virrey D. Francisco de Toledo á S. M. sobre asuntos de guerra, acompañando una relación de los yndios fronterizos, 20 de marzo de 1573," in MJL, vol. 1, pp. 100–103.

30. Ibid., p. 102. In this document Toledo declares the conquest of Martín Hurtado de Arbieto complete, when in fact this did not occur until 1582, as noted above.

31. Ibid., p. 103.

32. Alvarez Maldonado, "Relación verdadera," pp. 17ff.

33. Alvarez Maldonado (ibid., p. 65) names the Guarayos, which is a general term used by the Bauré (Arawak) converts or by those in contact with whites, which included all Indians who were independent or at war. The Bauré are a neighboring tribe related to the Mojo, and their present location is near the headwaters of the Verde and Blanco Rivers, that is, near what was the Chiquitos Mission, deep in the Bolivian jungle. Cf. Alfred Metraux, "Tribes of Eastern Bolivia and the Madeira Headwaters," in HSAI, vol. 3, pp. 396–97.

34. See Jiménez de la Espada, *Relaciones geográficas*, vol. 2, app. 3, p. 92.

35. The report states that the inhabitants of Tarma were accustomed to exchanging corn for salt with the jungle Indians, and the residents of Jauja "obtain chili peppers from the aforementioned peoples of the Andes, subjects of this valley, where plantains and coca grow" (Guacra Paucar, "Descripción," p. 88).

36. Jiménez de la Espada, *Relaciones geográficas*, vol. 2, app. 3, p. 94.

37. Ibid., p. 92.

38. Ibid., pp. 94–96.

39. Ibid., p. 95.

40. Ibid., p. 96.

41. Ibid., p. 95.

42. Ibid., p. 96.

43. Ibid.

44. Ibid., p. 95.

45. The term *pre-Andean*, introduced by Paul Rivet and Charles Tastevin for an exclusively linguistic purpose, nevertheless lends itself very well to a similar designation of the cultural area. Cf. Rivet and Tastevin, "Les langues," p. 857.

46. Jiménez de la Espada, *Relaciones geográficas*, vol. 2, app. 3, p. 96.

47. Ibid., p. 97.

48. Cf. Shell, *Grupos idiomáticos*, pp. 8–9.

49. Jiménez de la Espada, *Relaciones geográficas*, vol. 2, app. 3, p. 96.

50. Ibid.

51. Ibid.

52. Ibid. "[E]verywhere we have been they have given us everything we have needed, in great abundance, to us and to the Indians who are with us, approximately 30."

53. Font also uses the name *Marañón* and believes that it is the same river traveled by Diego de Córdoba Salinas and Pedro Ursúa, a common error in his time. Father Sobreviela in his 1791 map and M. E. de Rivero in his 1855 Junín map use the name *Cintiguailas* for the Mantaro River before it meets the Apurímac. Cf. Jiménez de la Espada, *Relaciones geográficas*, vol. 4, last appendix, p. 167.

54. Ibid., p. 148.

55. Ibid., pp. 147–48. Ancomayo, Acón, Angoyacu, Guadiana, Jauja, and Antiguo Marañón are all synonyms used at various times to refer to the Man-

taro River. Jiménez de la Espada quotes Cosme Bueno in his "Descripción de la provincia de Huanta del año 1767," in which he stated, "It still conserves the name Marañón, which it received at the beginning of the conquest, although in the Indian's language it conserves the name Angoyaco"; Bueno is referring to the Jauja or Mantaro River. Cf. Jiménez de la Espada, Relaciones geográficas, vol. 4, last appendix, p. 147.

56. Ibid., pp. 169–70.

57. Ibid., p. 172.

58. Ibid., p. 168.

59. Ibid., p. 173.

60. Ibid., pp. 177–78.

61. Ibid., pp. 180–81, 183.

62. Ibid., p. 187.

63. Ibid., pp. 192–93.

64. Maúrtua, *Exposición*, vol. 6, pp. 242–57.

65. Maúrtua, *Exposición*, vol. 2, pp. 104ff. Juan Recio de Leon, "Descripción del Paititi y provincias de Tipuani, Chunchos, por . . . Madrid, 19 de octubre de 1623," in MJL, vol. 6, pp. 242–57.

66. Balthasar Ramirez, "Descripción del reyno del Pirú del sitio, temple, provincias, obispados y ciudades; de los naturales de sus lenguas y trajes. Año de 1597," in MJL, vol. 1, pp. 281–363.

67. Diego de Torres, *Relatione breve del P. Diego de Torres della Compagnia di Giesú, procuratore della prouincia del Perú, circa il frutto che si raccoglie con gli indiani di quel regno . . . in Roma* (Written in 1603; published in Rome: Appresso Luigi Zannetti, 1903).

68. The first information about this expedition by Brother Jiménez is contained in Córdova Salinas, *Crónica*, book 2, chap. 30. Subsequent Franciscan historiography is based on Córdova Salinas. Cf. José Amich, *Compendio histórico de los trabajos, fatigas, sudores y muertes que los ministros evangélicos de la seráfica religión han padecido por la conversión de las almas de los gentiles, en la montaña de los Andes, pertenecientes a las provincias del Perú . . .* (Paris: Librería de Rosa y Bouret, 1854), pp. 20–21. See also Izaguirre, *Historia*, vol. 1, pp. 158–59. Contemporary Franciscan historian Odorico Saiz, relying exclusively on Córdova Salinas's information, believes that Jiménez was the first to establish evangelizing contact with the Campa. Cf. Odorico Saiz, "Los misioneros franciscanos en la Amazonía del Perú," *Mercurio Peruano* (Lima), year 17, no. 184 (July 1942), p. 335.

69. Izaguirre, *Historia*, vol. 1, pp. 181–84.

70. Córdova Salinas, *Crónica*, book 2, p. 127.

71. For a detailed history of the Bohórquez expedition, see Amich, *Compendio histórico*, pp. 22–24; and Izaguirre, Historia, vol. 1, pp. 186–89.

72. Córdova Salinas, *Crónica*. There is a more recent reprinting of this text, but in this work we use the original. Cf. Lino Canedo Gomez, *Crónica franciscana de las provincias del Perú, de Diego de Córdova Salinas* (Washington, D.C.: Academy of American Franciscan History, 1957).

73. Córdova Salinas, *Crónica*, book 2, pp. 206–7. Córdova Salinas refers to a great river, which, according to the Omagua, had "its origin toward Cuzco and its end at the Amazon. . . . [T]he *naturales* call it Yetau, and it has many names among them because of its riches as well as for the multitude of nations that it sustains, such as the Tipuna, the Guanaru, the Ozuna, the Morua, the Naunás, the Cononoma, [and] the Mariana."

74. Contreras, "Representación," pp. 61ff.

75. Ibid., p. 67.

76. Ibid., p. 62.

77. Ibid., pp. 62–63.

78. Ibid., p. 62.

79. Ibid. One might think of vestiges of the Cuzco insurrections of Toledo's time. In a letter from Franciscan missionary Manuel de Biedma to the comisario general of the Franciscan province of Peru, written from San Buenaventura de Savini in 1687, the term *pabate* appears: "Today I gave them a talk or reasoning on the zeal of Your Excellency and the love you had for them (which causes in them a reaction of wonder and operates as when mentioning the Apu or Pabate, which is the Prelate, Lord and Superior of all), for whose cause we were sent to found at the Perené"; AGOF, XL/39, fols. 162–63. Biedma is speaking of the Campa of the Upper Perené region. The word Contreras uses seems to be the same one, perhaps erroneously transcribed. Presently in the Campa Asháninka language, *paba* or *pahua* means "Lord, God, Father." It is only because of Biedma that we have more information about this mysterious mountain personage. The diary the missionary wrote in 1686 on the occasion of his journey from the Ucayali to the Perené contains information that was provided by the Cunibo guide and translator, information that is obviously related to that of Contreras. Here are Father Biedma's words: "Cayampay (the Cunibo guide) said that from there [the expedition was at that moment at the confluence of the Ene and the Perené], about thirty leagues up the Enne there was a large town called Puccetaguaro of Christian Indians who had fled from the sierra, about 8,000 of them, and that they were governed by a main *curaca* and four subaltern *caciques*" (Amich, *Compendio histórico*, p. 114). Naturally the name of the town mentioned by the guide is in the Cunibo language and is therefore completely different from the name given by Contreras.

80. Contreras, "Representación," pp. 69–70.

81. Father Manuel de Biedma in November 1686, after crossing the Tambo River, reached the point where the Ene meets the Perené. There he noted the presence of Campa, Camparite, Pirro, and Simirinche Indians. The agreement between Contreras and Biedma is clear: It is the same place and the same Indians, but they are designated by words of different origin. *Campa* and *Camparite* can be considered synonyms, as can *Pirro* and *Simirinche*. Cf. Amich, *Compendio histórico*, p. 114.

82. The three groups belong to the (western) Pano linguistic family, found mainly in the Ucayali Valley. The Panatahua are really unclassified linguistically,

but we risk calling them Pano based on the similarity of the ethnic name to those of the Pano tribes of the Jurúa and Purús River basins. Cf. Mason, "Languages," p. 263.

83. Amich, *Compendio histórico*, pp. 30–35.

84. Ibid., p. 35. See also Manuel de Sobreviela, "Varias noticias interesantes de las entradas que los religiosos de mi padre San Francisco han hecho á las montañas del Perú, desde cada uno de los partidos confinantes con la cordillera de los Andes para mayor esclarecimiento del mapa que se da á luz sobre el curso de los ríos Huallaga y Ucayali," *Mercurio Peruano* (Lima), no. 80 (9 October 1791), fols. 107–8. See also Manuel de Sobreviela, *Voyage au Pérou, faits dans les années 7191 á 1794 par les PP. Manuel de Sobreviela et Narcisso y Barcelo . . .* (Paris: J. G. Dentu, 1809), pp. 28–29. See also Izaguirre, *Historia*, vol. 1, pp. 197–98.

85. Izaguirre, *Historia*, vol. 1, pp. 207–8. In Amich, *Compendio histórico*, it is constantly repeated that Biedma knew the Campa language well. It is interesting to note that the old Christian missions among the American Indian populations left, in some cases, traces that are still evident, especially in the formal aspect of some rituals. Jehan Vellard in Paraguay gathered texts of prayers of the Mbwihá (Guaraní), in which the influence of the seventeenth- and eighteenth-century Jesuit *reducciones*, or settlements of converted Indians, is clearly recognizable. See Jehan A. Vellard, "Textes Mbwihá recueillis au Paraguay," *Jornal de la Société des Américanistes, Nouvelle Série* (Paris), vol. 29 (1937), pp. 373–86. Perhaps the same phenomenon is recognizable in some information provided by nineteenth-century French voyager Olivier Ordinaire, when he states that he heard the Campa of the Palcazú recite a sort of litany, which even in its tone reminded him of those used in the churches. See Olivier Ordinaire, *Du Pacifique à l'Atlantique par les Andes peruviennes et l'Amazone* (Paris: Libraire Plon, Nourrit et Cie., 1892), pp. 144–45.

86. For this reason Antonio Raimondi says that Biedma, although not the discoverer of the Tambo River, was the first to describe it in detail. Cf. Izaguirre, *Historia*, vol. 1, p. 283.

87. Izaguirre, *Historia*, vol. 1, p. 243. Naturally the names of the rivers were different. The name *Tambo* appears only in the second edition of Sobreviela's map, that is, in 1830. The name *Ucayali* began to be used by the Jesuit missionaries during the first half of the seventeenth century, whereas the Franciscans use the term *Paro* or *Parobeni*, perhaps of Piro origin. Franciscan Father Antonio Vital notes, "[The Jesuits] have given this Paro River the name of Ocayala" (Antonio Vital, "Carta del padre Antonio Vital al Rev. P. comisario . . . , San Miguel de Navarra, 18 de octubre de 1686," AGOF, XL/39, fols. 184–85). Strange stories, these of the names of places and towns. Why did the name *Ucayali* become widely used, whereas the name Paro did not survive other than in documents?

88. Amich, *Compendio histórico*, pp. 85–87. In the memoirs of the viceroy, duke of La Palata, there is no reference to Biedma's expeditions.

89. Amich, *Compendio histórico*, pp. 87–89. Izaguirre, *Historia*, pp. 248–52.

90. Amich, *Compendio histórico*, p. 95.

91. Cf. Amich, *Compendio histórico*, pp. 91ff. See also Sobreviela, "Varias noticias," p. 109; Izaguirre, *Historia*, vol. 1, pp. 255–56.

92. Sobreviela, in "Varias noticias," p. 109, bases his statement on Fernando Rodriguez de Tena, *Historia de la montañas y misiones del Perú* (Lima: 1780), book 1, p. 123.

93. Father Biedma recorded the information in a diary that he wrote, a summary of which is included here. Cf. Amich, *Compendio histórico*, p. 106.

94. Personal consultations with Franciscan historian Father Odorico Saiz of the Ocopa Monastery (Jauja) have shed light on this matter. Biedma's diary, according to Saiz, has been in Rome since 1857, along with other Franciscan documents from Peru, at the request of P. M. Civezza, who needed these sources for his *Storia universale delle missioni francescane* (Rome: 1857).

95. I thank Father Saiz for his consideration in providing me with textual copies of the aforementioned documents. Father Saiz faithfully transcribed the documents years ago during a research trip to the AGOF in Rome; therefore, the copies consulted for purposes of this research offer the greatest guarantee of accuracy. The following is a list of the documents I have reviewed:

(1) Manuel de Biedma, "Carta de . . . al comisario general desde San Buenaventura de Savini, 10 de noviembre(?) de 1685," AGOF, XL/39, fol. 135.
(2) Manuel de Biedma, "Carta de . . . al comisario general desde Comas, 23 de diciembre de 1685," AGOF, XL/39, fols. 135–38.
(3) Manuel de Biedma, "Carta de . . . al comisario general desde Andamarca, 25 de marzo de 1686," AGOF, XL/39, fols. 139–40.
(4) Manuel de Biedma, "Carta de . . . al comisario general desde San Buenaventura de Savini, 22 de abril de 1687," AGOF, XL/39, fol. 162.
(5) "Carta del comisario general al padre Manuel de Biedma," draft, undated and with no place noted, probably written in late 1685 or early 1686, AGOF, XL/39, fols. 137–38.
(6) Francisco de la Fuente, "Relación del viaje a los Cunibos por el capitán . . . , San Miguel de los Cunibos, 18 de setiembre de 1686," AGOF, XL/39, fols. 154–55.
(7) Francisco de Huerta, "Relación hecha a nuestro Reverendísimo Padre fray Felis de Como . . . , Andamarca, 29 de noviembre de 1686," AGOF, XL/39, fols. 171–78.
(8) Francisco de Huerta, Another untitled account of the same events, Andamarca, 29 November 1686, AGOF, XL/39, unpaginated.
(9) Bartolomé de Veraun, Copy of a letter describing the successful events of the expedition to the jungle, San Buenaventura, 23 October 1686, AGOF, XL/39, fols. 143–45.
(10) Antonio Vital, "Carta del padre Antonio Vital al Rev. P. comisario . . . , San Miguel de Navarra, 18 de octubre de 1686," AGOF, XL/39, fols. 184–85. (The place is without a doubt San Miguel de los Cunibos, as is clear from the text.)

96. Amich, *Compendio histórico*, pp. 104–5.

97. Ibid., p. 105.

98. Biedma "asked him earnestly to give him information on the names of all the rivers that they would encounter on the way and of all the people who inhabited them, and Don Felipe offered to do so with great pleasure. The venerable Father wrote them in a diary that he kept" (Amich, *Compendio histórico*, p. 106).

99. Cf. Julian H. Steward and Alfred Metraux, "Tribes of the Peruvian and Ecuadorian Montaña," in HSAI, vol. 3, pp. 557–67; Mason, "Languages," pp. 262–69.

100. Cf. Amich, *Compendio histórico*, pp. 107–14 passim.

101. There are two accounts by Huerta ("Relación" and an untitled account), but in reality the second, which is also unnumbered, is simply a letter that accompanies the first account, in which practical advice is given regarding the best manner of traveling through the places and the Indian hamlets located between Andamarca and the jungle. Quotes from Huerta will therefore refer to the first account (according to the order of our citation), and exceptions will be pointed out.

102. Huerta, "Relación," fol. 172.

103. Cf. Izaguirre, *Historia*, vol. 1, p. 257.

104. Huerta, "Relación," fols. 173–74.

105. Vital, "Carta," fols. 184–85. This letter, dated in San Miguel de Navarra on 18 October 1686, was written secretly by Vital, without the other members of the expedition knowing. Vital, against the wishes of the rest, did not head back toward the Perené but instead remained at the Ucayali to "defend" the new missions against Jesuit intrusion.

106. Fuente, "Relación del viaje," fols. 154–55.

107. Ibid., fol. 155.

108. Veraun, letter describing the expedition, fols. 143–45. There are two documents by Veraun, but all references are to this one unless otherwise noted.

109. Izaguirre, *Historia*, vol. 1, pp. 207–8.

110. Father Fernando Torre López, relying on linguist William Kindberg's supposition, believes that the name *Campa* can be attributed to a phonetic deformation by the Spaniards because they heard the sound "campa" frequently repeated in questions: *Paitiricampa incantiri?* (What could it be?). This hypothesis does not seem acceptable if we consider the following facts:

(1) Because a general term already existed for these Indians (*Andes* or *Antis*), the necessity to coin a new term based upon a phonetic deduction is not clearly shown. The phonetic deduction is readily reached by a modern-day linguist but was less obvious to a seventeenth-century Spanish speaker.

(2) Biedma uses the term *Campa* when he possesses a certain fluency in the language and therefore is capable of correctly using the indigenous self-denomination *Asháninka*.

This self-denomination is ignored in order to adopt the Pano term. All of this can be better understood if we consider that the Campa were completely "unconquered" at the time and that in 1687 Biedma himself asked that twelve Panatahua families be sent to the Perené (the heart of Campa territory) because the Panatahua were "Indians who knew how to use guns and were also skilled in navigating with rafts and canoes; they are reliable and . . . excellent trackers" (Biedma, "Carta de . . . San Buenaventura de Savini, 22 de abril de 1687," AGOF, XL/39, fol. 162). The missionaries' minimal familiarity with the Campa, combined with the good relationships they had already established with some of the Pano language groups, explains the preference they showed for the use of Pano ethnic terms.

111. The suggestion of analyzing this possibility is owed to Dr. Jehan Vellard.

112. Cf. Veraun, letter describing the expedition, fol. 143. "[O]nce we had approached them, Father Manuel de Biedma called to them . . . *in their Camba language*" (emphasis added). See also Samuel Fritz, "Description abrégée du fleuve Maragnon, et des missions établies aux environs de ce fleuve . . . ," in *Lettres édifiantes et curieuses, écrites des missions étrangéres* (Toulouse: Noel-Etienne Seus, 1810).

113. In Huerta's account, "Relación," fol. 174, the Tupi-Guaraní word *maloca* appears on several occasions to indicate the large communal house of the Cunibo. The same thing occurs in the account of Fuente, "Relación del viaje," fol. 154v, where the same term is used repeatedly with great accuracy.

114. Melchor de Navarra y Rocaful, "Autos sobre la delimitación de las misiones jesuitas y franciscanas del río Ucayali" (on paper bearing seal and years 1687 and 1688), AGOF, XL/39, fol. 195. In this document by the viceroy, the term appears to be already incorporated because information of Franciscan as well as Jesuit origin is included. However, in a report dated 1687 and written by a Franciscan from the Chanchamayo area, the word *Campa* is completely ignored and the term *Andes* is used instead. Perhaps the author of the document had not yet had contact with the members of the San Miguel expedition. Cf. Rodrigo Vazavil, "Información dada ante el general Dn. Alonso de la Cueva Messia, corregidor y justicia mayor de la provincia de Tarma y Chinchaycocha y su jurisdicción por su Magestad, a pedimento de M. R. P. predicador fray Rodrigo Vazavil del orden del señor San Francisco, sobre inquirir el mejor camino que se supiere para la entrada al Cerro de la Sal y montaña de los Andes. Ante Joseph de Roxas, escribano de su Magestad, Tharama, 6 de marzo de 1687," transcribed by Bernardino Izaguirre, in *Revista del Archivo Nacional del Perú* (Lima), vol. 2, no. 2 (1921), pp. 391–92.

115. These are names that are alternated and confused with Paro, Taraba, and *Enne* in the writings of Biedma, Huerta, and others.

116. Cf. ethnological map by Günter Tessmann, *Die Indianer Nordost-Perus* (Hamburg: Friederichsen, de Gruyter e Co., 1930).

117. Along the Curahuanía River (western tributary of the Ucayali), Biedma indicated the presence of the Ruanagua, who were always on the west bank; a

little farther south he encountered Mochobo. Along the western tributaries Chipani and Anacayari, Huerta also noted Mochobo groups. Along the Tahuanía, he pointed out the presence of Pichabo and Soboibo, and on the Cohenga River Father Huerta also noted Comabo. Comabo and Ruanagua groups were also found, according to Huerta, along the Urubamba, almost at its mouth. See figure 2 for more specific locations.

118. Veraun, letter describing the expedition, fol. 145. See also the account of Huerta, "Relación," fol. 176, stating that the Cunibo "go around completely naked; they do not spin or weave clothing; they wear only what they steal."

119. Vital, "Carta," fol. 185.

120. Huerta, "Relación," fols. 177v–178.

121. Huerta, untitled account, fols. 3v–4r. This is a type of missionary "raid" that began during this time to gather the Indians into settlements so as to indoctrinate them more easily. Force was used because it was impossible to use rhetoric to convince the Indians to leave their homes and fields. The missionaries needed "strong and spirited ministers dedicated to going with some men to pull them out of the forests and ravines and burn their houses so that they cannot easily return" (Biedma, "Carta de . . . Andamarca, 25 de marzo de 1686," AGOF, XL/39, fol. 140). Naturally most of these missions failed.

122. Amich, *Compendio histórico*, p. 120; Izaguirre, Historia, vol. 1, pp. 291–92.

123. Amich, *Compendio histórico*, p. 121; Izaguirre, Historia, vol. 1, pp. 294–95.

124. Dionisio Ortiz, *Reseña histórica de la montaña del Pangoa, Gran Pajonal y Satipo (1673–1930)* (Lima: Editorial San Antonio, 1961), pp. 151–54.

125. Biedma, "Carta de . . . Comas, 23 de diciembre de 1685," AGOF, XL/39, fol. 137v.

126. Biedma strongly favored the use of force to subjugate the Campa within certain areas, "having experienced that all the Andes of these principles are mainly traitorous, fickle, and changeable, and that when I tried subjugating them into towns, it was all erased by a one-night drinking binge or the devil" (Biedma, "Carta de . . . Andamarca, 25 de marzo de 1686," AGOF, XL/39, fol. 140).

127. Huerta, "Relación," fol. 175.

CHAPTER 3: CENTURY OF REBELLION

1. Fernando Pallares and Vicente Calvo, *Noticias históricas de las misiones de fieles é infieles del colegio de propaganda fide de San Rosa de Ocopa* (Barcelona: Imprenta de Magriña y Subirana, 1870), pp. 17–18. Cf. Francisco de San Joseph, "Memorial del P. francisco de San Joseph a S. M. Felipe V, 25 de noviembre de 1713," in IHM, vol. 2.

2. Francisco de San Joseph, "Informe hecho por el V. P. Fr. Francisco de San Joseph al Rmo. P. Fr. Joseph Sanz, comisario general de Indias de las misiones de infieles del Cerro de la Sal, con noticias muy singulares, para gloria de Dios nuestro Señor, y crédito de nuestra seráfica religión (1716)," in IHM, vol. 2, pp. 179–287.

3. Izaguirre, *Historia*, vol. 2, pp. 56–57.

4. Antonio Raimondi, *El Perú*, vol. 2 (Lima: Imprenta del Estado, 1876), p. 254.

5. Izaguirre, *Historia*, vol. 2, p. 59. See also Antonine S. Tibesar, "The Salt Trade among the Montaña Indians of the Tarma Area of Eastern Peru," *Primitive Man*, vol. 23 (1950), pp. 103–9; Antonine S. Tibesar, "San Antonio de Eneno: A Mission in the Peruvian Montaña," *Primitive Man*, vol. 25 (1952), pp. 23–29.

6. See Sobreviela, "Varias noticias," fol. 101, where a definition of the Pajonal is provided: "[T]he Gran Pajonal was discovered, named for the many grass fields (*pajonales*) that cover the hills around it. . . . Pajonal is a large area of mountainous country that extends more than 40 leagues north and 30 from west to east. On the north it is bordered by the Sacramento Plain, from which the Pachitea River separates it, and on the west by the extremely high peaks, from which many arroyos and rivers flow into the great Paro."

7. Izaguirre, *Historia*, vol. 2, p. 58. Ortiz, *Reseña histórica*, p. 38. In 1878 Charles Leclerc discovered in the Toledo archives an anonymous manuscript on the Campa language. In 1890 linguist Lucien Adam published it, with an introduction in which he expressed the hypothesis that the work might date from the second third of the eighteenth century, but that with regard to its author, he did not hazard a guess. Cf. Lucien Adam, *Arte de la lengua de los indios antis o campas. Varias preguntas, advertencias y doctrina cristiana conforme al manuscrito original hallado en la ciudad de Toledo por Charles Leclerc con un vocabulario metódico y una introducción comparativa* (Paris: J. Maisonneuve Libraire-Editeur, 1890), p. 2. At the 1904 International Congress of Americanists, Karl von den Steinen presented a paper in which he concluded that the "author of the manuscript must be Father Juan de La Marca." Cf. Karl von den Steinen, "Der Verfasser der Handschrift Arte de la Lengua de los Indios Antis ó Campas," 16th International Congress of Americanists, Stuttgart, 1906, pp. 603–5. See also Izaguirre, *Historia*, vol. 8, pp. 297–98.

8. Izaguirre, *Historia*, vol. 1, p. 81.

9. Raimondi, *El Perú*, vol. 2, p. 258; Izaguirre, *Historia*, vol. 2, p. 91.

10. Raimondi, *El Perú*, p. 258; Izaguirre, *Historia*, vol. 2, pp. 82–83.

11. Cf. Ortiz, *Reseña histórica*, p. 50. According to this author, the document was located in the archives of the Ocopa Convent. A census was taken of the Gran Pajonal three times between 1736 and 1739, recording a maximum of no more than about five hundred people. Cf. Alonso del Espíritu Santo, "Padrón de la gente que Dios Misericordioso se ha dignado alumbrar y atraer el conocimiento de nuestras verdades evangélicas testigo de esta maravilla yo su indigno sacerdote y ministro, fray Alonso del Espíritu Santo . . . a 15 de agosto de 1736," 6 fols. useful, BNSM. Alonso del Espíritu Santo, "Padrón de la nueva gente de Simaque que vió, habló y empadronó el hermano Cristóbal, doctrinado en Tampianique, a quien el infrascrito padre, informó y notició de dicha gente y encargó con el curaca Carate hiciese dicha diligencia, hallándome yo allí cerca en el pueblo de Tampianique, descansando de mis fatigas en la peregrinación a los Conivos y Simirinches y visitando al mismo tiempo los otros pueblos que se

fundaron el año pasado de 1735 . . . ," octubre de 1736," signed fray Alonso del Espíritu Santo, 6 fols. useful, BNSM. Francisco Simón Gazo, "Padrón de los indios christianos é infieles, que habitan los pueblos de Tampianique, Caponeaqui, Aporoqueaques, Sarsinquiaque, en el Paxonal. Escrito en 26 días del mes de noviembre del año del Señor 1739," 8 fols. useful as well as title, BNSM.

12. In a brief article in which I analyzed methodological viewpoints for the study of the Juan Santos movement (see "La rebelión de Juan Santos Atahualpa: Un movimiento mesiánico del siglo XVIII en la selva peruana," in *Actas y Trabajos*, 37th International Congress of Americanists, Mar del Plata, 1966), I also pointed out some morphological characteristics that introduce a possibility of broader comprehension. See also Alfred Metraux, "A Quechua Messiah in Eastern Peru," *American Anthropologist*, vol. 44 (1942), pp. 721–22; Vittorio Lanternari, *Movimientos religiosos de libertad y salvación de los pueblos oprimidos* (Barcelona: Seix Barral, 1965).

13. Steward and Metraux, "Tribes," p. 618.

14. Ibid., pp. 561 and 630.

15. Manuel de Biedma, "Carta de . . . al comisario general desde San Buenaventura de Savini, 22 de abril de 1687," AGOF, XL/39, fol. 159.

16. Ibid.

17. Izaguirre, *Historia*, vol. 2, pp. 84–88.

18. Ibid.; Raimondi, *El Perú*, vol. 2, p. 259.

19. For the native messianic movements of South America, see Alfredo Metraux, "The Guaraní," in HSAI, vol. 3, pp. 93–94; Luis Millones, "Un movimiento nativista del siglo XVI: El Taky Onkoy," *Revista Peruana de Cultura* (Lima), no. 3 (October 1964), pp. 134–40. For the messianism present in contemporary Andean society, see José María Arguedas, "Puquio una cultura en proceso de cambio," in *Estudios sobre la cultura actual del Perú* (Lima: Universidad Nacional Mayor de San Marcos, 1964), pp. 227–34.

20. Juan Bautista de La Marca, "Diario y padrón de la gente del Paxonal, que el P. fray . . . , actual misionero, congregó al gremio de Nuestra Santa Madre la iglesia católica apostólica romana. Año de 1733," BNSM, fols. 21–30, unpaginated, passim. The census carried out by Father La Marca at that time showed a total of 175 persons for this group.

21. Cf. Manuel Bajo, "Certificaciónes que da fray Manuel Bajo, misionero en las conversiones de Sonomoro, Pajonal y Pauja, de como se sacaron del río llamado Masajehenique, el año de 1736 las almas que se expresa en un padrón anexo, y se agregaron al inmediato pueblo de Quisopango . . . , setiembre de 1736," 3 fols., BNSM, C342.

22. Benito Troncoso de Lira y Sotomayor and Manuel de Albarran, "Información tomada a solicitud de los padres franciscanos, acerca de los alcances del levantamiento de Juan Santo Atahualpa, Tarma, 8 de octubre de 1745," 5 fols. useful, 1 blank, incomplete, BNSM. Francisco A. Loayza, *Juan Santos, el invencible,* manuscripts from 1742 to 1755 (Lima: Editorial Domingo Miranda, 1942), pp. 83–110. Cf. Izaguirre, *Historia*, vol. 2, p. 109.

23. Domingo García and Manuel del Santo, "Carta escrita por los padres fray Manuel del Santo y fray Domingo García, misioneros apostólicos del colegio de Santa Rosa de Ocopa, y misiones de infieles del Cerro de la Sal, al Rdo. padre fray Joseph Gil Muñoz, comisario de dichas misiones en la que le dan noticia de la entrada que hizo a ellas el escandaloso apóstata Juan Santos Atahualpa, Apuinga, Guainacapac, indio cristiano de la imperial ciudad del Cuzco . . . ," in IHM, vol. 2, pp. 115–20. Hereafter this document will be referred to by the following abbreviation: GSI.

24. Loayza, *Juan Santos*, pp. 96–97.

25. Anonymous, "Diario en el cual se da noticia individual de lo acaecido en el viaje o entrada, que por orden del Excelentísimo Señor virrey de estos reinos, el marqués de Villagarcía; se ejecutó por el mes de octubre del año de 1743, gobernando la Santa Iglesia nuestro santísimo padre Benedicto XVI rigiendo la monarquía de España nuestro católico Felipe V, que Dios guarde," in LJS, p. 38. Although unsigned, Loayza assumes this document was written by the secretary of the governor of the jungle, Don Benito Troncoso de Lira.

26. Loayza (*Juan Santos*, pp. 9–11) risks the hypothesis of a voyage by Santos to England, where he could have made contact with certain authorities to help him in his movement. In fact, the rebel makes frequent mention of English aid. Cf. GSI, p. 116.

27. José Patricio Arbeiza y Elizondo and Manuel de Barrenechea, "Carta de los oficiales reales a la corona de España. Caja de Pasco, 14 de marzo de 1744," in LJS, p. 50. According to Loayza (pp. 9–11), Santos would have reached Lambayeque from the north and the Napo River from the jungle.

28. Izaguirre, *Historia*, vol. 2, pp. 109–10.

29. Ibid., p. 110.

30. Kesha is a being that oscillates between cosmogonic divinity and cultural hero, sharing the two essences at the same time. Kesha is saved from the flood by sailing in the trunk of a palm tree and realizes that the earth has dried by throwing some palm seeds onto the ground. Cf. Fernando Torre López, "Fenomenología religiosa de la tribu Anti o Campa" (Ph.D. dissertation, Universidad Católica de Lovaina, Instituto Superior de Filosofía, 1965), p. 158. In the myths we gathered from the Gran Pajonal Campa, there appear paradigmatic figures that move in the same sphere as Kesha; this characteristic of some similar mythical figures (from a morphological point of view) has been noted among the Campa of the Ene River by linguist William Kindberg, whose notes were used in Torre López's work.

31. Ibid.

32. GSI, p. 117.

33. Izaguirre, *Historia*, vol. 2, p. 111, quoting a writing by Father Santiago Vásquez de Caicedo.

34. Loayza presents a series of facts to demonstrate that Juan Santos was a descendant of Atahualpa. He bases his hypothesis on documents from the General Archives of the Indies in Seville, Patronato Section, file 28, R. 56. Cf. Loayza, *Juan Santos*, p. 8.

35. GSI, p. 116.

36. Ibid., p. 117.

37. Izaguirre, *Historia*, vol. 2, p. 111.

38. Ibid., pp. 112–13.

39. GSI, p. 118.

40. Ibid.

41. Ibid., p. 116.

42. Ibid., p. 118.

43. If Santos's pacifist, conciliatory attitude now seems a bit naïve, it is because inevitably our mental behavior steers us toward interpretations of this nature. The trusting attitude of Atahualpa in Cajamarca has also appeared naïve to historiography. The examples of indigenous "naïveté" can be multiplied and are not limited to the New World.

44. GSI, p. 118.

45. Cf. Loayza, *Juan Santos*, p. 92.

46. At present the Asháninka do not raise pigs because this animal destroys cassava and plantain crops by digging holes to get at the roots; water stagnates in these holes and mosquitos hatch there. Even white and mestizo settlers now avoid raising pigs because they cause more harm than good on jungle farms. It is therefore logical to consider this sanitary, preventive measure by Santos as similar to the type of initiatives and "legislation" generally proposed by civic-religious leaders of certain populations.

47. GSI, pp. 115–20.

48. Ibid., p. 117.

49. In 1730 Gatica had accompanied Campa Mateo de Assia, another effective assistant of Santos, on the mission to contact the inhabitants of the Gran Pajonal, whom Father Juan de La Marca had organized. Cf. Izaguirre, *Historia*, vol. 2.

50. Izaguirre, *Historia*, vol. 2, p. 111.

51. GSI, p. 116. Exactly one year later Santos would fulfill this promise, and the mountain Indians would respond to his call.

52. Melchor de Navarra y Rocaful (duque de La Palata), "Relación del estado del Perú, en los ocho años de su gobierno que hace el duque de la Palata al Excmo. Señor Conde de La Moncloba, su subcessor en los cargos de virrey, gobernador y capitán general de estos reynos del Perú, Tierrafirme y Chile, de que tomó posesión el día 16 de agosto del año de 1689," in *Memorias de los virreyes que han gobernado el Perú durante el tiempo del coloniaje español* (Lima: Librería Central de Felipe Bailly, 1859), p. 240.

53. Regarding the Andean jungle contacts, see Emilio Mendizabal Losack, "La fiesta en Pachitea andina," *Folklore Americano* (Lima), year 13, no. 13 (1965), pp. 146–58 passim. See also the research carried out by John V. Murra, *Cuadernos de investigación: No. 1, Antropología* (Huánuco: Universidad Nacional Hermilio Valdizán, 1966); Iñigo Ortiz de Zuñiga, *Visita de la provincia de León de Huánuco en 1566*, edited by John V. Murra (Huánuco: Universidad Nacional Hermilio Valdizán, 1966).

54. Anonymous, "Diario," in LJS, pp. 20–38 passim.

55. Amich, *Compendio histórico*, pp. 188–89.

56. Ibid., p. 197.

57. For a brief summary of the external history of the rebellion, see Carlos Daniel Valcarcel Esparza, *Rebeliones indígenas* (Lima: Edit. PTEM, 1946).

58. GSI, p. 118.

59. Izaguirre, *Historia*, vol. 2, pp. 123–24; Ortiz, *Reseña histórica*, pp. 55–56.

60. Loayza, *Juan Santos*, pp. 86–87.

61. Ibid., pp. 10–14.

62. José Antonio de Mendoza, marqués de Villagarcía, "Relación del estado de los reynos del Perú que hace el Excmo. Sr. Marqués de Villagarcía al Excmo. Sr. Don José Manso de Velasco, conde de Superunda su sucesor en aquel virreynato, fecha en 24 de julio de 1745," in *Memorias de los virreyes que han gobernado el Perú durante el tiempo del coloniaje español*, vol. 3 (Lima: Librería Central de Felipe Bailly, 1859), pp. 382–83.

63. Izaguirre, *Historia*, vol. 2, pp. 128–30.

64. Ibid., p. 130.

65. Anonymous, "Diario," in LJS, pp. 47–48. Marqués de Villagarcía, "Carta del . . . al rey de España, Lima, 16 de agosto de 1744," in LJS, pp. 56–60. Ramón Urrutia y Las Casas, *Informe del intendente Urrutia sobre las ventajas que resultan de la apertura del camino y comunicación por el Chanchamayo, presentado al virrey del Perú en 1808* (Lima: Imprenta del Comercio, 1847), p. 75. Izaguirre, *Historia*, vol. 2, pp. 134–36.

66. Marqués de Ensenada, "Carta del . . . a Buenos Aires, Madrid, 21 de diciembre de 1744," in LJS, pp. 72–75.

67. Amich, *Compendio histórico*, pp. 193–94.

68. José Antonio Manso de Velasco, "Relación que suscribe el conde de Superunda, virrey del Perú, de los principales sucesos de su gobierno, de Real Orden de S. M. comunicado por el Excmo. Sr. Marqués de la Ensenada, su secretario del despacho universal, con fecha 23 de agosto de 1751, y comprehende los años desde 9 de julio de 1745 hasta fin del mismo mes en el de 1756," in *Memorias de los virreyes que han gobernado el Perú durante el tiempo del coloniaje español*, vol. 4 (Lima: Librería Central de Felipe Bailly, 1859), p. 101.

69. Amich, *Compendio histórico*, p. 194.

70. Ibid., pp. 195–96. Nevertheless, José de Llamas's statements prompt us to ponder the constant, though discreet, presence of the Jesuits in the entire movement. When Santos declared his intentions to Father Santiago Vásquez de Caicedo in 1742, he stated that in his kingdom there should not "be any clerics other than the Indians and the priests of the Society because these . . . [are] very beneficial to the republic" (Izaguirre, *Historia*, vol. 2, p. 112). A similar statement was made by a highland rebel captured by the Spaniards in 1743: Santos and his people "do not want Franciscan priests, but instead those of the Society" (Anonymous, "Diario," in LJS, p. 29).

71. Manso de Velasco, "Relación," pp. 101–3.

72. Izaguirre, *Historia*, vol. 2, pp. 140–41.

73. José Antonio Manso de Velasco (conde de Superunda), "Carta al rey de España, Lima, 31 de julio de 1746," in LJS, pp. 111–14.

74. Joseph de San Antonio, "Relación lastimosa de las crudelísimas muertes que dieron los apóstoles y gentiles de varias naciones a los PP. missioneros apostólicos del colegio de misiones de Ocopa y provincia de los Doce Apóstoles de Lima en el reyno del Perú. Guamanga, 5 de mayo de 1747," in IHM, vol. 2, pp. 291–96.

75. Izaguirre, *Historia*, vol. 2, pp. 145–46. In Amich, *Compendio histórico*, pp. 200–201, the Franciscan historian reports that Juan Santos regularly attended the masses celebrated by the priest and that, thanks to the rebel's direct intervention, his life was saved, for the Campa wanted to kill him.

76. Amich, *Compendio histórico*, p. 200.

77. Bueno, *Geografía*, p. 139. Izaguirre, *Historia*, vol. 2, p. 168.

78. Part of the "Memorial" is quoted directly in Izaguirre, *Historia*, but the author does not include the title of the manuscript; therefore we have entitled it Joseph de San Antonio, "Memorial del padre Joseph de San Antonio al rey de España, 11 de julio de 1750," AGI 72-2-31, in IHM, vol. 2, pp. 147–59.

79. Ibid., p. 157.

80. Ibid., p. 158.

81. Ibid., p. 157.

82. Amich, *Compendio histórico*, p. 204.

83. Loayza, *Juan Santos*, pp. 214–15, 233. Izaguirre, *Historia*, vol. 2, p. 163.

84. Urrutia y Las Casas, *Informe del intendente*, pp. 63–64. When General Llamas arrived in Quimirí, the town had been in rebel hands for almost eight years; in spite of this, the church had been maintained in order. We must note once more that these gestures on Santos's part confirm to us his profound religious sense, and it would be difficult to make of his movement a mere profane act of rebellion.

85. Manso de Velasco, "Relación," p. 305.

86. Izaguirre, *Historia*, vol. 2, p. 186.

87. Bueno, *Geografía*, pp. 46–47.

88. Francisco Alvarez de Villanueva, "Informes exactos del estado floreciente de las misiones de la gran pampa y montañas del Sacramento en el reino del Perú, por el colegio apostólico de religiosos franciscanos, con noticias individuales de sus derroteros, poblaciones, ríos y demás necesario al conocimiento de aquellos países. Años de 1765–1777," in MJL, vol. 12, pp. 278–91.

89. Ibid., pp. 298–99.

90. Ibid., pp. 303–9 passim.

91. Cf. Manuel de Sobreviela, "Diario del viaje que yo fray Manuel de Sobreviela, guardián del colegio de propaganda fide de Santa Rosa de Ocopa, hice a las conversiones de las montañas de Guanta, partido de la intendencia y obispado de Huamanga y a las fronteras de Tarma . . . (1788)," in IHM, vol. 7, pp. 84–86.

92. Izaguirre, *Historia*, vol. 7, pp. 110–12.

93. San Antonio, "Memorial," p. 153.

94. Ibid.

95. Amich, *Compendio histórico*, p. 12.

96. Cf. Alvarez de Villanueva, "Informes exactos," pp. 303–9 passim.

97. A summary of the hypotheses regarding Santos's death is contained in Loayza, *Juan Santos*, pp. 12–15. A. Carranza's data, quoted in Izaguirre, *Historia*, vol. 2, pp. 182–83, are not necessarily reliable because they are based on reports attributed to Carranza by Franciscan Father Hernández and date from nearly 150 years after the fact.

98. Izaguirre, *Historia*, vol. 2, p. 184.

99. A description of Juan Santos's grave is provided by Carranza and transcribed in Izaguirre, *Historia*, vol. 2, p. 183.

CHAPTER 4: THE WALLS CLOSE IN

1. Amich, *Compendio histórico*, p. 12.

2. Ramón Busquets and Cristóbal Rocamora, "Diario de la expedición del río de Santa Ana, que verifícaron los padres misioneros apostólicos, fray . . . , del colegio de Moquegua . . . , año de 1807," in MJL, vol. 12, pp. 207–27 passim.

3. Urrutia y Las Casas, *Informe del intendente*.

4. Ibid., pp. 77–78.

5. Pallares and Calvo, *Noticias históricas*, pp. 58–59.

6. Cf. Jorge Basadre, *Historia de la república del Perú*, vol. 1 (Lima: Edit. Cultura Antártica, 1949), pp. 298–320 passim.

7. Ibid., p. 331.

8. Lewis Herndon, *Exploration of the Valley of the Amazon* (Washington, D.C.: Taylor and Maury, 1854), p. 85.

9. Ibid., pp. 85–92 passim.

10. Ibid., p. 85.

11. Ibid., p. 206.

12. Ibid., p. 85.

13. Ibid., pp. 74–78, 210.

14. Antonio Raimondi, "Informe sobre la provincia litoral de Loreto, 1862," in LCCL, vol. 7, p. 217.

15. Belisario Barriga, "Exploración del valle de Chanchamayo. Año de 1868" (title added), in LCCL, vol. 2, pp. 445–50.

16. José Manuel Pereira, "Informe de la expedición exploradora de los valles de Chanchamayo, 1869," in LCCL, vol. 2, pp. 455–65.

17. John William Nystrom, *Argumento sobre Chanchamayo, sus primeras colonizaciones y los indios Chunchos* (Lima: Impr. y Lit. E. Prugue, 1870), pp. 16–18.

18. Pallares and Calvo, *Noticias históricas*, p. 69.

19. Ibid., p. 75. In 1869 a Franciscan priest, referring to the Asháninka, wrote "with the intention of opening a road to the Chanchamayo, and at the same [time] converting to the faith those poor savages, who are still submerged in the

darkness of error"; his language and attitude are the same as those of the European colonialists.

20. Ibid., chap. 2.

21. Nystrom, *Argumento*, pp. 18–19; John William Nystrom, "Relación del ataque Campa al correo Chanchamayo-Tarma, 1869," in LCCL, vol. 2, pp. 480–82.

22. Félix Giordano, "Memoria del ingeniero F. Giordano sobre la excursión que practicó en compañía del ministro italiano a los territorios orientales de Chanchamayo, 1875," in LCCL, vol. 11, pp. 221–24, 250–51.

23. Arturo Wertheman, *Informe de la exploración de los ríos Perené y Tambo* (Lima: Impr. del Estado, 1877), p. 2.

24. Luis Sabaté, *Viaje de los padres misioneros del convento del Cuzco a las tribus salvajes de los Campas, Piros, Cunibos, Sipibos en el año de 1874* (Lima: Tipogr. La Sociedad, 1877). Father Sabaté was accompanied by a party of Piro Indians, who on one occasion separated from the missionaries in order to carry out a raid against their Asháninka enemies. Two hundred years earlier, the Franciscans who were exploring the Tambo had watched passively as their Cunibo companions raided the Asháninka (see chapter 2).

25. Wertheman, *Informe de la exploración*, pp. 5–18 passim.

26. James Orton, *The Andes and the Amazon, or Across the Continent of South America* (New York: Harper and Brothers, 1875), p. 322.

27. Charles Wiener, *Pérou et Bolivie. Récit de voyage suivi d'études archéologiques et ethnographiques et de notes sur l'écriture et les langues de populations indiennes* (Paris: Hachette et Cie., 1880), p. 752.

28. Cf. Manuel de Almagro, *Breve descripción de los viajes hechos en América por la comisión científica enviada por el gobierno de S. M. C. durante los años de 1862 á 1866 . . .* (Madrid: Imprenta de M. Rivadeneyra, 1866); p. 130 reads as follows: "Three days earlier a Záparo died there and, timely warned, we extracted his skeleton, which we placed in a large box; we drilled holes in the box and towed it behind our raft, secured with a strong chain. The purpose of the holes was to establish a current of water inside the box to pull the soft substances off the bones. . . . We lost this interesting skeleton also [they had lost another one earlier], probably because of the superstition of the Indians; one night when we left the rafts to go to a hamlet of savages, the box disappeared."

29. Giuseppe Cocchiara, *Storia del folklore in Europa* (Turin: Edizioni Scientifiche Einaudi, 1954), pp. 271–73.

30. Olivier Ordinaire, *Les sauvages du Pérou* (Paris: E. Leroux Edit., 1888), pp. 19–20.

31. Ordinaire, *Du Pacifique*, pp. 103–7.

32. Ibid., pp. 139–42.

33. When we say that Ordinaire is the only person to date, we refer to up to 1950. Since 1950 other anthropologists have been studying the areas mentioned.

34. Ordinaire, *Du Pacifique*, pp. 144–46; Ordinaire, *Les sauvages*, pp. 11–17 passim.

35. Gabriel Sala, "Apuntes de viaje del P. Fr. Gabriel Sala. Exploración de los ríos Pichis. Pachitea y Alto Ucayali y de la región del Gran Pajonal, 1897," in IHM, vol. 10, pp. 470–71.

36. Ibid., p. 474.

37. Ibid., p. 475.

38. Ortiz, *Reseña histórica*, p. 111, quoting a 1922 article from the Mercurio Peruano.

39. Ibid., chap. 2.

40. Carlos Fry, "Diario de los viajes y exploración de los ríos Urubamba, Ucayali, Amazonas, Pachitea y Palcazú, por . . . 1886–1888," in LCCL, vol. 11, p. 413.

41. Sala, "Apuntes de viaje," p. 511.

42. Ortiz, *Reseña histórica*, p. 111.

43. Irving Goldman, "Tribes of the Uaupes-Caquetá Region," in HSAI, vol. 3, p. 768.

44. Julian Steward, "The Witotoan Tribes," in HSAI, vol. 3, p. 750.

45. Osambela, "El oriente del Perú," pp. 219–20.

46. Sala, "Apuntes de viaje," p. 565.

47. Ibid., p. 559.

48. Ibid., p. 560.

49. Ibid., p. 558.

50. Ibid., p. 559.

51. Ibid., pp. 559–60.

52. José B. Samanéz Ocampo, "Exploración de los ríos Apurímac, Ene, Tambo, Urubamba y Ucayali por . . . 1883–1884," in LCCL, vol. 11, p. 203. See also Mauricio Touchaux, "Apuntes sobre la gramática y el diccionario del idioma campa ó lengua de los Antis, tal como se usa en el río Apurímac," *Revista Histórica* (Lima), vol. 3, trim. 2 (1908), p. 132; Carlos Perez, "Informe de la expedición del río Azupizú en la confluencia de los ríos Pichis y Palcazú por el ingeniero . . . ," in LCCL, vol. 3, pp. 305–6.

53. Manuel Navarro, *La tribu Campa* (Lima: 1924), p. 23.

54. Carlos Larrabure y Correa, comp., *Colección de leyes, decretos, resoluciones y otros documentos oficiales referentes al Departamento de Loreto*, vol. 3 (Lima: Impr. La Opinión Nacional, 1905–9), pp. 132–134.

55. Ordinaire, *Du Pacifique*, p. 211.

56. Basadre, *Historia*, vol. 2, p. 326.

57. Ibid., vol. 2, p. 315.

58. Ibid., vol. 2, p. 325.

59. Gonzáles Prada, quoted in Basadre, *Historia*, vol. 2, p. 314.

60. Sala, "Apuntes de viaje," p. 404.

61. Ibid., p. 521.

62. Ibid., pp. 482–83.

63. Ibid., pp. 483–84.

64. Ibid., p. 488.

65. Ibid., p. 519.
66. Ibid., p. 528.
67. Ibid., p. 519.
68. Ibid., p. 521.
69. Ibid., p. 522.
70. Ibid.
71. Ibid., p. 520.
72. Ibid., p. 546.
73. Ibid., p. 541.
74. García Rosell, *Conquista de la montaña*, p. 50.
75. Sala, "Apuntes de viaje," p. 532.
76. See chapter 1.
77. Sala, "Apuntes de viaje," passim; Cipriani, *Informe del ingeniero*, passim.
78. Cipriani, *Informe del ingeniero*, p. 55.
79. Ibid., p. 57.
80. Ortiz, *Reseña histórica*, p. 110.
81. Basadre, *Historia*, vol. 2, pp. 363–77 passim. Cf. J. Capelo, *La vía central del Perú* (Lima: Impr. Masías, 1896); César Cipriani, "Viaje a la región de Pampa Hermosa, 1904," in LCCL, vol. 13, pp. 220–42; Pedro Portillo, "Exploración de los ríos Apurímac, Ene, Tambo, Ucayali, Pachitea y Pichis por el prefecto de Ayacucho . . . , año de 1900," in LCCL, vol. 3, pp. 463–550; Stiglich, *Informe del jefe*, passim.
82. Alberto Gridilla, "Los Campas," in *El cuarto centenario amazónico y la orden franciscana*, Colección descalzos, no. 4 (Lima: Gráfica Scheuch S. A., 1942), pp. 75–77.
83. Cocchiara, *Storia del folklore*, p. 513.
84. Arnald Van Gennep, "Etudes d'ethnographie sud-américaine," *Journal de la Société des Américanistes* (Paris), vol. 11 (1919), pp. 121–33.
85. Paul Mercier, *Histoire de l'anthropologie* (Paris: Presses Universitaires de France, 1966), pp. 83–85.
86. Ibid.
87. Cf. Nordenskjold, "Explorations," passim.
88. Tessmann, *Die Indianer*.
89. Ibid., p. 102.
90. Ibid., p. 30.
91. Ibid., p. 102.
92. Ibid., pp. 101–2.
93. Ibid.
94. Ibid., p. 100.
95. Jacques Lambert, *L'America Latina: Strutture sociali e istituzioni politiche* (Rome: Editori Riuniti, 1966), pp. 102–4.
96. Ibid., pp. 104–5.
97. Ibid., pp. 128–32.
98. Ibid., pp. 114–24 passim.

99. Ibid., p. 107; latifundia are "large estates of lands partially worked with archaic methods."

100. Ortiz, *Reseña histórica*, pp. 163–64, mentions the Supreme Resolution of 1925, which authorized the apostolic prefect of the Ucayali, rather than the departmental prefecture, to receive jungle-land–acquisition applications. The missionaries were likewise charged with enforcing compliance with all governmental decrees.

101. Ibid., pp. 158–59.

102. Ibid., p. 159.

103. Ibid., p. 196.

104. Ibid., pp. 186–87.

105. Ibid., p. 256.

106. Gridilla, "Los Campas," p. 75.

107. Ortiz, *Reseña histórica*, p. 225.

108. The kinship system has an important foundation in the reciprocity of the exchange of sons through marriage. My daughter will bring home a son-in-law, who will help me in my work and defend me.

109. Ortiz, *Reseña histórica*, p. 252.

110. Ibid., p. 256.

111. Ibid., p. 241.

112. Meggers, "Ambiente y cultura"; see chapter 1 of my book, where this subject is discussed.

113. Cf. Ortiz, *Reseña histórica*, pp. 178–79, 212.

114. Ibid., p. 239. Missionary action in the Peruvian jungle has followed the historical rhythm with its political, economic, and social connotations; therefore it is to be expected that from this point on, the missions acquire a new structure in accordance with the latest doctrinarian contributions of the church in the social field and with its pronouncements about colonialism.

115. Gridilla, "Los Campas," p. 77.

116. Ibid., p. 58.

117. Ibid.

118. Maxime Kuczynski-Godard, *La colonia del Perené y sus problemas médico sociales* (Lima: Ediciones La Reforma Médica, 1939), p. 29.

119. Maxime Kuczynski-Godard and Carlos Enrique Paz Soldan, *La selva peruana: Sus pobladores y su colonización en seguridad sanitaria* (Lima: Ediciones de la Reforma Sanitaria, 1939), pp. 13–14.

120. Ibid., pp. 19–20.

121. Ibid., p. 9.

122. Valid critiques of western missionary methods have been expressed by those of the East in general and have been collected by Father Thomas Ohm in a book, which, though it refers concretely to Asia, is of great significance for indigenous America. Ohm states that in Asia there are many people "who for a long time have viewed the missions as the harbingers and hunting dogs of imperialism and a path to conquest and colonization." He adds that "the harshest

criticism is directed against the missionary methods of preachers. . . . They blame them for condemning their religions without knowing enough about them, for making untrue statements, and for constantly giving false interpretations of non-Christian religions. It is sufficient to recall the matter of the worship of idols, when there is no Asian who worships idols; we speak of polytheism where no such thing exists; we demonstrate the powerlessness of the gods by saying that they cannot help us in anything, but our saints do not help us either; we also lack tact; we have no consideration for other religions and no qualms about criticizing them." Cf. Thomas Ohm, *Crítica de Asia sobre el cristianismo de Occidente* (Buenos Aires: Edic. Desclée de Brouwer, 1950), pp. 137–39.

123. Cf. Eliade, *Il sacro*, pp. 79–93 passim; René Guénon, *Oriente e occidente* (Turin: Edizioni Studi Tradizionali, 1965), passim.

124. This version of the myth was recorded during fieldwork on the Gran Pajonal in the summer of 1967. In the Spanish translation, we have tried to be as faithful as possible to the synthetic and linear style of the Campa version.

125. Mircea Eliade, "Time and Eternity in Indian Thought," in *Man and Time*, Papers from the Eranos Yearbook (New York: Pantheon Books, 1957), p. 173.

126. Vladimir Propp, *Morfología della fiaba* (Original edition published in Russian in 1928; Turin: G. Einaudi Edit., 1966), p. 3.

127. Eliade, *Trattato di storia*, p. 469.

128. Ananda K. Coomaraswamy, *Hindouisme et bouddhisme* (Paris: Gallimard, 1949), p. 18. Note the current position of the Catholic Church: "Myth is a universal phenomenon of the human race . . . and is present in all religions to a greater or lesser degree"; Secretariatus pro non christianis, *Towards the Meeting of Religions: Suggestions for Dialogue* (Rome: Vatican Polyglot Press, 1967), passim.

129. Raffaele Pettazzoni, *Miti e leggende*, 4 vols. (Turin: UTET, 1963), pp. 10–11.

130. Mircea Eliade, "Structure et fonction du mythe cosmogonique," in *La naissance du monde* (Paris: Éditions du Seuil, 1959), p. 471.

131. Ibid., p. 490.

132. Eliade, *Il sacro*, pp. 79–80.

133. Ibid., p. 80.

134. Gustave Van Der Leeuw, "Primordial Time and Final Time," in *Man and Time*, Papers from the Eranos Yearbook (New York: Pantheon Books, 1957), p. 332.

135. Ibid., pp. 81–82.

136. Ibid., pp. 332–37.

137. Ibid., p. 336.

138. Eliade, *El mito*, pp. 108–11.

139. These means, in the case of the Campa Asháninka, do not exclude armed action; but it will always be an action supported and guaranteed by an archetypal event known through myth or made known by the shaman, who has received it in his communications with the ultrasensitive world.

140. Eliade, *El mito*, p. 101.

141. Ibid., p. 111.

142. Cited in Van Der Leeuw, "Primordial Time," p. 332.

143. Cf. Eliade, *Trattato di storia*, pp. 465–69. See also René Guénon, *Il simbolismo della croce* (Turin: Edizioni Studi Tradizionali, 1964), pp. 5–6. With regard to the concept of religious error as a breaking of rules or a lack of precaution and fear, it is interesting to observe that originally the Latin word religio meant an attitude: "selective caution." Cf. Karl Kerenyi, *La religione antica nelle sue linee fondamentali* (Bologna: Nicola Zanichelli Edit., 1940), chap. 3 passim.

144. Van Der Leeuw, "Primordial Time," p. 333.

145. Guénon, *Il simbolismo*, p. 5.

146. Rom. 1:20.

147. For the water symbolism we rely mainly on Eliade, *Trattato di storia*, pp. 193–221 passim.

148. Ibid., p. 195.

149. Eliade, *Structure et fonction*, pp. 473–74.

150. Naturally, whites are not included in the cosmogonic myth or in the myths regarding the origin of animals, which explains how most animals were, *in illo tempore*, men later transformed by Oriátziri because of a primordial "sin-error."

151. A Pajonalino myth explains how Kontáwo, at once shaman hero and trickster (see Paul Radin, Carl Gustav Jung, and Karl Kerenyi, *Il briccone divino* [Milan: V. Bompiani, 1965], for a morphological study of this type of character), manages to trick the Nónki with the help of the tiger, thus triumphing over death and disease.

152. This association also has validity on a historical level, as does that of the plantains, elements that cannot be considered "autochthonous" in the strict sense of the word.

153. Bronislaw Malinowski, *Estudios de psicología primitiva* (translation of *Myth in Primitive Psychology*) (Buenos Aires: Paidos, 1963), p. 33.

154. *Shiripiári* (shaman) means "chewer of tobacco," that is, of the initiation plant par excellence, which confers exceptional knowledge and powers.

155. Van Der Leeuw, *La religión*, pp. 65–74 passim.

156. Cf. Joseph Campbell, *El héroe de las mil caras* (Mexico City and Buenos Aires: Fondo de Cultura Económica, 1959), pp. 70–77; Joseph Campbell, *Le maschere di Dio* (Milan: V. Bompiani, 1962), chap. 6 passim; Propp, Morfología, passim; Mircea Eliade, *El chamanismo y las técnicas arcaicas del éxtasis* (Mexico City and Buenos Aires: Fondo de Cultura Económica, 1960), passim.

157. Campbell, *Le maschere*, p. 303.

158. Only individuals who are killed in combat are abandoned to the action of the vultures.

159. Campbell, *Le maschere*, p. 261.

160. Campbell, *Le maschere*, pp. 264–65; for a discussion of shamanism and psychopathology, see Eliade, *El chamanismo*, pp. 35–42.

161. Eliade, *Il sacro*, pp. 76–77; see also Eliade, *El mito*, passim, which deals concretely with the topic of history and the traditional concept of time.

162. Time in which the *shiripiári* moves in his role as such.

163. Eliade, "Time and Eternity," pp. 173–75.

164. Eliade, *El mito*, passim.

165. Eliade, "Time and Eternity," p. 174.

166. Ibid., pp. 174–75.

167. In Hindu terms it is the Pralaya.

168. Eliade, *El mito*, pp. 170–75.

169. According to Eliade, the shaman hero always appears with the morphological traits of the trickster.

170. There are many rules concerning hunting and gathering. Plants have an "owner," who may be offended if the plants are abused; the same is true for animals and insects.

171. See Eliade, *Il sacro*, p. 78, which reads, "[F]rom the viewpoint of profane existence, man does not recognize responsibilities beyond those to himself and society. For him, the Universe is not a true Cosmos, a living and articulated unit; it is the pure and simple sum of material reserves and physical energies of the planet, and the great concern of modern man is to not foolishly waste the economic resources of the globe."

172. Eliade, *Il sacro*, chap. 2 passim; Eliade, *El mito*, passim.

173. Eliade, *El mito*, p. 119.

174. The term *millenarianism* has been introduced into the lexicon of ethnologists and historians with a broader meaning than the original Judeo-Christian one, which referred concretely to the "millennium" as a period of one thousand years. Cf. Sy1via L. Thrupp, ed., *Millennial Dreams in Action*, Comparative Studies in Society and History, suppl. 2 (The Hague: Mouton and Co., 1962), passim; Eliade, *The Two and the One*, chap. 3 passim. For a brief history of the millenarian and apocalyptic tradition in Jewish and Christian thought, see Robert Kaufman, *Millénarisme et acculturation* (Brussels: L'Institut de Sociologie de l'Université Libre de Bruxelles, 1964), chap. 1 passim.

175. Thrupp, *Millennial Dreams*, p. 27.

176. See chapter 1, the meaning of trade.

177. Measles, the cold or flu (*karnantzi*), and smallpox (*apátawo*) are all diseases against which the shaman cannot fight. The Campa know perfectly well that these illnesses were brought by the whites, and the indigenous people believe that only by eliminating the carriers of the diseases will there be hope of being saved.

178. I recorded this myth from Pashúka and Coronado in 1964.

179. Van Der Leeuw, *La religión*, pp. 104–6. With regard to the messianism of Juan Santos Atahualpa, a great influence of Christian thought is evident in the movement. Mircea Eliade has found this to be the case in general for all forms of native millenarianism (see *The Two and the One*, chap. 3; and "Cargo Cults and Cosmic Regeneration," in Thrupp, *Millennial Dreams*).

180. From a historical perspective, the relationship between this Campa divinity and the Andean divinity Pachacamac is interesting. The fact that the myth attributes the functions of cultural hero and benefactor to a mythological character from the Andean world is also quite significant because it alludes to

the important role that the cordillera cultures had in the diffusion of several cultural elements. The statement that it is not a *chori* or *virakocha* divinity in a sense confirms its exogenous origin because it is an "unnecessary" statement.

181. See chapters 2 and 3.

182. Cf. Rudolf Otto, *Il sacro* (Milan: Feltrinelli Edit., 1966), chap. 4.

183. See chapter 1 on the importance of trade. The Campa man is frequently away from home on trading trips, and the danger of an abandonment of his social duties is very real.

184. See chapter 1 for the meaning of the term *ayúmpari*.

185. The morphology of this myth fits perfectly with the myth of the hero adventure, which is universal in scope. See the study by Campbell, *El héroe*, particularly the chapters "The Initiation" and "The Return."

186. To the Pajonalino Campa Asháninka, death from measles is one of the worst because one's destiny in the life after death is uncertain and unknown, and the dead person definitely will not have access to the places that, according to tradition, provide lodging to the "souls." Measles, the demonic woman, abducts the men to keep them in a state of permanent slavery.

187. The birds Hankátzi and Ttamíri may possibly belong to the genus *Crax*; the Herótzi has been impossible for us to identify. For an analysis of the types of magical flight, see Propp, *Morfología*, particularly chapter 3.

188. Otto, *Il sacro*, p. 153.

189. Campbell, *El héroe*, p. 211.

190. Ibid., p. 216.

191. Carlos Beas and Stefano Varese, "Consideraciones acerca de la investigación de los símbolos religiosos prehispánicos," Mesa Redonda de Ciencias Prehistóricas y Antropológicas, Instituto Riva-Agüero, Lima, October 1965.

192. Cf. Van Der Leeuw, "Primordial Time," p. 336.

193. With regard to the meaning of the plane, it is interesting to note among the Pajonalino Campa Asháninka the same reaction as that of the inhabitants of the Central Highlands of New Guinea (see Lanternari, *Movimientos religiosos*, pp. 250–51). When the first plane landed in Oventeni in 1938, the Campa were so frightened that the missionaries had to convince them not to shoot their arrows at the machine (Ortiz, *Reseña histórica*, p. 433). Presently one can observe replicas of small planes, made of reeds, on the peaks of some indigenous homes in Oventeni.

194. Lanternari, *Movimientos religiosos*, p. 242.

195. Ibid., p. 263.

196. Cited in Léopold Flam, "Le sacré et la désacralisation dans la pensée contemporaine," in *Le Pouvoir et le sacré*, Annales du Centre d'Etude des Religions, vol. 1 (Brussels: Université Libre de Bruxelles, 1962), p. 183.

197. Van Der Leeuw, *La religión*, p. 258.

Bibliography

Some citations include abbreviations from the list located at the beginning of the notes section.

ARCHIVED MANUSCRIPTS

Bajo, Manuel. "Certificaciones que da fray Manuel Bajo, misionero en las conversiones de Sonomono, Pajonal y Pauja, de como se sacaron del río llamado Masajehenique, el año de 1736 las almas que se expresa en un padrón anexo, y se agregaron al inmediato pueblo de Quisopango . . . , setiembre de 1736." BNSM.

Biedma, Manuel de. Five original letters. AGOF.

"Breve noticia ó diario: Cuarta expedición que salió de Manoa, el 28 de junio del presente año, dirigida al río Tambo, con destino a conducir la remesa de las conversiones del Ucayali, y procurar la pacificación de los infieles Campas, Pangoa, 8 de setiembre de 1816." BNSM.

"Censo o patrón general del partido de Tarma en la actual visita que está haciendo de él el gobernador intendente de la provincia de este nombre ha mandado extender previos los datos oportunos de su seguridad y exactitud, Cerro de Yuricocha, setiembre de 1797." BNSM.

Espíritu Santo, Alonso del. "Padrón de la gente que Dios Misericordioso se ha dignado alumbrar y atraer el conocimiento de nuestras verdades evangélicas testigo de esta maravilla yo su indigno sacerdote y ministro, fray Alonso del Espíritu Santo . . . a 15 de agosto de 1736." BNSM.

———. "Padrón de la nueva gente de Simaque que vió, habló y empadronó el hermano Cristóbal, doctrinado en Tampianique, a quien el infrascrito padre informó y notició de dicha gente y encargó con el curaca Carate hiciese dicha diligencia, hallándome yo allí cerca en el pueblo de Tampianique, descansando de mis fatigas en la peregrinación a los Conivos y Simirinches y visitando al mismo tiempo los otros pueblos que se fundaron el año pasado de 1735 . . . , octubre de 1736." BNSM.

"Expedición emprendida y felizmente concluida por los PP. de Ocopa, con el objeto de abrir comunicación desde el colegio de las misiones de Manoa, por la vía de Andamarca, siguiendo el curso de los ríos Pangoa, Tambo y Ucayali, cuya empresa se dio principio en 1814, y se concluyó en 1815 en los términos que constan del diario siguiente." BNSM.

Fuente, Francisco de la. "Relación del viaje a los Cunibos por el capitán . . . , San Miguel de los Cunibos, 18 de setiembre de 1686." AGOF.

Gazo, Francisco Simón. "Padrón de los indios christianos é infieles, que habitan los pueblos de Tampianique, Caponeaqui, Aporoqueaques, Sarsinquiaque, en el Paxonal. Escrito en 26 días del mes de noviembre del año del Señor, 1739." BNSM.

Huerta, Francisco de. "Relación hecha a nuestro Reverendísimo Padre fray Felis de Como lector jubilado pre. or. de su Magestad Padre Perpetuo de las santtas provincias de Milan y dosse apostoles de Lima y comisario general de todos los Perú, de la entrada y sucessos a las Santas Comberciones de San Francisco Solano en los gentiles Conibos hecha por el Pe. Por. fray Francisco de Huerta precidente de dichas Santas Comberciones, Andamarca, 29 de noviembre de 1686." AGOF.

———. Another untitled account of the same events, Andamarca, 29 de noviembre de 1686. AGOF.

"Información tomada a solicitud de los padres franciscanos, acerca de los alcances del levantamiento de Juan Santos Atahualpa, Tarma, 8 de octubre de 1745." BNSM.

Jesús, Juan de. "Memoria de los muchos religiosos sazerdotes, legos, donados, terzenos, españoles, mestisos, indios christianos y sirvientes de las cuatro converziones de Jauxa. Tarma, Guanuco, y Tulumayo que han muerto por la fee en distintos tiempos en las dichas quatro convensiones para gloria de Dios y credito de la religión de N. P. S. Francisco. Año de 1783." BNSM.

La Marca, Juan Bautista de. "Carta del P. . . . al comisario de las conversiones, en Ocopa, fray Francisco de San Joseph, San Thadeo, 11 de noviembre de 1730." BNSM.

———. "Borradores de cartas del P. misionero Juan de La Marca al virrey marqués de Castel Fuerte y al P. presidente de las conversiones, año de 1732." Accompanied by a description entitled "Plano del paraje de San Fermín del Ene, en el río Perené conversiones de nuestro seráfico padre San Francisco. Año de 1732." BNSM.

———. "Diario y padrón de la gente del Paxonal, que el P. fray . . . , actual misionero, congregó al gremio de Nuestra Santa Madre la iglesia católica apostólica romana. Año de 1733." BNSM.

Navarra y Rocaful, Melchor de. "Autos sobre la delimitación de las misiones jesuitas y franciscanas del río Ucayali. Años de 1687 y 1688." AGOF.

Veraun, Bartolomé de. Copy of a letter from Captain . . . to Governor Francisco de Elso y Arbizu, San Buenaventura, 23 October 1686. AGOF.

———. Copy of a letter describing the successful events of the expedition to the jungle, San Buenaventura, 23 October 1686. AGOF.

Vital, Antonio. "Carta del padre Antonio Vital al Rev. P. comisario . . . , San Miguel de Navarra, 18 de octubre de 1686." AGOF.

OTHER TEXTS

Adam, Lucien. *Arte de la lengua de los indios antis o campas. Varias preguntas, advertencias y doctrina cristiana conforme al manuscrito original hallado en la ciudad de Toledo por Charles Leclerc con un vocabulario metódico y una introducción comparativa*. Paris: J. Maisonneuve Libraire-Editeur, 1890.

Allen, William, and Judy Holshouser. "Land Use Patterns among the Campa of the Alto Pachitea, Perú." Unpublished manuscript, personal communication, 1970.

Almagro, Manuel de. *Breve descripción de los viajes hechos en América por la comisión científica enviada por el gobierno de S. M. C. durante los años de 1862 á 1866. . . .* Madrid: Impr. de M. Rivadeneyra, 1866.

Alvarez de Villanueva, Francisco. "Informes exactos del estado floreciente de las misiones de la gran pampa y montañas del Sacramento en el reino del Perú, por el colegio apostólico de religiosos franciscanos, con noticias individuales de sus derroteros, poblaciones, ríos y demás necesario al conocimiento de aquellos países. Años de 1765–1777." In MJL, vol. 12.

———. *Relación histórica de todas las misiones de los PP. franciscanos en las Indias y proyecto para nuevas conversiones en las riberas del afamado río Marañón, memorial dirigido a S. M. el rey D. Carlos III, 28 de mayo de 1781*. Madrid: Librería de V. Suárez, 1892.

Alvarez Maldonado, Juan. "Relación verdadera del discurso y subceso de la jornada y descubrimiento que hizo desde el año de 1567 hasta el de 1569." In MJL, vol. 6.

Amich, José. *Compendio histórico de los trabajos, fatigas, sudores y muertes que los ministros evangélicos de la seráfica religión han padecido por la conversión de las almas de los gentiles, en la montaña de los Andes, pertenecientes a las provincias del Perú. . . .* Paris: Librería de Rosa y Bouret, 1854.

Anonymous. "Relación de la ciudad de Guamanga y sus términos. Año de 1586." In JERG, vol. 1.

———. "Diario en el cual se da noticia individual de lo acaecido en el viaje o entrada, que por orden del Exocelentísimo Señor virrey de estos reinos, el marqués de Villagarcía; se ejecutó por el mes de octubre del año de 1743. . . ." In LJS.

Arbeiza y Elizondo, José Patricio, and Manuel de Barrenechea. "Carta de los oficiales reales a la corona de España. Caja de Pasco, 14 de marzo de 1744." In LJS.

Armas Medina, Fernando de. *Cristianización del Perú*. Seville: Escuela de Estudios Hispano-Americanos de Sevilla, 1953.

Arriaga, Pablo Joseph de. "La extirpación de la idolatría en el Perú, Lima, 1621." In *Colección de libros y documentos referentes a la historia del Perú*, vol. 1. Lima: Impr. Sanmarti y Cia, 1920.

Arrieta, Valentín. "Informe y descripción. Guamanga, 12 de junio de 1782." In IHM, vol. 5.

Arroyo, Francisco. "Recorrido de los ríos Apurímac y Ene por los PP. y Juan Pérez." In BSG, vol. 53 (1936).

Ballon-Landa, Alberto. *Los hombres de la selva*. Lima: Ofic. Tipogr. La Opinión Nacional, 1917.

Barriga, Belisario. "Exploración del valle de Chanchamayo. Año de 1868" (title added). In LCCL, vol. 2.

Basadre, Jorge. *Historia de la república del Perú*. 3 vols. Lima: Edit. Cultura Antártica, 1949.

Beas, Carlos, and Stefano Varese. "Consideraciones acerca de la investigación de los símbolos religiosos prehispánicos." Mesa Redonda de Ciencias Prehistóricas y Antropológicas, Instituto Riva-Agüero, Lima, October 1965.

Bodley, John H. "Campa Social Organization." Unpublished manuscript, personal communication, 1969.

———. "The Last Remaining Independent Campa." *Peruvian Time*, vol. 29, no. 1498 (5 September 1969).

———. "Campa Socio-Economic Adaptation." Ph.D. dissertation, University of Oregon, 1970.

———. "A Transformative Movement among the Campa of Eastern Peru." *Anthropos*, vol. 67 (1972), pp. 220–28.

———. *Tribal Survival in the Amazon: The Campa Case*. IWGIA Documents, no. 5. Copenhagen: International Work Group for Indigenous Affairs, 1972.

Bolivar, Gregorio de. "Relación de la entrada del padre fray Gregorio de Bolivar, en compañía de Diego Ramírez de Carlos, á las provincias de indios Chunchos, en 1621." In MJL, vol. 8.

Brinton, Daniel G. *La raza americana*. Buenos Aires: Edit. Nova, 1946.

Brown, Michael, and Eduardo Fernández. *War of Shadow: The Struggle for Utopia in the Peruvian Amazon*. Berkeley: University of California Press, 1991.

Bueno, Cosme. *Geografía del Perú virreynal (siglo XVIII)*. Lima: D. Valcárcel, 1951.

Busquets, Ramón, and Cristóbal Rocamora. "Diario de la expedición del río de Santa Ana, que verificaron los padres misioneros apostólicos, fray . . . , del colegio de Moquegua . . . , año de 1807." In MJL, vol. 12.

Cabello de Balboa, Miguel. "Carta del P. Miguel Cabello de Balboa al virrey, marqués de Cañete, sobre la conversión de los indios Chunchos, 11 de setiembre de 1594." In MJL, vol. 8.

Campbell, Joseph. *El héroe de las mil caras*. Mexico City and Buenos Aires: Fondo de Cultura Económica, 1959.

———. *Le maschere di Dio*. Milan: V. Bompiani, 1962.

Cantoni, Remo. *Illusione e pregiudizio*. Milan: Casa Ed. Il Saggiatore, 1967.

Capelo, J. *La vía central del Perú*. Lima: Impr. Masías, 1896.

Carballo Alonso, Pablo. "Informe que manifiesta los progresos desde el año de 1791 en el que le dio principio a su restauración, y el estado en que al presente se hallan. . . ." In "Documentos para el estudio de la historia de las misiones franciscanas en el Perú oriental," by Rodolfo Shuller. *Revista Histórica* (Lima), trim. 2, vol. 3 (1908).

Carneiro, Robert L. "Slash-and-Burn Agriculture: A Closer Look at Its Implications for Settlement Patterns." In *Men and Cultures*. Selected Papers of the 5th International Congress of Anthropological and Ethnological Sciences, September 1956. Philadelphia: University of Pennsylvania Press, 1960.

———. "Little-Known Tribes of the Peruvian Montaña." In *Bulletin of the International Committee on Urgent Anthropological and Ethnological Research*, no. 5. Vienna: Heine-Geldern Edit., 1962.

Carranza, Albino. "Geografía descriptiva y estadística industrial de Chanchamayo." In BSG, vol. 4, año 4, nos. 1–3 (1894).

Carrasco, Francisco. "Principales palabras del idioma de las tribus de infieles antis, piros, conibos, sipibos." In BSG, vol. 11 (1901).

Castelnau, Francis de. *Expédition dans les parties centrales de l'Amérique du Sud, de Rio de Janeiro a Lima, et de Lima au Para; exécutée par ordre du government français pendant les anées 1843 a 1847*. 15 vols. Paris: P. Bertrand, 1850–59.

Cátedra Nuestra Selva. *Antropología lingüística de la Amazonía*. Publicación no. 2. Lima: Universidad Nacional Mayor de San Marcos, Facultad de Ciencias Económicas y Comerciales, 1964.

Chantre y Herrera, José. *Historia de las misiones de la Compañá de Jesús en el Marañón Español por . . . , 1637–1767*. Madrid: Impr. de A. Avriol, 1901.

Chirif, Alberto, and Carlos Mora. *Atlas de comunidades nativas*. Lima: Sistema Nacional de Apoyo a la Movilización Social, 1976.

Chrostowki, Marshall S. "Environment, Resource Potential, and Campa Cultural Patterns in the Gran Pajonal." In *Actas y Memorias*, 39th International Congress of Americanists, Lima, August 1970.

Chrostowski, M., and W. Denevan. *The Biogeography of the Savanna Landscape: The Gran Pajonal of Eastern Peru*. Savana Research Series, no. 16. Montreal: McGill University, 1970.

Cipriani, César. "Viaje a la región de Pampa Hermosa, 1904." In LCCL, vol. 13.

———. *Informe del ingeniero sobre la ruta Perené-Ucayali*. Ministerio de Fomento, Junta Consultiva del Ferrocarril al Oriente. Lima: Impr. del Estado, 1906.

Cirlot, Juan Eduard. *Diccionario de símbolos tradicionales*. Barcelona: L. Miracle Edit., 1958.

Cocchiara, Giuseppe. *Storia del folklore in Europa*. Turin: Edizioni Scientifiche Einaudi, 1954.

Combe, Ernesto de la. "Informe que presenta el coronel don . . . á la Sociedad Geográfica, dándole cuenta de su expedición al río Azupizú y del camino que á él conduce." In BSG, vol. 1, nos. 10–12 (1892).

Comité Interamericano de Desarrollo Agrícola. *Tenencia de la tierra y desarrollo socio-económico del sector agrícola, Perú*. Washington, D.C.: Unión Panamericana, 1966.

Conklin, Harold. *El estudio del cultivo de roza*. Estudios monográficos, no. 11. Washington, D.C.: Unión Panamericana, 1963.

Contreras, Fernando. "Representación de Fernando Contreras a S. M. sobre la reducción de los Aucaya, Austria-América, nueva provincia de los Minarvas, 10 de mayo de 1651." In MJL, vol. 5.

Coomaraswamy, Ananda K. *Hindouisme et bouddhisme*. Paris: Gallimard, 1949.

Córdova Salinas, Diego de. *Crónica de la religiosissima prouincia de los Doze Apóstoles del Perú, de la orden de nuestro Seráfico P. S. Francisco de la Regular Obseruancía; con relación de las prouincias que della an salido, y son sus hijas. Compuesta por su historiador el P. Fray Diego de Cordua Salinas, predicador y padre dela mesma prouincia natural de la ciudad de Lima, metrópoli del Perú . . .*, book 2. Lima: Jorge López de Herrera, 1651. Modern edition, with introduction and notes by Lino G. Canedo. Washington, D.C.: Academy of American Franciscan History, 1957.

Dávila Brizeño, Diego. "Relación de don Diego Dávila Brizeño, corregidor de Guarocheri, al virrey del Perú don Hernando de Torres y Portugal, conde de Villar, en que se describe la provincia de Yauyos, enero de 1586" (our title). In JERG, vol. 1.

Delgado, Eulogio. "Vocabulario del idioma de las tribus campas." In BSG, vol. 5, nos. 10–12; vol. 6, nos. 1–12 (1896–97).

Denevan, William M. "Campa Subsistence in the Gran Pajonal, Eastern Peru." *Geographical Review* (New York), vol. 61, no. 4 (1971).

Dirks, Servais. "Explorations du fleuve des Amazones, faites par les franciscains du Pérou (1633–1650)." International Congress of Americanists, Brussels, 1879.

Dumont, Jean Paul. "El occidente y los bárbaros." *Anuario Indigenista* (Mexico City), vol. 30 (December 1970).

Duncan, Otis Dudley. "The Ecosystem Concept and the Problem of Air Pollution." In *Environment and Cultural Behavior: Ecological Studies in Cultural Anthropology*, edited by Andrew Vayda. New York: Natural History Press, 1969.

Eberhardt, Charles C. *Indians of Peru*. Miscellaneous Collections, vol. 52. Washington, D.C.: Smithsonian Institution, 1907.

Eliade, Mircea. *El mito del eterno retorno: Arquetipos y repetición*. Buenos Aires: Emecé Editores, 1952.

———. *Trattato di storia delle religioni*. Turin: Edizioni Einaudi, 1954.

———. "Time and Eternity in Indian Thought." In *Man and Time*. Papers from the Eranos Yearbook. New York: Pantheon Books, 1957.

———. "Structure et fonction du mythe cosmogonique." In *La naissance du monde*. Paris: Éditions du Seuil, 1959.

———. *El chamanismo y las técnicas arcaicas del éxtasis*. Mexico City and Buenos Aires: Fondo de Cultura Económica, 1960.

———. "Cargo Cults and Cosmic Regeneration." In *Millennial Dreams in Action*, edited by Sylvia L. Thrupp. Comparative Studies in Society and History, suppl. 2. The Hague: Mouton and Co., 1962.

———. *The Two and the One*. London: Harvill Press, 1965.

———. *Il sacro e il profano*. Turin: Edit. Boringhieri, 1967.

Elick, John. "An Ethnography of the Pichis Valley Campa of Eastern Peru." Ph.D. dissertation, University of California, Los Angeles, 1969; University Microfilms, Ann Arbor.

Ensenada, Marqués de la. "Carta del . . . a Buenos Aires. Madrid, 21 de diciembre de 1744." In LJS.

Fanon, Frantz. *Peau noire, masques blancs*. Paris: Edit. du Scuil, 1952.

Farabee, William Curtis. "Indian Tribes of Eastern Peru." In *Papers of the Peabody Museum of American Archaeology and Ethnology*, vol. 10. Cambridge: Harvard University, 1922.

Fast, Pedro W. *Distribución geográfica de 30 naciones aborígenes en la Amazonía peruana*. Lima: Ministerio de Educación Pública, 1961.

Flam, Léopold. "Le sacré et la désacralisation dans la pensée contemporaine." In *Le Pouvoir et le sacré*. Annales du Centre d'Etude des Religions, vol. 1. Brussels: Université Libre de Bruxelles, 1962.

Fritz, Samuel. "Description abrégée du fleuve Maragnon, et des missions établies aux environs de ce fleuve. . . ." In *Lettres édifiantes et curieuses, écrites des missions étrangéres*. Toulouse: Noel-Etienne Seus, 1810.

Fry, Carlos. "Diario de los viajes y exploración de los ríos Urubamba, Ucayali, Amazonas, Pachitea y Palcazú, por . . . 1886–1888." In LCCL, vol. 11.

———. *Navegación fluvial peruana*. Lima: Impr. de Gómez y Ledesma, 1890.

Galt, Francisco L. "Informe del cirujano de la Comisión Hidrográfica del Amazonas." *El Peruano* (Lima), year 31, vol. 2 (1873).

García, Domingo, and Manuel del Santo. "Carta escrita por los padres fray Manuel del Santo y fray Domingo García, misioneros apostólicos del colegio de Santa Rosa de Ocopa, y misiones de infieles del Cerro de la Sal, al Rdo. padre fray Joseph Gil Muñoz, comisario de dichas misiones en la que le dan noticia de la entrada que hizo a ellas el escandaloso apóstata Juan Santos Atahualpa, Apuinga, Guainacapac, indio cristiano de la imperial ciudad del Cuzco. . . ." In IHM, vol. 2.

García Rosell, Ricardo. *Conquista de la montaña. Sinópsis de los descubrimientos, expediciones, estudios y trabajos llevados a cabo en el Perú para el aprovechamiento y cultura de sus montañas*. Lima: Tipogr. La Prensa, 1905.

Geertz, Clifford. "Two Types of Ecosystems." In *Environment and Cultural Behavior: Ecological Studies in Cultural Anthropology*, edited by Andrew Vayda. New York: Natural History Press, 1969.

Gennep, Arnald Van. "Etudes d'ethnographie sud-américaine." *Journal de la Société des Américanistes* (Paris), vol. 11 (1919).

Gil de Taboada y Lemos, Francisco. "Relación de gobierno del Excmo. Señor Virrey del Perú . . . , presentada á su sucesor el Excmo. Señor Baron de Vallenari.

Año de 1796." In *Memorias de los virreyes que han gobernado el Perú durante el tiempo del coloniaje español*, vol. 6. Lima: F. Bailly, 1859.

Giordano, Félix. "Memoria del ingeniero F. Giordano sobre la excursión que practicó en compañía del ministro italiano a los territorios orientales de Chanchamayo, 1875." In LCCL, vol. 11.

Goldman, Irving. "Tribes of the Uaupes-Caquetá Region." In HSAI, vol. 3.

Golewsky, Stanislaw. "El Gran Pajonal." In BSG, vol. 50 (1933).

Gonzales, Bernardino. "Ojeada sobre la montaña." Serie de artículos publicados por . . . el año de 1886. In IHM, vol. 10.

Grandidier, Ernest M. *Voyage dans l'Amérique du Sud: Pérou et Bolivie*. Paris: M. Lévy, 1861.

Gridilla, Alberto. "Los Campas." In *El cuarto centenario amazónico y la orden franciscana*. Colección descalzos, no. 4. Lima: Gráfica Scheuch S. A., 1942.

Grubb, Kenneth George. *The Lowland Indians of Amazonia*. London: Word Dominion Press, 1927.

Guacra Paucar, Felipe. "La descripción que se hizo en la provincia de Xauxa por la instrucción de S. M. que a la dicha provincia se envió de molde, mayo de 1582." In JERG, vol. 1.

Guénon, René. *Il simbolismo della croce*. Turin: Edizioni Studi Tradizionali, 1964.

———. *Oriente e occidente*. Turin: Edizioni Studi Tradizionali, 1965.

Guillaume, Herbert. *The Amazon Provinces of Peru as a Field for European Emigration*. London: Wyman and Sons, 1888.

Gurvitch, Georges. *Los marcos sociales del conocimiento*. Caracas: Monte Avila Editores, 1969.

Gutierrez, Ruperto. "Informe del comandante . . . 1868" (my title). In LCCL, vol. 2.

Herndon, Lewis. *Exploration of the Valley of the Amazon*. Washington, D.C.: Taylor and Maury, 1854.

Hervas y Panduro, Lorenzo. *Catalogo delle lingue conosciute e notizia della loro affinitá, e diversitá, opera del signor abate. . . .* Cesena: Gregorio Biasini, 1784.

Instituto Nacional de Planificación, Dirección Nacional de Estadística y Censos, República del Perú. *Sexto censo nacional de población*. Lima: INP, 1965.

Izaguirre, Bernardino. "Descripción histórico-etnográfica de algunas tribus orientales del Perú." In BSG, vol. 44 (1927).

———, comp. *Historia de las misiones franciscanas y narración de los progresos de la geografía en el oriente del Perú*. 14 vols. Lima: Talleres Tipogr. de la Penitenciaría, 1922–29.

Jiménez de la Espada, Marcos, comp. *Relaciones geográficas de Indias*. 4 vols. Madrid: Tipogr. M. Hernandez, 1881–97.

Kaufmann, Robert. *Millénarisme et acculturation*. Brussels: L'Institut de Sociologie de l'Université Libre de Bruxelles, 1964.

Kerenyi, Karl. *La religione antica nelle sue linee fondamentali*. Bologna: Nicola Zanichelli Edit., 1940.

Kuczynski-Godard, Maxime. *La colonia del Perené y sus problemas médico sociales*. Lima: Ediciones La Reforma Médica, 1939.

———. *La vida en la Amazonía peruana*. Lima: Libr. Internacional, 1944.

Kuczynski-Godard, Maxime, and Carlos Enrique Paz Soldan. *La selva peruana: Sus pobladores y su colonización en seguridad sanitaria*. Lima: Ediciones de la Reforma Sanitaria, 1939.

Laing, R. D. *La política dell' esperienza*. Milan: Feltrinelli, 1968.

———. "Lo obvio." In *Dialéctica de la Liberación*. Mexico City: Siglo XXI Edit., 1969.

Lambert, Jacques. *L'America Latina: Strutture sociali e istituzioni politiche*. Rome: Editori Riuniti, 1966.

Lanternari, Vittorio. *Movimientos religiosos de libertad y salvación de los pueblos oprimidos*. Barcelona: Seix Barral, 1965.

Larrabure y Correa, Carlos, comp. *Colección de leyes, decretos, resoluciones y otros documentos oficiales referentes al Departamento de Loreto*. 18 vols. Lima: Impr. La Opinión Nacional, 1905–9.

Lathrap, Donald. "The Hunting Economics of the Tropical Forest of South America: An Attempt at Historical Perspective." In *Man the Hunter*, edited by R. Lee and I. De Vore. Chicago: Aldine Publishing, 1968.

———. *The Upper Amazon*. London: Thames and Hudson, 1970.

Lehnertz, Jay F. "Cultural Struggle on the Peruvian Frontier: Campa-Franciscan Confrontations, 1595–1752." Master's thesis, University of Wisconsin, 1969.

Lévi-Strauss, Claude. "El problema de la invariancia en antropología." *Diógenes* (Buenos Aires), year 7, no. 31 (September 1960).

Loayza, Francisco A. *Juan Santos, el invencible.* Manuscripts from 1742 to 1755. Lima: Editorial D. Miranda, 1942.

Loukotka, Chestmir. *Clasificación de las lenguas sudamericanas.* Edición Lingüística Sudamericana, no. 1. Prague: 1935.

Lowie, Robert H. "The Tropical Forest: An Introduction." In HSAI, vol. 3.

Malinowski, Bronislaw. *Estudios de psicología primitiva.* Buenos Aires: Paidos, 1963.

Mannheim, K. *Ideology and Utopia*. London: 1948. Cited in *Illusione e pregiudizio*, by Remo Cantoni. Milan: Casa Ed. II Saggiatore, 1967.

Manso de Velasco, José Antonio (conde de Superunda). "Carta al rey de España, Lima, 31 de julio de 1746." In LJS.

———. "Relación que suscribe el conde de Superunda, virrey del Perú, de los principales sucesos de su gobierno, de Real Orden de S. M. comunicado por el Excmo. Sr. Marqués de la Ensenada, su secretario del despacho universal, con fecha 23 de agosto de 1751, y comprehende los años desde 9 de julio de 1745 hasta fin del mismo mes en el de 1756." In *Memorias de los virreyes que han gobernado el Perú durante el tiempo del coloniaje español*, vol. 4. Lima: F. Bailly, 1859.

Marcoy, Paul. See Saint-Cricq, Laurent.

Markham, Clements R. *Expeditions into the Valley of the Amazons, 1539, 1540, 1639*. London: Hakluty Soc., 1859.

Mason, Alden J. "The Languages of South American Indians." In HSAI, vol. 6.

Maúrtua, Víctor M., comp. *Exposición de la república del Perú presentada al Excmo. Gobierno Argentino en el juicio de límites con la república de Bolivia, conforme al tratado de arbitraje del 30 de diciembre de 1902*. 2 vols. Barcelona: Impr. de Henrich y Comp., 1906.

———, comp. Juicio de límites entre el Perú y Bolivia. 15 vols. Barcelona: Impr. de Henrich y Comp., 1906.

Meggers, Betty J. "Ambiente y cultura en la cuenca del Amazonas: Revisión de la teoría del determinismo ambiental." In *Estudios sobre ecología humana*. Estudios Monográficos, no. 3. Washington, D.C.: Unión Panamericana, 1960. (The original English version of this article was published in 1956.)

Meillet, A., and Marcel Cohen, eds. *Les langues du monde*. Société Linguistique de Paris, Centro National de la Recherche Scientifique. Paris: H. Champion, 1952.

Mendizabal Losack, Emilio. "La fiesta en Pachitea andina." *Folklore Americano* (Lima), year 13, no. 13 (1965).

Mendoza, José Antonio de, (marqués de Villagarcía). "Relación del estado de los reynos del Perú que hace el Excmo. Sr. Marqués de Villagarcía al Excmo. Sr. Don José Manso de Velasco, conde de Superunda, su sucesor en aquel virreynato, fecha en 24 de julio de 1745." In *Memorias de los virreyes que han gobernado el Perú durante el tiempo del coloniaje español*, vol. 3. Lima: F. Bailly, 1859.

Mercier, Paul. *Histoire de l'anthropologie*. Paris: Presses Universitaires de France, 1966.

Metraux, Alfred. "A Quechua Messiah in Eastern Peru." *American Anthropologist*, vol. 44 (1942).

———. "The Guaraní." In HSAI, vol. 3.

———. "Tribes of Eastern Bolivia and the Madeira Headwaters." In HSAI, vol. 3.

———. *Religions et magies indiennes d'Arnérique du Sud*. Paris: Gallimard, 1967.

Ministerio de la Reforma Agraria. *Avances y proyecciones de la Reforma Agraria*. Lima: November 1970.

Murra, John V. *Cuadernos de investigación: No. 1, Antropología*. Huánuco: Universidad Nacional Hermilio Valdizán, 1966.

Navarra y Rocaful, Melchor de, (duque de La Palata). "Relación del estado del Perú, en los ocho años de su gobierno que hace el duque de La Palata al Excmo. Señor Conde de la Moncloba, su subcessor en los cargos de virrey, gobernador y capitán general de estos reynos del Perú, Tierrafirme y Chile, de que tomó posesión el día 16 de agosto del año de 1689." In *Memorias de los virreyes que han gobernado el Perú durante el tiempo del coloniaje español*. Lima: F. Bailly, 1859.

Navarro, Manuel. *La tribu Campa*. Lima: 1924.

Nordenskjold, Otto. "Explorations chez les indiens Campas dans le Pérou." *Meddelande fran Geografiska Foreningen i Göteborg* (Gothenburg, Sweden), vol. 3 (1924).

———. *Sudamerika. Ein Zukunftland der Menschheit*. Stuttgart: 1927.

Nystrom, John William. "Relación del ataque Campa al correo Chanchamayo-Tarma, 1869." In LCCL, vol. 2.

———. *Argumento sobre Chanchamayo, sus primeras colonizaciones y los indios chunchos*. Lima: Impr. y Lit. E. Prugue, 1870.

Oficina Nacional de Evaluación de Recursos Naturales (ONERN), República del Perú. *Colonización del río Apurímac*. Lima: ONERN, 1961.

———. *Estudio de Moscoc-Llacta*. Lima: ONERN, 1961.

———. *Tingo María–Tocache*. Lima: ONERN, 1962.

———. *Uctubamba-Bagua*. Lima: ONERN, 1963.

———. *Medio Urubamba*. Lima: ONERN, 1964.

———. *Koosñipata–Alto Madre de Dios-Manú*. Lima: ONERN, 1965.

———. *Pachitea*. Lima: ONERN, 1966.

———. *Perené*. Lima: ONERN, 1966.

———. *Camisea*. Lima: ONERN, 1967.

———. *Yurimaguas*. Lima: ONERN, 1967.

———. *Alto Mayo*. Lima: ONERN, 1968.

———. *Bajo Mayo–Huallaga Central*. Lima: ONERN, 1968.

———. *Chiriyacu-Nieva*. Lima: ONERN, 1968.

———. *Tambo–Gran Pajonal*. Lima: ONERN, 1968.

———. *Tocache-Campanilla*. Lima: ONERN, 1968.

———. *Santiago-Morona*. Lima: ONERN, 1970.

———. *Villa Rica–Pachitea*. Lima: ONERN, 1970.

Ohm, Thomas. *Crítica de Asia sobre el cristianismo de Occidente*. Buenos Aires: Edic. Desclée de Brouwer, 1950.

Orbigny, Alcides d'. *Voyage dans l'Amérique méridionale.* 5 vols. Paris: Pitois-Levrault, 1836–40.

Ordinaire, Olivier. *Les sauvages du Pérou*. Paris: E. Leroux Edit., 1888.

———. *Du Pacifique à l'Atlantique par les Andes peruviennes et l'Amazone*. Paris: Libraire Plon, Nourrit et Cie., 1892.

Oricain, Pablo José. "Compendio breve de discursos varios sobre diferentes materiales y noticias geográficas comprehensivas a este obispado del Cuzco que claman remedios espirituales. Andaguaylillas en 1790." In MJL, vol. 11.

Ortiz, Dionisio. *Monografía de Chanchamayo*. Lima: Edit. San Antonio, 1958.

———. *Reseña histórica de la montaña del Pangoa, Gran Pajonal y Satipo (1673–1930)*. Lima: Edit. San Antonio, 1961.

Ortiz de Zuñiga, Iñigo. *Visita de la provincia de León de Huánuco en 1566*. Edited by John V. Murra. Huánuco: Universidad Nacional Hermilio Valdizán, 1966.

Orton, James. *The Andes and the Amazon, or Across the Continent of South America*. New York: Harper and Brothers, 1875.

Osambela, Claudio. "El oriente del Perú." In BSG, vol. 6, nos. 1–6 (1896).

Pallares, Fernando, and Vicente Calvo. *Noticias históricas de las misiones de fieles é infieles del colegio de propaganda fide de San Rosa de Ocopa*. Barcelona: Impr. de Magriña y Subirana, 1870.

Pereira, José Manuel. "Informe de la expedición exploradora de los valles de Chanchamayo, 1869." In LCCL, vol. 2.

Perez, Carlos. "Informe de la expedición del río Azupizú en la confluencia de los ríos Pichis y Palcazú por el ingeniero. . . ." In LCCL, vol 3.

Pettazzoni, Raffaele. *Miti e leggende*. 4 vols. Turin: UTET, 1963.

Poeppig, Eduard Friedrich. *Eduard Poeppig's Reise in Chile, Peru und auf dem Amazonenstrome*. Stuttgart: F. A. Brockhaus Komm. ABt. Antiquarium, 1960.

Porras Barrenechea, Raúl. "Esquema para una bibliografía amazónica." *Mercurio Peruano* (Lima), year 17, vol. 24, no. 180 (1942).

———. Speech. In *El Perú y la Amazonía*. Lima: SPI, 1961.

———. *Fuentes históricas peruanas*. Lima: Instituto Raúl Porras B., 1963.

Porres, Diego de. "Memorial del padre fray Diego de Porres a S. M. pidiendo mercedes por sus servicios, año de 1582." In MJL, vol. 1.

Portillo, Pedro. "Exploración de los ríos Apurímac, Ene, Tambo, Ucayali, Pachitea y Pichis por el prefecto de Ayacucho . . . , año de 1900." In LCCL, vol. 3.

Prince, Carlos. *Idiomas y dialecto indígenas del continente Hispano Sud-Americano*. Lima: Ministerio de Fomento, 1905.

Propp, Vladimir. *Morfologia della fiaba*. Original edition published in Russian in 1928. Turin: G. Einaudi Edit., 1966.

Radin, Paul, Carl Gustav Jung, and Karl Kerenyi. *Il briccone divino*. Milan: V. Bompiani, 1965.

Raimondi, Antonio. "Informe sobre la provincia litoral de Loreto, 1862." In LCCL, vol. 7.

———. *El Perú*. 4 vols. Lima: Impr. del Estado, 1874, 1876, 1879, 1902.

Ramirez, Balthasar. "Descripción del reyno del Pirú del sitio, temple, provincias, obispados y ciudades; de los naturales de sus lenguas y trajes. Año de 1597." In MJL, vol. 1.

Recio de Leon, Juan. "Descripción del Paititi y provincias de Tipuani, Chunchos, por . . . Madrid, 19 de octubre de 1623." In MJL, vol. 6.

Rey Riveros, Edmundo. "El censo y los aborígenes selvícolas de nuestra Amazonía." *Revista Militar del Perú* (Lima), nos. 613, 633, 634 (July, August, and September–October 1956; reprinted 1957).

Rivet, Paul, and Charles Tastevin. "Les langues du Purus, du Juruá et des régions limitrophes. I, le groupe arawak pré-andin." *Anthropological Papers*, vol. 73, no. 8 (undated).

Rodriguez, Manuel. *El Marañón y Amazonas. Historia de los descubrimientos, entradas y reducción de naciones. Trabajos malogrados de algunos conquistadores, y dichosos de otros assi temporales, como espirituales en las dilatadas montañas y mayores ríos de la América*. Madrid: Impr. de A. Gonzales de Reyes, 1684.

Rowe, John Howland. "The Distribution of Indians and Indian Languages in Peru." *Geographical Review* (New York), vol. 37, no. 2 (1947).

Sabaté, Luis. *Viaje de los padres misioneros del convento del Cuzco a las tribus salvajes de los Campas, Piros, Cunibos, Sipibos en el año de 1874*. Lima: Tipogr. La Sociedad, 1877.

Sahlins, Marshall. *Tribesmen*. Upper Saddle River, N.J.: Prentice Hall Inc., 1968.

Saint-Cricq, Laurent. *Voyage a travers l'Amérique du Sud de l'Océan Pacifique a l'Océan Atlantique*. Paris: 1869.

Saiz, Odorico. "Los misioneros franciscanos en la Amazonía del Perú." *Mercurio Peruano* (Lima), year 17, no. 184 (July 1942).

Sala, Gabriel. "Apuntes de viaje del P. Fr. Gabriel Sala. Exploración de los ríos Pichis, Pachitea y Alto Ucayali y de la región del Gran Pajonal, 1897." In IHM, vol. 10.

Samanéz Ocampo, José B. "Exploración de los ríos Apurímac, Ene, Tambo, Urubamba y Ucayali por . . . 1883–1884." In LCCL, vol. 11.

San Antonio, Joseph de. "Relación lastimosa de las crudelísimas muertes que dieron los apóstatas y gentiles de varias naciones a los PP. misioneros apostólicos del colegio de misiones de Ocopa y provincia de los Doce Apostóles de Lima en el reyno del Perú, Guamanga, 5 de mayo de 1747." In IHM, vol. 2.

———. "Memorial del padre . . . al rey de España, 11 de julio de 1750" (no original title). AGI 72-2-31. In IHM, vol. 2.

San Joseph, Francisco de. "Memorial del P. . . . a S. M. Felipe V, 25 de noviembre de 1713." In IHM, vol. 2.

———. "Informe hecho por el V. P. Fr. Francisco de San Joseph al Rmo. P. Fr. Joseph Sanz, comisario general de Indias de las misiones de infieles del Cerro de la Sal, con noticias muy singulares, para gloria de Dios nuestro Señor, y crédito de nuestra seráfica religión (1716)." In IHM, vol. 2.

Schlaeppi, Federico. "El río Perené." In BSG, vol. 52 (1935).

Schwab, Federico. *Bibliografía etnológica de la Amazonía peruana*. Lima: Comp. de Impresiones y Publicidad, 1942.

Secretariatus pro non christianis. *Towards the Meeting of Religions: Suggestions for Dialogue*. Rome: Vatican Polyglot Press, 1967.

Shell, Olive A. *Grupos idiomáticos de la selva peruana*. Publicaciones del Instituto de Filología de la Facultad de Letras. Estudios, no. 7. Lima: Universidad Nacional Mayor de San Marcos, 1958.

Shuller, Rodolfo. "Documentos para el estudio de la historia de las misiones franciscanas en el Perú oriental." *Revista Histórica* (Lima), trim. 2, vol. 3 (1908).

Sobreviela, Manuel de. "Diario del viaje que yo fray Manuel de Sobreviela, guardián del colegio de propoganda fide de Santa Rosa de Ocopa, hice a las conversiones de las montañas de Guanta, partido de la intendencia y obispado de Huamanga y a las fronteras de Tarma . . . (1788)." In IHM, vol. 7.

———. "Varias noticias interesantes de las entradas que los religiosos de mi padre San Francisco han hecho á las montañas del Perú, desde cada uno de los partidos confinantes con la cordillera de los Andes para mayor esclarecimiento del mapa que se da á luz sobre el curso de los ríos Huallaga y Ucayali." *Mercurio Peruano* (Lima), no. 80 (9 October 1791).

———. *Voyage au Pérou, faits dans les années 1791 à 1794, par les PP. Manuel de Sobreviela et Narcisso y Barcelo. . . .* Paris: J. G. Dentu, 1809.

Steinen, Karl von den. "Der Verfasser der Handschrift Arte de la lengua de los indios Antis ó Campas." 16th International Congress of Americanists, Stuttgart, 1906.

Steward, Julian. "The Witotoan Tribes." In HSAI, vol. 3.

———. "South American Cultures: An Interpretative Summary." In HSAI, vol. 5.

———, ed. *Handbook of South American Indians*. 7 vols. Washington, D.C.: Smithsonian Institution, 1946–59.

Steward, Julian, and Louis C. Faron. *Native Peoples of South America*. New York: McGraw-Hill Co., 1959.

Steward, Julian H., and Alfred Metraux. "Tribes of the Peruvian and Ecuadorian Montaña." In HSAI, vol. 3.

Stiglich, Germán. *Informe del jefe de la comisión exploradora de las regiones del Ucayali, Fiscarrald y Madre de Dios*. Lima: SPI, 1904.

Tello, Julio C. "Algunas conexiones gramaticales de las lenguas campa, ipurina, moxa, baure, amuesha, goajira, del grupo o familia arawak o maipuru." *Revista Universitaria* (Lima), year 7, vol. 1 (1913).

Tessmann, Günter. *Die Indianer Nordost-Perus*. Hamburg: Friederichsen, de Gruyter e Co., 1930.

Thrupp, Sylvia L., ed. *Millennial Dreams in Action*. Comparative Studies in Society and History, suppl. 2. The Hague: Mouton and Co., 1962.

Tibesar, Antonine S. "The Salt Trade among the Montaña Indians of the Tarma Area of Eastern Peru." *Primitive Man*, vol. 23 (1950).

———. "San Antonio de Eneno: A Mission in the Peruvian Montaña." *Primitive Man*, vol. 25 (1952).

Toledo, Francisco de. "Relación de los yndios de guerra que están en las fronteras de los yndios christianos de la governación del reyno del Pirú. In carta del virrey D. Francisco de Toledo á S. M. sobre asuntos de guerra, acompañando una relación de los yndios fronterizos, 20 de marzo de 1573." In MJL, vol. 1.

———. "Provisión del virrey don Francisco de Toledo concediendo á Martín Hurtado de Arbieto, á su petición, los privilegios de conquistador. Arequipa, 4 de noviembre de 1575." In MJL, vol. 7.

Torre López, Fernando. "Fenomenología religiosa de la tribu Anti o Campa." Ph.D. dissertation, Universidad Católica de Lovaina, 1965.

Torres, Diego de. *Relatione breve del P. Diego de Torres della Compagnia di Giesú, procuratore della prouincia del Perú, circa il frutto che si raccoglie con gli indiani di quel regno . . . in Roma*. Written in 1603. Published in Rome: Appresso Luigi Zannetti, 1903.

Touchaux, Mauricio. "Apuntes sobre la gramática y el diccionario del idioma campa ó lengua de los Antis, tal como se usa en el río Apurímac." *Revista Histórica* (Lima), vol. 3, trim. 2 (1908).

Tovar, Antonio. *Catálogo de las lenguas de América del Sur*. Buenos Aires: Edit. Sudamericana, 1961.

Troncoso de Lira, Benito. "Información jurada de seis testigos parciales para desvirtuar las inculpaciones que se habían hecho a los PP. franciscanos como causantes de la sublevación de Juan Santos Atahualpa." In LJS.

Urrutia y Las Casas, Ramón. *Informe del intendente Urrutia sobre las ventajas que resultan de la apertura del camino y comunicación por el Chanchamayo, presentado al virrey del Perú en 1808*. Lima: Impr. del Comercio, 1847.

Valcarcel, Luis E. *Etnohistoria del Perú antiguo*. Lima: Universidad Nacional Mayor de San Marcos, 1959.

Valcarcel Esparza, Carlos Daniel. *Rebeliones indígenas*. Lima: Edit. PTEM, 1946.

Valenzuela, Francisco. "Información de servicios de . . . años de 1578–1592." In MJL, vol. 7.

Van Der Leeuw, Gustave. *La religion dans son essence et ses manifestations*. Paris: Payot, 1955.

———. "Primordial Time and Final Time." In *Man and Time*. Papers from the Eranos Yearbook. New York: Pantheon Books, 1957.

Varallanos, José. *Historia de Huánuco*. Buenos Aires: Impr. López, 1959.

Varese, Stefano. "La rebelión de Juan Santos Atahualpa: Un movimiento mesiánico del siglo XVIII en la selva peruana." In *Actas y Trabajos*, 37th International Congress of Americanists, Mar del Plata, 1966.

———. "Antropología, política y neutralidad." *Amaru* (Lima), no. 7 (July–September 1968).

———. *La Sal de los Cerros*. Lima: Universidad Peruana de Ciencias y Tecnologías, 1968.

———. "Dos versiones cosmogónicas Campa: Esbozo analítico." *Revista del Museo Nacional* (Lima), vol. 36 (1970).

———. *Estudio sondeo de seis comunidades Aguaruna del Alto Marañón*. Lima: Dirección de Comunidades Campesinas, Ministerio de Agricultura, 1970.

———. *The Forest Indians in the Present Political Situation of Peru*. IWGIA Documents, no. 8. Copenhagen: International Work Group for Indigenous Affairs, 1972.

———. "Inter-ethnic Relations in the Selva of Peru." In *The Situation of the Indians in South America: Contribution to the Study of Inter-ethnic Conflict in the Non-Andean Regions of South America*, edited by W. Dostal. Geneva: World Council of Churches, 1972.

———. "La misión, las sociedades nativas y su liberación." In *Antropología y teología en la acción misionera*. Bogota: Vicariato Apostólico de Iquitos, Indo-American Press Service, 1972.

———. "Relaciones interétnicas en la selva del Perú." In *La situación indígena en América del Sur*, edited by Walter Dostal. Montevideo: Tierra Nueva, Biblioteca Científica, 1972.

———. "Au sujet du colonialisme ecologique." *Les Temps Modernes* (Paris), no. 316 (April 1973).

———. *La Sal de los Cerros: Una aproximación al mundo Campa*, 2d ed. Retablo de Papel Ediciones. Lima: Instituto Nacional de Investigación y Desarrollo de la Educación, 1973.

———. "La selva: Viejas fronteras, nuevas alternativas." *Participación* (Lima), no. 5, year 3 (1974).

———. *Las minorías etnicas y la comunidad nacional*. Lima: Ediciones del Centro de Estudios de Participación Popular, 1974.

———. "Celebración del desencuentro." In *A los quinientos años del choque de dos mundos: Balance y perspectiva*, compiled by Adolfo Colombres. Buenos Aires: Ediciones del Sol, 1989.

Varese, Stefano, and Sergio Chang. *Las sociedades nativas de la selva: Diagnóstico socio-económico preliminar del área rural peruana*. Reporte oficial. Lima: Sistema Nacional de Apoyo a la Movilización Social, Dirección General de Organizaciones Rurales, 1972.

Vargas Ugarte, Rubén. *Historia del Perú, fuentes*. Lima: 1939.

———. *Historia general del Perú*. Virreynato, vols. 3–5. Lima: Edit. C. Milla B., 1966.

Vasquez de Espinoza, Antonio. *Compendio y descripción de las Indias Occidentales*. Washington, D.C.: Smithsonian Institution, 1948.

Vayda, Andrew, ed. *Environment and Cultural Behavior: Ecological Studies in Cultural Anthropology*. New York: Natural History Press, 1969.

Vazavil, Rodrigo. "Información dada ante el general Dn. Alonso de la Cueva Messia, corregidor y justicia mayor de la provincia de Tarma y Chinchaycocha y su jurisdicción, por su Magestad, a pedimento de M. R. P. predicador fray Rodrigo Vazavil del orden del señor San Francisco, sobre inquirir el mejor camino que se supiere para la entrada al Cerro de la Sal y montaña de los Andes. Ante Joseph de Roxas, escribano de su Magestad, Tharama, 6 de marzo de 1687." Document published by B. Izaguirre. *Revista del Archivo Nacional del Perú* (Lima), vol. 2, no. 2 (1921).

Velasco, Juan de. *Historia del reino de Quito (1789)*. Quito: Impr. del Gobierno, 1841–44.

Vellard, Jehan A. "Textes Mbwihá recueillis au Paraguay." *Jornal de la Société des Américanistes, Nouvella Série* (Paris), vol. 29 (1937).

Villagarcía, Marqués de. "Carta del marqués de Villagarcía al rey de España. Lima, 16 de agosto de 1744." In LJS.

Viñaza, Conde de la. *Bibliografía española de las lenguas indígenas de América*. Madrid: 1892.

Von Hassel, Jorge M. *Apuntes de viaje en el oriente peruano*. Lima: Impr. San Pedro, 1905.

———. "Las tribus salvajes de la región amazóníca del Perú." In BSG, vol. 17 (1905).

Weiss, Gerald. "The Cosmology of the Campa Indians of Eastern Peru." Ph.D. dissertation, University of Michigan, 1969.

———. "Campa Cosmology." *Ethnology* (Pittsburgh), vol. 11, no. 2 (April 1972).

Wertheman, Arturo. Informe de la exploración de los ríos Perené y Tambo. Lima: Impr. del Estado, 1877.

Wiener, Charles. *Pérou et Bolivie. Récit de voyage suivi d'études archéologiques et ethnographiques et de notes sur l'écriture et les langues de populations indiennes.* Paris: Hachette et Cie., 1880.

Zavala, Miguel J. "Vocabulario de la lengua campa." In *La vía central del Perú*, by J. Capelo. Lima: Impr. Masías, 1896.

Index